Hostile Habitats
Scotland's Mountain Environment

editors
Nick Kempe
Mark Wrightham

A hillwalkers' guide to the landscape and wildlife

SCOTTISH MOUNTAINEERING TRUST

Published with support from Scottish Natural Heritage

SCOTTISH
NATURAL
HERITAGE

Published in Great Britain by the Scottish Mountaineering Trust, 2006
2nd Edition 2018

ISBN 978-1-907233-25-8
A catalogue record for this book is available from the British Library

Because of their connections with Scottish Natural Heritage, the editors have waived their rights to any fees or royalties due from this publication

This book is published by the Scottish Mountaineering Trust, a charitable trust. Revenue from all books published by the Trust is used for the continuation of its publishing programme and for charitable purposes associated with Scottish mountains and mountaineering. For more information see <https://smt.smc.org.uk>

Front Cover: Morning light on Buachaille Etive Mor *Cubby Images*

Title Page: The summit ridge of Stob Ghabhar *Tom Prentice*

Some maps are derived from Ordnance Survey OpenData™
© Crown copyright and database right 2018

Production: Scottish Mountaineering Trust (Publications) Ltd
Design & Graphics: Tom Prentice
Colour separations: Core Image, East Kilbride
Printed & bound by Latitude Press Limited

Distributed by Cordee, 11 Jacknell Road, Dodwells Bridge Industrial Estate, Hinkley, Leicestershire LE10 3BS
(t) 01455611185, (f) 01455635687, (w) www.cordee.co.uk

Contents

Introduction

Approaching the South Peak of The Cobbler

When Hostile Habitats first appeared, there were few books on any aspect of Scotland's mountain environment aimed at hillwalkers and climbers. The First Edition appeared to tap an unmet need with sales higher than anyone had anticipated. An excerpt from the book was even used by the Scottish Qualification Authority in a Standard Grade biology exam – we hope it enthused some young people to learn more about our hills! This new edition has been fully updated to reflect changes in understanding and expanded to meet that demand and interest.

While designed to dip into, rather than read in one go, its purpose is to enable hill goers to get more out of even the most demanding of days. The landscapes and wildlife of the mountains, and the traces left by humans on their slopes and summits, are inseparable features of every journey into the hills and there is always a time before or after struggling with the elements, navigating in a whiteout or stretching for that elusive hold to appreciate this.

Scottish mountaineering has been served by an extensive literature, from guidebooks and technical manuals to poetry and autobiography, but until recently this barely touched on the mountain environment. Lots has changed since the first edition and there are now a range of guides aimed at the layperson on specific aspects of the mountain environment as well as many on-line resources, including data bases which can tell you where many of the things described in the identification guide can be seen. Identification guides have also improved considerably and many now make it much easier to work out what you might see in the hills. Such guides though still tend to focus on 'what' rather than 'why', although the presence of a particular species is of greater interest when its place in the wider ecosystem is understood. This book distils this information into a single accessible source dedicated to the Scottish hills. Each chapter of the book describes a different aspect of the mountain environment. In each case, underlying principles and processes are explained, along with their historical context, to illustrate why the mountain environment is the way it is, and why particular rocks, landforms or species occur in particular places. The emphasis is on the more common and visible features, but intriguing rarities are also highlighted.

The chapters are followed, as appropriate, by practical identification guides to the more common rocks, landforms, animals, plants and human traces. This also stresses visible features, with differing implications for each subject. The entries relating to plants, for example, note conspicuous flowers but also highlight other 'vegetative' characteristics, dead or alive, which may be all that can be seen for much of the year. The entries relating to mammals, by contrast, include traces such as trails or droppings, which are often more likely to be seen than the animal itself.

This book has been written primarily for hillwalkers and mountaineers, although it will also be of interest to others who visit the Scottish mountains. Accordingly, a familiarity with the geography of these hills and at least the better-known Munros and Corbetts has been assumed. By contrast, no particular knowledge of natural history should be required, and the book explains relevant technical terms and concepts. The lower altitudinal limit of the mountain environment is open to interpretation, and the scope of this book is taken to include everything above the level of enclosed and more intensively managed farmland. This excludes the fields which comprise the first few hundred metres of some hill outings, particularly in the Southern Highlands, but includes everything beyond the boundary wall or fence. This usually marks some degree of transition to vegetation, and a general environment, of more natural upland character. The lower slopes of some hills include extensive fenced areas which are otherwise indistinguishable from the open hill, particularly on the 'common grazings' of crofting communities in the west. Areas of this type are included.

In Britain, 'montane' and 'alpine' are used interchangeably to refer to land above the potential tree line. Elsewhere, however, 'montane' is applied to the upper part of the forest zone. In an international spirit, and to emphasise the ecological commonality with summits elsewhere in the world, the area above the tree line is referred to as the 'alpine zone'.

In trying to introduce a vast and fascinating subject, it has inevitably been difficult to decide what should be included or omitted. The 'further reading' section suggests additional information sources for those wishing to delve further.

Acknowledgements

The authors and editors would like to acknowledge the help and support of the many friends and colleagues who have commented on drafts or provided other types of technical assistance. We would particularly like to thank Colin Ballantyne, Louise Brimelow, Barbara Brodie, James Carew, Mike Dodd, Philip Entwhistle, Mairi Gillies, James Gordon, Steve Gouldstone, Mary Gregory, Adrian Hall, Mark Hancock, Dave Horsfield, Pete Inness, Robyn Ireland, David Jarman, Andrew Kitchener, Angus Macdonald, Fergus MacTaggart, Carl Mitchell, Stephen Moran, Gill Nisbet, Elizabeth Pickett, Alina Piotrowska, Mo Richards, Samantha Rider (British Trust for Ornithology), Chris Rollie, Lorna Stewart, Martin Twiss, Adam Watson, and the many people who have provided photos.

We are grateful to Graham Bartlett (Met Office) and Chris Quine (Forest Research) for the use of climate data. Special thanks must go to former SMT Publications Manager Tom Prentice for his advice, support and hard work. The Scottish Mountaineering Trust would also like to acknowledge the support of Scottish Natural Heritage, which made the first edition of the book possible.

Overview

Sgurr a' Choire Ghlais, Strathfarrar

The Munros and Corbetts are the foundation for Scottish mountaineering, with its rich subculture and human history of triumph, trial and tribulation. These hills also play a small but significant part in the lives of many who never set foot on their slopes, forming part of an image of Scotland that is treasured by those who live here and those who visit. Any who doubt this need only consider the references that are liberally sprinkled through Scottish literature, celebrating the 'heather braes' and the 'hills of home'. The mountains also underpin the rural economy through outdoor recreation, tourism, agriculture, forestry, deer stalking and grouse shooting.

The hills of Scotland are of modest height by comparison with the Alps, Andes or Himalaya, and it is not for nothing that these are sometimes known as the 'Greater Ranges'. This comparison is, however, misleading, as Scotland's mountains derive their own particular distinction from the combination of their latitude and their position on Europe's Atlantic fringe. The resulting conditions confine tree growth to relatively modest altitudes, and the extent of land above the treeline, which many might regard as the touchstone of the mountains, is comparable with much higher ranges further south, such as the Tatra and Pyrenees. Scotland's mountains combine the influence of a mild, wet 'oceanic' climate with some features of colder, drier ranges of the European mainland, and are a melting pot for wildlife of temperate and arctic zones. Although it has not always been managed sustainably, this natural environment is an asset of international value.

Scientific descriptions tend to isolate particular aspects of the mountain environment and this book adopts a similar approach based on the building blocks of climate, geology, landforms, wildlife and human traces. This separation is only, however, a practical convenience, as these elements are closely interlinked, and the more important or conspicuous relationships are noted at key points throughout the book.

Chapter 1 considers the climate of Scotland's mountains, which is all-pervasive, leaving its imprint on every other aspect of the upland environment. The climate orchestrated the glaciations which carved the hills to something approaching their present forms, and continues to drive relentless weathering and erosion. The mountain climate also creates opportunities and defines limits for all upland plants and animals, including ourselves.

The large-scale geography of the Scottish hills is determined by their geological foundations, which are described in **Chapter 2**. The principal mountain areas are defined, in broad terms, by the presence of hard, resistant rocks, while a number of prominent glens, including Glen Tilt and the Great Glen, correspond to major fault lines. These foundations have been sculpted by a variety of processes, which are discussed in **Chapter 3**. These have included weathering and the movement of debris by ice, wind and water, which act in different ways and to differing extents, according to the underlying rock and pre-existing landform. This combination of factors has created the diverse present-day topography of the mountains, with ground of widely varying altitude, slope and aspect, clothed by bare rock, frost-shattered debris or glacial deposits.

The chemical composition of the underlying rock combines with the local climate and topography to exert a strong influence on the vegetation cover, which is described in **Chapter 4**. This is a two-way process, and the development of vegetation is intertwined with the evolution of the land surface, forming deep blankets of peat, stabilising screes or interacting with other types of mobile rock debris to form terraces and vegetation stripes.

The vegetation of the Scottish mountains is the ecological foundation that supports all other upland wildlife. An extraordinary diversity of invertebrates lives in, on and around upland plants, often depending closely on individual species. This neglected universe of animal life is considered in **Chapter 5** and forms its own ecosystem populated by hunters, hunted and the scavengers that clean up afterwards.

Plants and invertebrates also underpin the birds, mammals and other vertebrates of the Scottish hills, which are described in **Chapters 6** and **7**. The distributions of many upland birds and mammals are closely linked to vegetation, which variously provides food, shelter or cover. The influence of large herbivores, conversely, is imprinted on the vegetation of the hills and does much to determine the balance between woodland, heather moorland and grassland on their lower slopes. Topography and local landform are of direct importance to many upland animals, and stalkers well know that deer move into lee corries during severe weather, while ptarmigan take refuge in summit boulder fields. The conjunction of climate and topography is the undoing of wind-blown insects that are trapped on spring snowfields, and is crucial for the snow buntings that prey upon them.

Human activities influence almost all other aspects of the mountain environment and feature, to varying degrees, in most chapters of this book. **Chapter 8** provides an overview of some of the traces we have left in the uplands, with a particular emphasis on those whose presence or purpose are less obvious. The climate, geology and topography of mountain regions impose clear limits on human land use and settlement, which are well seen by anyone flying over the Highlands on a clear day. This book considers climate, geology, landforms, wildlife and human activity as a logical progression, but in practice they all interweave in a Gordian knot with no single point of entry.

Human imprints have gradually accumulated on Scotland's mountains as a result of successive phases of land use, which have reflected social, economic and political factors as well as environmental constraints. The pace of change has been particularly rapid in recent centuries, beginning with the infamous clearance of subsistence agriculture from many glens in the wake of the Jacobite rising of 1745. This traumatic episode heralded a brief phase of large scale sheep farming, which was in turn succeeded by the widespread development of Victorian sporting estates geared to the stalking of red deer and the shooting of red grouse. A variety of new land uses emerged during the 20th century and have resulted in further profound changes to the uplands, including: the post-war proliferation of large-scale hydro schemes; the spread of vast commercial conifer plantations, and more recently, new forms of renewable energy generation. The mountains are also subject to more insidious human influences from further afield, and the well-documented effects of global warming may, in the longer term, lead to pronounced changes in our upland wildlife.

The growth of both conservation and recreation is changing the terms on which society engages with the mountains. These relatively recent social trends have shifted the balance between production and enjoyment or, in the words of the environmental historian T.C.Smout, between 'use and delight'. These activities now make substantial contributions to the economy of Scotland's remoter areas, and a number of national and international conservation designations seek to protect those aspects of the mountain environment which are considered to be of particular value. One of the clearest indications of this perceptual shift is the growing value that is attributed to wild land areas, which partly reflects a low intensity of land use. **Chapter 9** considers some key issues for the future management of Scotland's mountains.

Upland vegetation is linked to climate, geology and landform. The extensive three-leaved rush heath on the Cairngorm plateau reflects wind exposure and the unstable granite soils

Ciste Dhubh from the east. Over the last 4,500 to 6,000 years, former woodland has declined and blanket peat has expanded, against a background of natural climate change and changing human use of the land

The mountain environment is constantly changing in response to the slow grind of geology and landform evolution, which is difficult if not impossible to relate to human timescales. In *On a Raised Beach*, Hugh MacDiarmid hints at the enormity and inexorability of these processes:

"...these stones are at one with the stars.
It makes no difference to them whether they are high or low,
Mountain peak or ocean floor, palace, or pigsty.
There are plenty of ruined buildings in the world but no ruined stones."

Natural long-term climatic change can also alter the abundance and distribution of different types of vegetation and other wildlife, and can wipe the slate clean through extensive glaciation, although this is thankfully infrequent. Our own sweaty endeavours are of very modest significance against this epic backdrop, and this liberating state of affairs may contribute to the appeal of mountaineering.

Outdoor recreation is important to a growing number of people, who are also part of the mountain environment, if only transiently. Against the background of natural processes and other human activities, recreation is a comparatively minor influence on the Scottish uplands. This is not, however, to suggest that any adverse effects can be ignored, and we all share a responsibility to leave this heritage undiminished, or enriched, for those who will follow. This should require little exhortation, because for those who encounter it at close quarters, Scotland's mountain environment itself provides both inspiration and motivation.

Mountain Climate

Jonathan Gregory and Richard Essery

Tom Prentice

Introduction

For better or worse, Scotland's mountain weather imposes itself on every day that we spend in the hills, and can range from glorious sunshine to life-threatening blizzards, often within the space of a few hours. The art of reading the weather is an essential skill of mountaineering.

The climate is the average behaviour of the weather, and has shaped the landscape over millions of years. The climate also strongly influences upland wildlife and the activities of residents and visitors. Its importance is reflected in names such as Fuar Tholl (cold hole), Sgorr Gaoith (peak of the winds) and Beinn a' Ghlo (mountain with a veil of mist). This chapter describes how Scotland's mountain climate works and how it interacts with the wider mountain environment.

The global climate system

The energy to drive the weather comes from the sun, which is a prodigious energy source. The solar energy input to the climate system is 7000 times more than the total generated by humans from all energy sources (fossil fuels, nuclear and renewables). This incoming energy is not evenly distributed, and varies between latitudes, seasons and times of day. It is also unevenly absorbed, with considerable variation between land and water, white snow and dark vegetation, and north and south facing slopes. The climate system, comprising the atmosphere and ocean, reduces these contrasts by moving heat away from regions where more is absorbed.

The most important factor affecting delivery of the sun's energy is latitude. In the tropics, the sun is high in the sky and supplies on average about six times more heat per square metre of ground than at higher latitudes, where the sun's rays are slanting and there is more reflective cloud, snow and ice. Scotland lies at around 55° N, and on the sole basis of incoming solar energy would be about 50° C colder than at the equator. Under these circumstances, an equatorial temperature of, say, 25° C would translate to a crisp -25° C in the Highlands. However, owing to heat transport, the actual temperature differences are only about half this size.

The phenomenon called the greenhouse effect is a further important influence on the surface temperature. A greenhouse lets in sunlight but inhibits heat loss, so keeping the inside warm. The atmosphere behaves similarly, due to the insulating properties of gases which are present in comparatively small quantities, including carbon dioxide and water vapour. Global average surface temperature is about 15° C, but without the natural greenhouse effect it would be about -18° C.

Depressions and fronts

Scotland lies in mid-latitudes, roughly equidistant from the equator and the North Pole. In these latitudes, the north-south temperature gradient combines with the rotation of the earth to create a prevailing wind which blows roughly from the west. Small meanders in this prevailing westerly flow are magnified by energy derived from horizontal temperature contrasts, especially between warm tropical and cold polar air masses, to form areas of low atmospheric pressure known as mid-latitude depressions.

These depressions frequently form over the western Atlantic, and tend to be particularly intense during the winter, due to the compounding effects of the temperature contrast between the cold land and the relatively warm ocean along the east coast of North America. These weather systems are blown eastwards by a band of strong high-altitude westerly winds called the jet stream, although the depressions move more slowly than the wind and usually take several days to cross the ocean. The continual passage of depressions makes our weather very changeable. Since the jet stream tends to pass close to Scotland, their influence is felt more strongly and frequently in northern Britain.

Depressions are associated with sharp boundaries between warm and cold air masses which are known as fronts, by a military analogy which was developed in Norway after the First World War. The interface between the cold and warm air which gives rise to a depression usually develops into a warm front at the leading edge of the warm air mass, and a cold front at its trailing edge, and these pass over the country in turn. Warm air is less dense than cold air, and the movement of both types of front forces warm air, at all levels from the ground upwards, to ascend over cold air. When damp air rises to higher altitudes, the associated cooling results in condensation of its moisture content, and fronts are therefore associated with clouds and precipitation. Although most cloud and rainfall is associated with fronts, clouds can also develop at other times because of local evaporation from damp ground.

Frontal cloud can take various forms depending on the altitude at which it occurs. While cloud at lower altitude consists of water droplets, high cloud is colder and is formed from ice crystals. Very small droplets or crystals are kept aloft by continual turbulence within the cloud, and precipitation occurs when these particles get big enough literally to fall out of the sky. The highest cloud is the wispy cirrus, whose characteristic vague edges reflect the relatively slow evaporation of ice when turbulence mixes the cloud with the clear air. Lower frontal

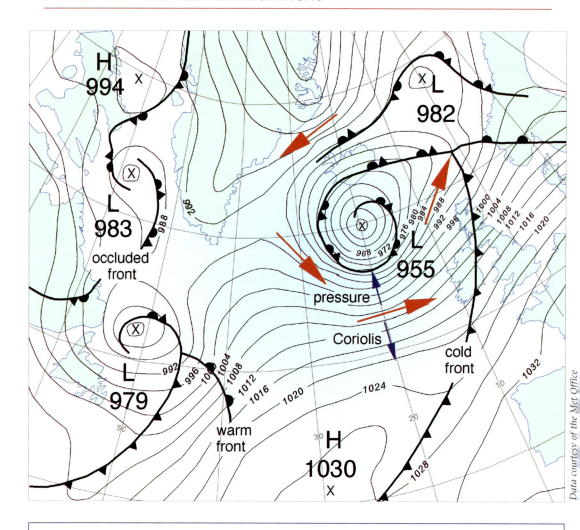

Data courtesy of the Met Office

A map of sea level atmospheric pressure at midnight on 15th January 2003. The contours of pressure (isobars) are marked in millibars with 'H' and 'L' indicating high and low pressure centres; a deep low pressure centre (depression) lies south of Iceland. The symbols denoting warm, cold and occluded fronts point in the direction in which the front is moving.

In this map, a warm front has recently passed over Scotland and a cold front is moving over the country. The wind direction is indicated by red arrows. The wind does not blow directly from high to low pressure, but circulates anticlockwise round low pressure centres, because moving objects in the northern hemisphere have a tendency to veer right due to the rotation of the Earth (the Coriolis effect). While the wind is blowing anticlockwise around the depression, the pressure force pulling inwards is nearly balanced by the Coriolis force pushing outwards (blue arrows), causing the airflow to circle the depression.

Winds near ground level actually blow slightly inwards towards the depression, rather than directly along the isobars, due to friction at the surface. Closely spaced isobars mean strong pressure gradients and high winds, and on the day shown there were gusts of up to 80 mph in the Highlands.

cloud, by contrast, often produces a featureless sheet and is responsible for continuous rain or snow.

Astute hillgoers can identify the nature of approaching fronts from the sequence in which these cloud formations appear. The boundary between warm and cold air is tilted, with the cold air underneath. This means that the leading edge of a cold front is near the earth's surface, with successively higher cloud and precipitation behind it, while the first signs of a warm front are high cloud, succeeded by lower cloud and precipitation, with the warm air arriving at the surface last of all. Cold fronts move relatively fast and can catch up with preceding warm fronts, creating so-called occluded fronts, which are boundaries between cold air masses at the ground, with warmer air aloft. An occluded front may be marked by a modest change in temperature, also accompanied by cloud and precipitation. The succession of fronts, of various types, is largely responsible for Scotland's changeable weather.

Depressions also influence the strength and direction of the wind, which meanders anticlockwise around low pressure centres and clockwise around areas of high pressure. Scotland consequently experiences changing wind strengths and directions as a depression goes past. Winds from different directions bring contrasting conditions. Southerly winds are generally warm and northerly generally cold, while easterly winds tend to be cold in winter and warm in summer. For example, winds from the east brought bitterly cold temperatures and widespread snowfall to the UK in the winter of 2009 – 2010. On account of the average course taken by the depressions, however, the prevailing wind is somewhat south of west. The characteristics of this airflow have very important implications for Scotland's climate.

The climate of Scotland

The prevailing westerly airstream strongly influences the general climate of this country. This airflow is generally moist, because winds blowing over the ocean evaporate water, leading in turn to frequent cloud cover and high annual rainfall. Scotland's climate is also very windy, particularly in the west, as the ocean presents no physical obstruction to check the force of the Atlantic gales. These general effects are greatly amplified in the hills.

The prevalence of westerly winds also means that extreme temperatures are rare. It takes a lot of heat to warm up the ocean, which is therefore cooler in summer than the air over land. During the winter, conversely, the ocean is warmer than the land and releases heat stored in the summer, as a ceramic hob continues to heat the saucepan after it has been switched off. Winds coming from the Atlantic therefore moderate the seasons, keeping Scotland relatively cool in summer and warm in winter compared with other places on the same latitude.

This combination of factors defines what is sometimes referred to as an 'oceanic' climate, and the natural vegetation of Scotland is characterised by many plants, including the ubiquitous heather, which are closely associated with these conditions.

Scotland's climate history

The most important factor influencing climate, over geological timescales, is the movement of continents. Scotland has experienced very different climates in the past, for example when it lay in tropical latitudes around 300 million years ago. The most obvious marks of climate change on the mountain landscape derive, however, from the Ice Age of the last 2.6 million years.

This period has been associated with numerous climate shifts, which are believed to be driven by cyclic variations in the Earth's orbit and axis of rotation. Cold phases, or 'glacials', were characterised by the expansion of ice cover across much of North America and northern Eurasia. The cooling was reinforced by two important positive feedbacks from the climate system. The growing ice cover reflected energy from the sun, causing a reduction in surface temperature, and the atmospheric carbon dioxide concentration fell, for reasons not yet wholly understood, reducing the greenhouse effect. These processes combined to encourage further ice accumulation. Warmer ice-free epochs, or 'interglacials', have occurred during this period at intervals of around 100,000 years, and our present climate represents one such interlude.

The last glaciation reached its maximum extent in Scotland about 26,000 years ago, when all but the southernmost part of the British Isles was covered by an immense ice sheet which retreated, with some temporary reversals, over the following 11,000 years. The receding ice left behind a landscape transformed by glacial erosion, with numerous corries, glacial troughs and other spectacular features. Periods of less extensive glaciation, during which temperatures remained generally cold, gave rise to so-called 'periglacial' conditions, associated with intense freeze-thaw activity. These have resulted in numerous smaller scale features which are common in the Scottish hills.

The present interglacial, called the Holocene, has enjoyed a relatively stable climate, but this has not been without variation. The climate of about 6000 years ago is referred to as the 'Holocene optimum' because summer in the Northern Hemisphere was somewhat warmer than now. Subsequent climatic trends, along with human activities, have greatly reduced the extent of woodland, helping to establish the open upland landscapes of the present day.

The mountain climate

Mountainous terrain tends to create its own weather, greatly amplifying some of the characteristics of our mild, wild and wet climate. Between 1883 and 1904, the Victorian observatory on the summit of Ben Nevis provided a unique opportunity to directly observe mountain weather, and William Kilgour's *Twenty Years on Ben Nevis* provides a remarkable anecdotal account of the elements at work. Scotland's mountain climate continues to be monitored by a number of weather stations, including the automated installation on the summit of Cairn Gorm, and the resulting data has added greatly to our understanding.

Pressure

Some of the most important climatic effects of mountains are linked to the decline in atmospheric pressure with altitude. Atmospheric pressure is caused by the weight of overlying air and averages 1016 millibars (mbar, or hectopascals, which are exactly the same) at sea level, decreasing by 10mbar, or about 1%, for every 100m of altitude gain. At the altitude of Ben Nevis (1344m), the average atmospheric pressure is about 860mbar, meaning that each lungful contains only 85% of the amount of air (including oxygen) that it does at sea level. As the pressure falls, the air becomes less dense, so pressure declines more slowly as altitude increases. For comparison, the average pressures at the altitudes of Mont Blanc (4807m) and Everest (8850m) are 560mbar and 320mbar respectively.

The variation of pressure with altitude does not show in the isobars plotted on weather maps, which are 'corrected' to sea level. The variation in sea-level pressure

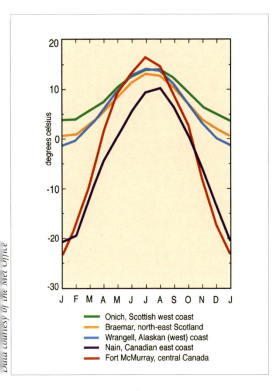

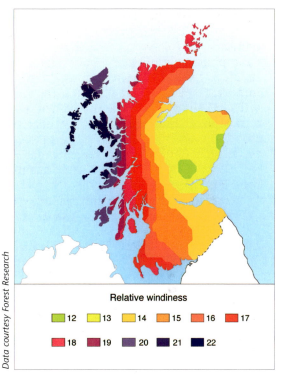

Data courtesy of the Met Office

Data courtesy Forest Research

Onich, Scottish west coast
Braemar, north-east Scotland
Wrangell, Alaskan (west) coast
Nain, Canadian east coast
Fort McMurray, central Canada

Relative windiness

| 12 | 13 | 14 | 15 | 16 | 17 |
| 18 | 19 | 20 | 21 | 22 |

Left: Seasonal temperature variation (average of 1931-1960) at locations on Scottish latitudes. The influence of Atlantic airflow moderates the climate across all Scottish mountain areas, and a comparable effect is seen for Wrangell in Alaska. Fort McMurray lies close to the Birch Mountains in central Canada, while Nain lies on the Newfoundland coast, where the prevailing winds are coming off the land rather than the ocean. In both instances, the climate is much more extreme with a very high annual temperature range.

Right: Variation in windiness across Scotland. This map refers to exposed sites at sea level; windiness increases by 2 units for every 100m of altitude and decreases by up to 9 units in sheltered glens. Scores of 12 and 22 correspond to mean annual wind speeds of approximately 7mph and 16mph respectively.

due to the passage of high- and low-pressure mid-latitude weather systems is much smaller than the variation of pressure with altitude. The lowest pressure ever recorded in a mid-latitude depression over the Atlantic was 916mbar, during the storm of January 1993 which led to the break-up of the oil tanker Braer off Shetland. A pressure of 936mbar was recorded at Stornoway Airport on Christmas Eve 2013, the lowest recorded over land in the British Isles since 1886.

Temperature

The reduction in pressure at Munro height does not create a physiological problem for hillwalkers, and is only directly apparent from the bulging of water bottles when these are taken up a mountain. The reduction in pressure is, however, largely responsible for the decrease in temperature with altitude, which

Cool air condensing in the valleys can generate memorable temperature inversions for hillwalkers on the tops the following day, as in this view from Beinn Alligin to Liathach

is much more obvious on the hill.

As warm air rises, the pressure on it reduces and it consequently expands. In doing so it has to push against the prevailing atmospheric pressure. This takes energy and cools the warm air down. The rate of decline of pressure with altitude thus sets the rate at which temperature falls, called the lapse rate.

In dry air, the lapse rate is 1° C per 100m of altitude, but in moist air, as is usual in Scotland, the temperature does not fall so quickly. Air near the surface is generally moist because of evaporation, and more water vapour can be contained in air at higher temperatures. If the warm moist air rises and cools, some of the vapour condenses. This process releases energy as heat. The net lapse rate in saturated air is consequently around 0.6° C per 100m. The actual lapse rate in the Scottish mountains is generally somewhere between these extremes, and can be greatly compounded by the effects of wind chill.

The lapse rate can be less than 0.6° C per 100m if other factors heat the air above or cool it below. This can occur on clear nights when the ground tends to cool down more than the air, producing an inversion in the lower atmosphere so that the temperature increases with height, reversing the usual situation. This happens particularly in valleys, where a cold layer can build up near the ground. Some of the water in the cooling air condenses into small droplets, creating fog, and those fortunate enough to be on ridges and summits on the following morning may look down on glens filled with cloud. The clear cold nights favourable to temperature inversions are most likely to occur during the winter months, and when high pressure systems prevail.

Spectacular inversions are experiences to savour. In *Mountaineering in Scotland*, W.H.Murray describes a winter ascent of Tower Ridge in which: 'The corrie was roofed by an even fleece of cloud, which lapped against the wall of the ridge several hundred feet below and ran down the full length of the Allt a' Mhuillin glen, where the surface was sunset-fired. The red-gold of the sky, coming so suddenly after hard climbing along an ice-clad wall, literally stopped my breath.'

The typical mountain temperature gradient is not only important to hillwalkers, but also to vegetation, which changes considerably with altitude. This ecological principle is common to mountain areas throughout the world, although Scotland's oceanic climate shifts the zones of vegetation downhill by comparison with most other mountains of similar latitude.

Wind

Wind is a prominent and often memorable feature of Scotland's mountains, and is associated with the shifting patterns of high and low air pressure discussed earlier. The strongest winds are associated with the deepest, most energetic, depressions, and consequently occur in winter.

Rough features on the ground, such as boulders and trees, obstruct and slow down the air moving over them, and winds thus get stronger with height above the surface. Winds can therefore be two or three times greater on tops than they are in open, low country at the same time, and tend to be particularly high on exposed ridges and isolated peaks, where the air experiences relatively little resistance from the ground. The automatic weather station on the summit of Cairn Gorm holds the record for the highest wind speed in the UK, of 176 mph on 3 January 1993. Wind is also accelerated on being forced up over a mountain, leading to higher speeds on windward slopes and marked differences across a summit ridge. On a much smaller scale, there may be drastic differences in the microclimate on windward and lee sides of a boulder or outcrop.

The shape of individual mountains can strongly influence wind speed if, for example, winds are funnelled into suitably aligned bealachs. The air flow can separate from the surface when descending steep lee slopes, giving generally lighter but highly variable winds on one side of the hill. This effect may result in blustery winds coming from unpredictable directions in corries which might otherwise be expected to be sheltered, as many climbers will have experienced on Ben Nevis and in the Northern Corries. Some of the strongest gusts, as opposed to average wind speeds, occur in this way.

In addition to obstructing the large-scale flow of the atmosphere, mountains can generate local winds on their slopes. Cooling at night creates dense air which runs downhill as katabatic winds, and the stagnation of this cold air in sheltered hollows can make such places a chilly choice for a campsite.

High winds can directly affect mountain slopes and summits by scouring away loose soil or gravel, to be redeposited in lee sites. Wind exposure is a major influence on mountain vegetation, both by direct physical battering and more indirect effects linked, for example, to the distribution of snow. High winds also make life difficult for upland animals, which usually cope by avoidance, and only humans choose to be on high ground in such conditions.

Cloud and rain

Air is forced to rise when it blows over high ground, and if it is cool and damp, condensation will readily occur. The topography of mountain areas thus accentuates the effects of the procession of incoming fronts, resulting in low cloud (or 'hill fog') and rain on high ground. It is common for the skies to be clear over the relatively flat Hebrides, while hills on the mainland are covered in cloud, and most hillwalkers will be able to recall memorable drenchings in the mountains on days when the weather in the lowlands was merely bad.

Cloud may also result from other processes which cause air to be lifted, and which can be accentuated in the Scottish hills. Such circumstances can arise during sunny conditions when water evaporates from damp ground into warm air. As this air rises and cools, the moisture condenses into puffy clouds, which are initially of benign appearance but develop into taller and darker rainclouds. These clouds are promoted by mountainous terrain, because slopes facing the sun heat up quickly and because the forced ascent of air over the hills adds to the influence of warming. The fact that such cloud is not uniform is an indication of the complex variation of the land surface and the chaotic behaviour of the atmosphere. High pressure conditions may, however, keep a 'lid' on the ascending air, so that the condensation produces a lumpy sheet of cloud. Since sunshine drives the evaporation, these clouds and the associated showery rain or thunderstorms

Lenticular clouds over Gars-bheinn, Cuillin of Skye. The smooth and elongated shapes of the clouds show that moist air is being forced to rise as it flows over the mountains

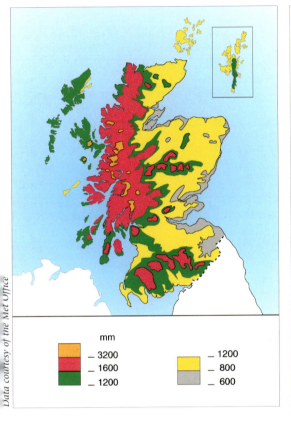

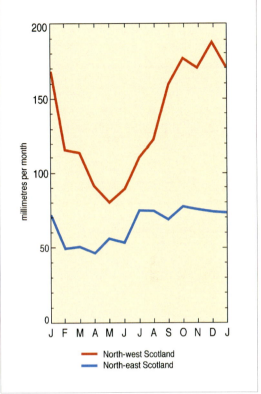

Left: Average annual precipitation across Scotland. Precipitation is much greater over western mountain areas, which have about twice the annual rainfall of more eastern ranges.

Right: The annual precipitation cycle for northern Scotland. The data are averages from several rain gauges in each of the regions over 1931-1988. The uneven seasonal distribution of precipitation arises because more intense depressions occur during the winter, but evaporation from the ocean surface is greater under warm conditions. Precipitation is consequently relatively high in the autumn and low in the spring.

are more common in summer, and tend to build up during the day and dissipate in the evening. Summer days in the hills may often therefore start fine and have glorious evenings, with less pleasant hours in between.

Under certain conditions, mountains can trigger the formation of characteristic lens-shaped, or lenticular, clouds. This happens if there is a layer of damp air between drier layers. On being forced up over high ground, moisture in this layer condenses to produce cloud, which evaporates again as the air descends on the lee side. If there is more than one moist layer, the same phenomenon may happen at several levels, causing a stack of lenticular clouds known, for obvious reasons, as a 'pile of plates'. Sometimes the air continues to bounce up and down as it streams

Andy Nisbet

Snow tends to be rapidly redistributed from windward to lee slopes and has been scoured from this exposed slope to reveal the compacted footprints of a previous visitor

away downwind of the mountain, producing a succession of such clouds at regular intervals in its wake. Lenticular clouds are distinctive because they do not appear to move. In fact, the layers of air are moving along like conveyor belts, with condensation and evaporation occurring at stationary points through which the layers pass. This type of cloud can form when strong winds are blowing continuously in one direction across the mountains and increasing with height. Favourable conditions are more common in winter and when a front is near.

These processes, alone and in combination, result in very frequent cloud cover and high rainfall over the mountains, and precipitation from high frontal cloud often falls into low cloud on the hills, stimulating further condensation. Air passing eastward across the Scottish mountains releases a lot of its moisture over western hills, so the east of the country is in a rain shadow and is drier and less cloudy. This is demonstrated by precipitation data from Onich, Dalwhinnie and Braemar, which record annual rainfall of 2000mm, 1200mm and 900mm respectively. The rain shadow effect can also be seen on the scale of individual mountains, which tend to have a higher cloudbase on lee slopes than on the windward side, where the air is relatively moist.

It is also warmer to the east of the hills because with less cloud there is more sunshine, and because of the so-called föhn effect. This phenomenon arises because of the difference in lapse rates between moisture-laden rising air on the windward side and drier descending air to leeward, resulting in an overall increase in the temperature of air as it crosses mountain areas. The föhn effect can be very important in higher mountain ranges, but is also significant in Scotland – in westerly conditions in summer it can make the east coast of Scotland the warmest place in Britain.

The wet climate of the Scottish hills drives various processes of landscape change, and numerous rivers gradually transport the mountains to the sea. Not surprisingly, the high rainfall is also reflected in mountain vegetation, with an abundance of plants characteristic of high humidity and wet peaty soils. Against this background, however, the climatic contrast between western and eastern upland areas is associated with highly visible differences in vegetation and land use, which are explored in later chapters.

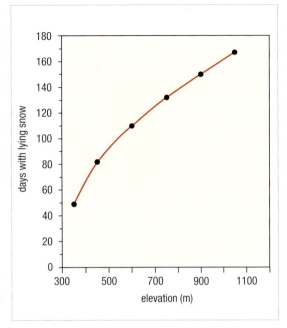

Numbers of days with lying snow observed at Dalwhinnie (351 m above sea level) and on the surrounding hills during the winter of 1992-1993.

Snow

Scotland's particular combination of latitude and oceanicity means that snow is essentially confined to the winter months and the summer and winter hills seem like two different ranges of mountains. Whether precipitation arrives at the earth's surface as rain or snow depends on the air temperature and humidity, and the majority of the rain which falls in mid-latitudes forms as snow and melts on its way down. Snow is obviously more likely to fall and lie on the mountains, because it is colder than in the glens.

The annual duration of snow cover in the Highlands increases by roughly 15 days for every 100m of ascent. North-facing and gentler slopes experience cooler and more humid conditions and tend to retain snow for longer. This effect is compounded by our strong winter winds, which very efficiently redistribute both falling and fallen snow. Blowing snow settles in sheltered topographic features such as lee slopes, corries and smaller hollows, which are typically north- to east-facing. This combination of factors ensures that the pattern of snow-lie is extremely uneven in spatial terms, but broadly consistent from year to year, and isolated snow patches survive well into the summer on some shady lee slopes and in hollows. In particularly favoured locations, such as Garbh Choire Mor on Braeriach, snow patches can survive throughout the year.

The snowpack is built up in layers by successive winter storms, and is gradually compacted by processes of metamorphism which cause the crystals to become rounded and pack more closely. This happens more rapidly at higher temperatures

Rime ice attaching to exposed grass on the northern flanks of Meall an t-Seallaidh, Southen Highlands

and in moister conditions, and is augmented by the effects of strong winds, which shatter and pack the surface crystals to form areas of hard windslab. Snow is not the only source of surface ice, which can also be deposited as frost, or by the freezing of rain or water on the ground. Freezing fog deposits soft feathery ice crystals, known as rime, on the upwind side of rocks, plants and structures such as cairns or fence posts. These accumulations can be very substantial and Kilgour reported that on Ben Nevis: "Fog-crystals presented a most interesting and fantastic spectacle … These crystals have been seen to grow to a length of about six feet".

Snow is a poor conductor of heat and there can be a large temperature difference between the base and the surface of the snowpack. This temperature gradient is important to mountaineers as it encourages the formation of depth hoar, a layer of large and loosely bonded crystals at the base of the snowpack which contributes to the development of avalanche hazard. It is also, however, important to some plants and animals, providing a protective blanket while blizzards rage above. Particular types of vegetation are associated with areas of high snow cover.

Sunshine

The amount of sunshine falling on slopes is strongly influenced by their aspect and angle, which are highly variable in mountain landscapes. When the sun is low in winter, steep south-facing slopes can receive more sunshine than level ground. North-facing and gentle slopes experience correspondingly cooler conditions and higher humidity and this is often reflected by their vegetation.

Under cloudless skies, the energy from the sun reaching ground level increases by approximately 1.5% per 100m increase in altitude, because it has passed through less atmosphere on the way. High levels of solar radiation are consequently a major feature of higher altitudes in many of the Greater Ranges, and some alpine plants are specifically adapted to cope with this. The relatively modest height of Scottish hills, however, means that such altitudinal effects are relatively small. Indeed, incoming solar energy actually decreases with altitude under typical Scottish conditions because of the greater cloud cover.

Climate change

Global climate change has become an issue of worldwide public concern in recent years. Due mostly to combustion of coal, oil and natural gas, the atmospheric concentration of carbon dioxide has increased more rapidly in the past century than at any previous time in the last 22,000 years, and is higher now than it has been for at least 800,000 years. A higher concentration of carbon dioxide means a stronger greenhouse effect and a warmer climate. Global average surface temperature has increased by about 0.8°C since the 19th century, and the last 30-year average is probably the warmest for more than 1000 years in the Northern Hemisphere. Unlike the slow climate changes earlier in the Holocene and during the Ice Age, this warming has not been caused by variations in the Earth's orbit or axis. It is highly likely that most of the warming over the last 50 years has been caused by the increase in greenhouse gas concentrations due to human activities.

There is considerable uncertainty about what may happen during the 21st century, but a lot depends on future emissions of greenhouse gases, and various scenarios suggest a further rise in global average surface temperature of up to about 5°C. For comparison, the difference in global average temperature between cold phases during the Ice Age and the present day is of the magnitude of a few degrees. To have a 50% chance of keeping global warming below 2°C compared with the late 19th century, the maximum amount of carbon dioxide that can be emitted is no more than about thirty years' worth at the current rate.

For Scotland, climate modelling predicts a greater warming in summer than in winter, along with reduced summer precipitation and increased winter precipitation (with less falling as snow). Overall the extent and duration of snow and ice cover will probably diminish. Climate change could also affect the mountain environment in a number of other ways, shifting the altitudinal zones of vegetation uphill and resulting in the loss of mountain species which are close to the limits of their range in Scotland. Extreme precipitation is also expected to become more frequent, providing greater impetus to certain natural processes of landscape change, such as debris flows and the downstream movement of material by rivers. In the higher mountains, the general recession of glaciers is expected to continue.

In 1992, the international community resolved to stabilise greenhouse gas concentrations at levels that would prevent dangerous interference with the climate system. Since then, negotiations have continued in pursuit of this aim. Substantial climate change is already inevitable over the coming century, but decisions and actions taken in 2015 and the following few years will have a very large effect on the long-term future of the global climate, and of Scotland's mountain environment.

Geological Foundations

Kathryn Goodenough

The magnificent granite face of Cir Mhor, Arran

Introduction

The mountains of Scotland have been shaped by a variety of processes, but under-pinning them all is the country's rich and complex geological heritage. Scotland's geological history spans two-thirds of the lifetime of the Earth, and reflects a range of past environments from dry deserts to the ocean floor. For much of that time, Scotland has been mountainous, but some of our past mountain ranges were at least Alpine, and possibly Himalayan, in scale. This chapter will describe the main types of rock that make up Scotland's mountains and the processes by which they came into being.

Plate tectonics

In order to appreciate the history of Scotland's mountains, it is important to understand some fundamental geological processes, of which the most important is plate tectonics. The ground on which we walk is not static and the outer layer of the Earth, or lithosphere, including the crust and part of the upper mantle, con-sists of several separate plates. These plates are up to 100km thick in the centres of the continents, but beneath the ocean they are typically about 10 km in thick-ness. The material beneath the plates, the asthenosphere, is solid but behaves rather like plasticine, and can flow, over geological timescales, carrying the plates with it. Where two plates come together, they can move slowly past each other in various directions, often causing earthquakes as they grind together. Plates which underlie oceans are relatively dense, and can sink below other plates at subduc-tion zones. Under these circumstances, the subducting crustal plates melt as they descend, producing magma that may be erupted from volcanoes at the surface. If, by contrast, two continental plates collide, they do not sink into the mantle. Instead, the crustal material crumples up, squeezing and deforming the rocks to create mountain ranges, a process which is currently active in the Himalaya. When neighbouring plates move apart, molten rock wells up from the mantle to form new crust, creating volcanoes such as those seen on Iceland.

Scotland presently lies in the centre of the European continental plate and is geologically stable, with few earthquakes and no volcanoes. However, this has not always been the case, and Scotland's rocks record a turbulent past with long periods of intense geological activity. Until a little over 400 million years ago, Scotland was joined to Greenland and lay on a separate continental plate from England. This dramatic history is recorded in a wide variety of rock types across the Scottish uplands.

Igneous, metamorphic and sedimentary rocks

There are essentially three main types of rocks: igneous, metamorphic and sedimentary. Igneous rocks are formed by the cooling and solidification of molten rock, or magma. The first rocks formed on Earth were of this type and igneous rocks are continuing to form in areas of volcanic activity all over the world. Magma may be erupted onto the surface or may solidify underground, resulting in two broad types of igneous rock, which are respectively termed 'extrusive' and 'intrusive'.

The precise rock type that forms depends upon the chemical composition of the magma and the length of time that it takes to cool (see Rock identification (p46-53). Magma that emerges onto the Earth's surface cools very quickly and only small crystals have time to grow. Extrusive igneous rocks are therefore typically fine-grained, such as the basalt of the Quiraing on Skye or the rhyolite of Buachaille Etive Mor. At the other extreme, some intrusive rocks result from the very slow cooling of a large body of magma, so that large crystals grow. Such rocks are coarse-grained, like the gabbro of the Skye Cuillin or the granite of the Cairngorms. If the magma is intruded up cracks in the crust towards the surface, but cools and solidifies before it gets there, the cooling time will fall between these two extremes and a medium-grained rock will result. In this case, the body of rock will often have a sheet-like shape because it formed within a crack, and may be either vertical (a dyke) or horizontal or gently sloping (a sill).

The other two broad rock types are derived from pre-existing rocks. Metamorphic rocks form when igneous or sedimentary rocks are buried deep within the Earth's crust, for instance during a mountain building event. The rocks are changed or metamorphosed by intense heat and pressure, so that existing minerals are broken down and new ones grow in their place. Not surprisingly, these depend on the particular temperature and pressure of metamorphism, and on the chemical composition of the original rock. Rocks that were rich in mud and clay, for example, contain abundant aluminium and encourage the formation of minerals such as mica, which forms prominent crystals that are flat and sheet-like. This process can also result in the development of new textures; for example, when mica crystals form under pressure, the flat sheets will lie parallel to each other, giving the rock a pronounced breaking direction or cleavage. Examples of metamorphic rocks in Scotland include the Lewisian gneisses of the North-west Highlands and the mica schists that underlie much of the Central Highlands.

Sedimentary rocks form when existing rocks are brought to the surface and eroded by wind, water or ice. The resulting sand, mud, and rock fragments are eventually redeposited as sediments in a variety of environments, including

In this view north-west from Conival, the quartzites of Na Tuadhan on Beinn an Fhurain have been buckled and folded as they were moved westwards along thrusts in the Moine Thrust zone

rivers, lakes or the sea floor. These deposits are compressed as they accumulate, and a variety of processes cause the grains to become cemented together. Sedimentary rocks are soft compared with igneous and metamorphic rocks, and are consequently less important in Scotland's mountain areas. Key exceptions, however, are the Torridonian sandstones and Cambrian quartzites of the North-west Highlands.

Faults and thrusts

Tectonic activity within the Earth's crust can affect the physical structure of existing rocks, often on a very large scale, and they can fracture and move against each other along lines known as faults. Similar phenomena occur on many different scales and may be observed in rocks that can be held in the hand or on cliffs hundreds of metres high. The appearance of Scotland's mountain landscape is controlled by major faults, in particular the Highland Boundary Fault, which runs from Stonehaven down to the Mull of Kintyre, separating the Highlands from the much softer rocks of the Midland Valley. During mountain building events, layers of rock can be thrust over each other like snow being cleared by a snowplough, and this process is recorded in the Moine Thrust Zone of the North-west Highlands.

Scotland's geological history

The geological history of Scotland is long, varied and amazingly complicated, and the rocks of our mountains range in age from 55 million to 3,000 million years. The oldest of these are the Lewisian gneisses of the North-west Highlands, which are also among the most ancient rocks in Europe. This complex series of metamorphic rocks originated as granites and has recently been dated by analysis of tiny zircon crystals. Uranium in these crystals decays at a known rate to form certain isotopes of lead, and precise measurement of these indicates when the crystal was formed. These results suggest that the original rocks were formed as granites almost 3,000 million years ago, and at that time these may have been part of completely different continental masses.

These rocks developed into the Lewisian gneisses through a long and convoluted history which extended over 1,500 million years, one third of the age of the Earth. It is difficult to disentangle events during this great expanse of time, but it is clear that the granites were buried and metamorphosed during several mountain building events related to the collision of ancient continents. New igneous rocks also continued to form during this period. These included a distinctive suite of dark coloured, iron-rich dolerite sheets known as the Scourie Dykes, and a series of pink granite sheets. Both rock types can be seen cutting through the granitic gneisses in many places; particularly good examples can be seen around the shores of Loch Torridon. It is clear that by about 1,650 million years ago, all the continental masses had come together in a final collision, and the Lewisian gneisses looked much as they do today. These rocks, which are referred to as a single unit, record as long a span of time as the entire remainder of Scotland's geological history.

By around 1,000 million years ago, the last range of mountains had been eroded away and the Lewisian gneisses were exposed at the Earth's surface. At that time, Scotland and North America were part of the same great supercontinent and lay south of the equator. The land was still devoid of life and the surface of this continent was a barren landscape over which broad rivers flowed. These rivers carried with them sand and pebbles that had been eroded from a mountain range to the

west, possibly in modern-day Canada. As the rivers spread out they gradually dumped their loads of sediment, and thick layers of sand and pebbles accumulated to a depth of several kilometres, forming the Torridonian sandstone that can be seen in the north-west today. At the same time that the Torridonian was being laid down on land, sand and mud eroded from the land surface were gradually accumulating in the seas to the east, at the margin of the continent. This was the unremarkable beginning of the Moine rocks, which today form many of Scotland's most remote mountains to the north and west of the Great Glen.

The next bit of Scotland's history is rather confused, and the evidence is fragmented and obscured. The deposition of the Torridonian and Moine rocks ceased about 900 million years ago, but exactly what caused this is uncertain; was there yet another continental

Intermediate Gully, Raeburn's Buttress, Ben Nevis; such features generally correspond to faults in the surrounding rock

Scotland's Mountain Environment

Time period	Millions of years ago	What happened in Scotland's mountains?
Quaternary	present – 2.6	Glaciation shaped the mountains
Neogene	2.6 – 24	As global temperatures decreased, sea levels gradually fell, and further uplift brought Scotland's mountains to roughly their current heights above sea level
Palaeogene	24 – 65	As the North Atlantic began to open, volcanoes developed down the west coast of Scotland. The Scottish landmass began to rise relative to sea level
Cretaceous	65 – 142	Scotland was largely an exposed landmass surrounded by shallow seas
Jurassic	142 – 205	Much of Scotland was still high ground, but shallow seas flooded the west coast and the Moray Firth area. Ammonites and belemnites, sharks and plesiosaurs swam in the seas, and dinosaurs roamed the shores
Triassic	205 – 248	Most of Scotland remained as a dry landmass
Permian	248 – 290	Scotland was largely dry and desert-like, with some volcanic activity
Carboniferous	290 – 354	Erosion of the Caledonian mountain chain continued. Central Scotland formed a low-lying area where sediments were deposited in lakes, rivers and swamps, punctuated by periodic volcanic activity
Devonian	354 – 417	Sediments eroded from the Caledonian mountain chain were deposited on the floor of large lakes, in which lived many primitive fish and other creatures. Volcanic eruptions were common, with major calderas at Glencoe and Ben Nevis. Beneath the volcanoes, magma crystallised in chambers to form granites
Silurian	417 – 443	Collision of the continents that included England and Scotland, building the Caledonian mountain chain and metamorphosing the Moine rocks. Rocks in the present-day Northern Highlands and Southern Uplands were pushed over each other, forming thrust zones. Magma, rising into the base of the mountain chain, cooled and crystallised to form granites
Ordovician	443 – 495	First mountain-building event, with a volcanic island chain colliding with the Scottish margin and leading to the metamorphism of the Dalradian rocks. Sediments eroded from the mountain chain were deposited on the ocean floor
Cambrian	495 – 545	Scotland lay on the margin of an ancient ocean, with quartzites formed as beach sand, and limestones and mudstones laid down offshore. Early life, including trilobites, inhabited the ocean
Proterozoic	545 – 2500	Scotland lay within a supercontinent, which was stretched and eventually pulled apart to form a major ocean. The Torridonian, Moine and Dalradian rocks were laid down as sediments
Archaean	Before 2500	Formation of the Lewisian gneisses

collision, and another mountain building event? By about 700 million years ago, Scotland was situated within a major continent that was gradually being pulled apart by tectonic forces, leading to the formation of an ocean. The rocks deposited between about 700 and 540 million years ago are extremely varied. Sands and muds were formed in the ocean, but there was also at least one extensive period of glaciation and a major episode of volcanism as the continent was stretched to breaking point. The resulting complex group of rocks is now known as the Dalradian, and underlies much of the Southern and Central Highlands.

Deposition of the Dalradian rocks appears to have ceased around, or not long after, 500 million years ago, in the late Cambrian period. At that time, much of Scotland was under the sea, on the edge of a major continent called Laurentia. The youngest Dalradian rocks, which now form the Southern Highlands, were laid down in fairly deep water. Other sediments were deposited at the same time on beaches and in tidal lagoons on the continental margin, and these became the quartzites and limestones of the North-west Highlands.

The next hundred million years were to be of crucial importance in the history of Scotland's mountains. 500 million years ago, a wide ocean separated Scotland and England, but that ocean was gradually narrowing as the oceanic crust sank beneath the continent of Laurentia at a subduction zone. This meant that the continent that contained England was moving rapidly northwards towards Scotland. At this time, the Scotland that we know today did not exist as a single entity, and the present-day Highlands were probably a series of small slivers of continental crust that may have been widely separated from each other.

About 470 million years ago, a chain of volcanic islands within this ocean collided with the edge of the Laurentian continent, crumpling up the rocks at the margin and burying them beneath a chain of mountains, where they were metamorphosed. In this way, the sands and muds at the continental margin were changed into the Dalradian schists of the Southern and Central Highlands. However, this Grampian mountain-building event was relatively small in scale, and many of the rocks of the Northern Highlands were unaffected.

A far more major mountain building event occurred some 430 million years ago, when England collided with Scotland. At about the same time, the Scandinavian continent also came up next to the Scottish margin, squeezing the rocks still further. This important event is known as the Caledonian orogeny, and formed a mountain range that may have been comparable in scale to the Alps. At this time, the rocks of the Northern and Western Highlands were buried, folded and deeply metamorphosed. The Moine rocks, which had formed on the edge of the ancient continent some 500 million years earlier, were forced about a hundred kilometres westwards over the top of the Lewisian gneisses and Torridonian sandstones. The immense fracture in the Earth's crust over which these rocks moved is known as the Moine Thrust and is a major structure that controls much of the geology of the Northern Highlands. The line that marks where the Moine Thrust comes to the surface runs from Loch Eriboll on the north coast down to Skye. West of this boundary are virtually undeformed Torridonian sandstones, together with quartzites and limestones of Cambrian age, which lie on the ancient Lewisian gneisses. To the east of the thrust, by contrast, are highly deformed and metamorphosed Moine rocks.

Other significant faults were also active at this time, and movement along the Great Glen brought the present day Central and Northern Highlands adjacent to each other. The collision of England and Scotland also had repercussions further to the south. As the two continents moved together, sediments from the disappearing ocean floor were swept up and squeezed between the two continents. The resulting stack of sediments, largely sandstones, now forms the Southern Uplands.

Following this major mountain-building event, volcanoes developed across much of what is now Scotland, as beneath the thickened crust of the mountain belt the mantle melted to form magma. The lavas that were formed through eruption from these volcanoes are only preserved in a few places, notably including Ben Nevis and Glen Coe. However, deep beneath the volcanoes, magma cooled slowly to form large bodies of granite. After hundreds of millions of years of erosion, these granites are now seen at the surface forming mountains such as the Cairngorms.

By the time this volcanic event had ceased, the rocks of most of the Highland mountains had formed. Scotland was once again in the centre of a great supercontinent, which was to exist for over 300 million years. A brief period of further volcanism around 350 million years ago formed the hills of the Midland Valley, such as the Campsie Fells. However, the last great event in the geological story of Scotland's mountains did not occur until about 60 million years ago. At this time, North America was breaking away from Europe as the Atlantic slowly opened. A series of massive volcanoes developed along the line of the break, roughly corresponding to what is now Scotland's north-western coast. Each volcano only lasted for a relatively short period, with less than a million years of discontinuous activity, before being rapidly eroded to expose the magma chamber beneath. These magma chambers today form some of Scotland's most dramatic mountains on Arran, Mull and Rum, and the mountaineer's paradise – the Skye Cuillin. The rise of hot buoyant magma beneath the earth's surface also led to uplift of the continental masses on the Atlantic margins. The evidence of this process can still be seen across the Scottish hills, and is described in the next chapter.

Scotland's mountains thus have a long and complex geological history, and this sketch can only provide a brief overview. This legacy is directly reflected in the landscapes of different mountain areas, which are now considered in more detail.

North-west Highlands and Western Isles

The north-western part of the Scottish mainland, west of the Moine Thrust, together with the Western Isles, forms a geologically distinct unit. The Inner Hebrides, by contrast, are geologically much younger and are therefore considered later. In all, the geology of the North-west Highlands and the Western Isles encompasses something like 2,500 million years of Earth history – an unimaginable amount of time.

The oldest rocks in Scotland are the Lewisian gneisses, which take their name from Lewis. These rocks make up the entirety of the Western Isles, forming the spectacular mountain scenery of North Harris and South Uist, as well as the lower hills of the other islands. The largest area of Lewisian gneiss on the mainland extends from just north of Stac Pollaidh to Cape Wrath, although there are many smaller gneiss areas between Loch Broom and Loch Hourn, and on the Sleat peninsula of Skye. Lewisian gneiss country typically consists of low hills separated by lochs, and few high mountains are formed entirely of this rock. The most prominent gneiss hills on the mainland include Ben Stack and some of the peaks of Letterewe and Fisherfield, with these rocks achieving one of their highest points on the remote summit of A' Mhaighdean.

The Lewisian gneisses form what is known as the basement of the North-west Highlands, but for many hillwalkers and mountaineers, the most important rocks in this area are those that overlie the gneisses. Most of the dramatic peaks that march along the coast from Applecross to Cape Wrath are composed of Torridonian sandstones.

The jury is still out on how this part of Scotland might have looked when the Torridonian sandstones were being laid down, about 1,000 million years ago. For many years it was thought that they were formed from debris carried by streams cascading down the steep sides of a rocky rift valley, which was probably a few tens of kilometres wide. More recently, it has been suggested that they were

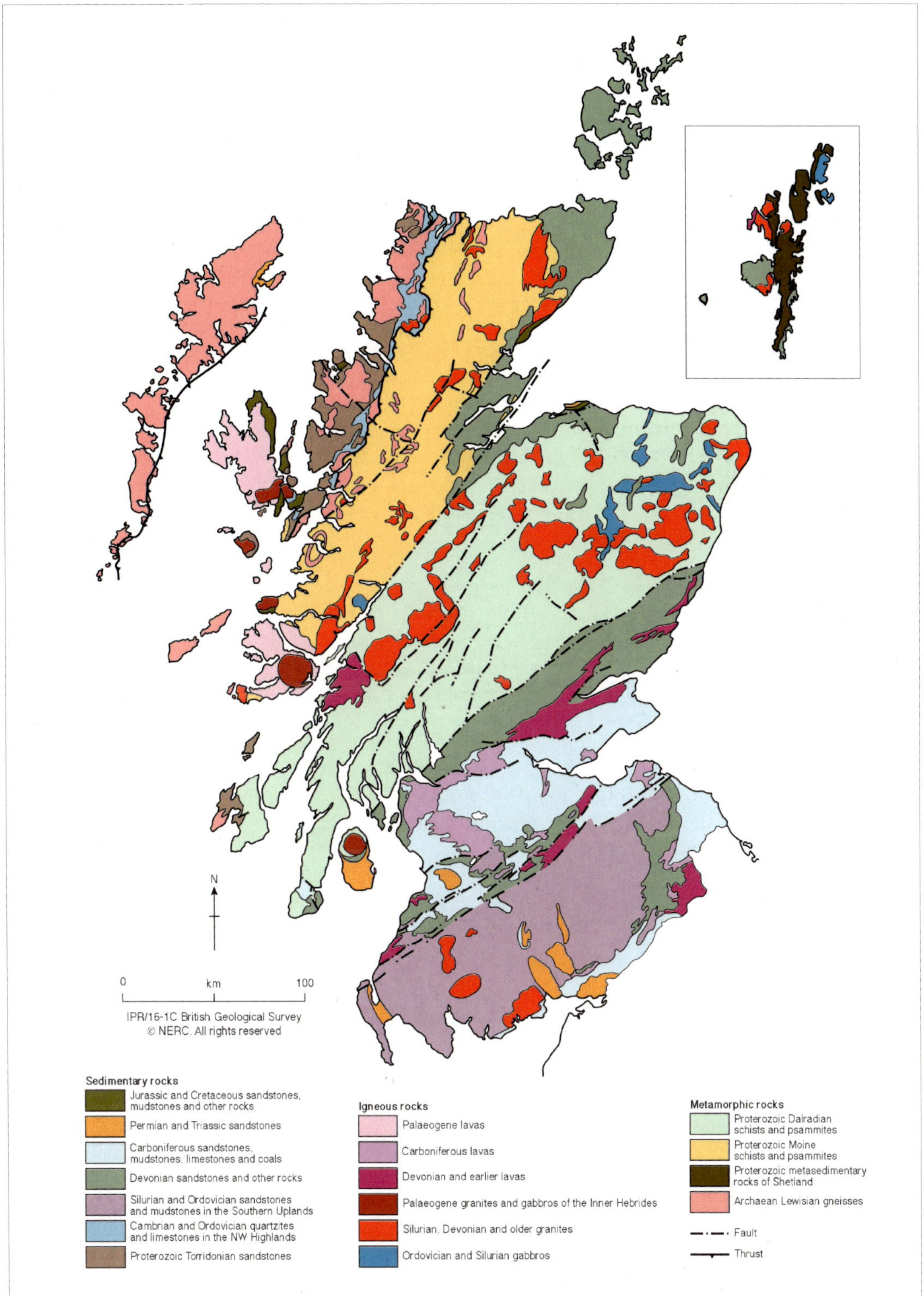

IPR/16-1C British Geological Survey
© NERC. All rights reserved

Sedimentary rocks

- Jurassic and Cretaceous sandstones, mudstones and other rocks
- Permian and Triassic sandstones
- Carboniferous sandstones, mudstones, limestones and coals
- Devonian sandstones and other rocks
- Silurian and Ordovician sandstones and mudstones in the Southern Uplands
- Cambrian and Ordovician quartzites and limestones in the NW Highlands
- Proterozoic Torridonian sandstones

Igneous rocks

- Palaeogene lavas
- Carboniferous lavas
- Devonian and earlier lavas
- Palaeogene granites and gabbros of the Inner Hebrides
- Silurian, Devonian and older granites
- Ordovician and Silurian gabbros

Metamorphic rocks

- Proterozoic Dalradian schists and psammites
- Proterozoic Moine schists and psammites
- Proterozoic metasedimentary rocks of Shetland
- Archaean Lewisian gneisses

- —·—·— Fault
- ——▼—— Thrust

carried here by rivers flowing from a mountain belt hundreds of kilometres to the west. Much of the basis for this argument rests on a structure in the rocks called cross-bedding, which represents fossilised ripples that formed on the ancient river bed. Careful study of these ripples can reveal the direction from which the rivers flowed. Cross-bedding is very clear in the rocks of the Torridonian mountains, where the surfaces of ancient sand dunes and ripples have been exploited by erosion to form the gently sloping, rounded ledges on which scramblers ascend to the summit of Stac Pollaidh or cross the Am Fasarinen pinnacles of Liathach. These rocks are also criss-crossed by a network of vertical cracks, known as joints, that have been gradually opened up by erosion. These joints probably formed as the original thickness of sandstone was gradually removed over millions of years, releasing the pressure on the rocks and allowing them to crack.

The Torridonian sandstones form a pile of mostly unvaried, coarse-grained red rocks, reaching almost a thousand metres in thickness on peaks such as An Teallach and Beinn Alligin. At the base, where they rest on the Lewisian gneiss, the sandstones are generally full of pebbles that would have been lying on the land surface as the sands were deposited. Good examples can be seen at the foot of Suilven and on the lower slopes of Slioch. In places, the thick pile of sandstones is interrupted by a finer-grained layer of mudstone. These layers tend to erode more easily, forming the prominent horizontal breaks in the cliffs that encircle peaks such as Liathach and Beinn Dearg Mor.

The names of many mountains in the north-west reflect their geology. There are abundant 'red' hills and peaks, such as Maol Chean-dearg, Sgorr Ruadh and Ruadh-stac Mor, which are all largely made up of Torridonian sandstone. But there are also several hills named 'white' or 'grey', including Canisp, which translates as 'white hill', Sgurr Ban, meaning 'white peak', and Liathach; 'the grey one'. Those who gave these names were not just observing snow lingering on the tops, for these hills, along with many others from Arkle to Beinn Damh, are capped by angular blocks of hard, white Cambrian quartzite, contrasting strongly with the red Torridonian sandstones.

Deposition of the Torridonian sandstones ceased around 900 million years ago, and the Cambrian quartzites were laid down around 380 million years later. North-west Scotland was then part of a major continent that also included North America and Greenland, and sediments deposited on the margins of this continent during the intervening period are preserved in other parts of the Highlands. However, in the north-west there is no record of any rocks formed between the Torridonian sandstones and Cambrian quartzites. The sharp boundary between the two rock-types, which can be seen particularly clearly on Beinn Eighe's Triple Buttress, is an 'unconformity' – a line that represents a long period of 'missing' geological time.

The Cambrian quartzites were formed at a time when early life was just beginning to flourish on Earth. The lower quartzites contain a type of cross-bedding that preserves the pattern of ancient tidal ripples. These rocks do not contain signs of life, but in younger quartzites, higher up in the succession, flat surfaces are often covered with many tiny knobbles. These are the surface expression of 'pipes', the fossilised burrows of ancient sand worms. A good place to see these pipes is on the ascent of Conival, and they are clearly visible on the rock steps that are ascended to gain the corrie above Gleann Dubh, on the normal route to the summit.

The Cambrian quartzites are the youngest rocks commonly seen on mountain

Outcrops at the summit of Cul Mor. Reddish-brown cross-bedded sandstones of the Torridon Group are overlain by pale grey Cambrian quartzites.

peaks in the north-west, but there are some areas, particularly around Loch Assynt and Durness, where the rocks that were laid down on top of the quartzites can still be seen. These are chiefly softer mudstones and limestones that have been eroded away from the summits, and record a period of deeper sea levels about 500 million years ago, when the quartzite beaches were drowned. Trilobite fossils have been found in a few places within the mudstones, which are known as the Fucoid Beds. One of these localities lies on the eastern slopes of Beinn Eighe, although hammering the rocks to look for fossils is not encouraged! Near the summit of Beinn Eighe, on the approach to Ruadh-stac Mor, there is a small area covered in relatively lush grass rather than the bare blocks of quartzite. This green area is underlain by a small patch of the Fucoid Beds that has not yet been eroded away, and is one of the few places where hillwalkers and climbers may encounter these rocks. The Durness limestones, which lie above the Fucoid Beds, are also seen only in low-lying areas, on the north coast around Durness and in the Traligill valley, the starting point for the ascent of Ben More Assynt.

Many of the mountains of the North-west Highlands are thus made up of a simple three-part sequence of gneiss, sandstone and quartzite that represents some 2,500 million years of Earth history. However, the situation is not always so straightforward. Why is the peak of Conival formed of quartzite, when the valley below contains limestone that should lie above the quartzite? How can Lewisian gneiss, generally only seen at low levels, appear on top of younger quartzites close to the summit of Mullach Coire Mhic Fhearchair? The answer lies with the major structure that has shaped much of the geology of Northern Scotland; the Moine Thrust.

During the Caledonian Orogeny around 430 million years ago, massive

Steeply dipping Moine psammites on the Forcan Ridge above Glen Shiel. The arete-like form of the ridge has resulted from glacial erosion parallel to the layering of these rocks.

compressive forces created by continental collision piled up the existing rocks to form a great mountain range. The Moine rocks of the Northern Highlands were forced westwards over the rocks below, along the plane of the major fracture in the earth's crust known as the Moine Thrust. The real interest with regard to the peaks of the North-west Highlands lies in what happened beneath this area. The compressive forces generated by the continental collision could not be accommodated by movement on a single plane of weakness, and a series of smaller thrusts lies parallel to and below the main fracture, in what is known as the Moine Thrust Zone. These thrusts tended to develop along layers of softer rocks such as the Fucoid Beds and in some places they have folded the existing rocks into a variety of contorted shapes.

The Moine Thrust Zone forms a belt of variable width immediately west of the Moine Thrust itself, and runs down the north-western side of Scotland from Loch Eriboll to the southern part of Skye. Several of the major peaks of this area lie within the thrust zone, from Foinaven down to the Coulin Forest. Foinaven itself consists of a great mass of quartzite that has been thickened by a series of small thrusts, and the Moine Thrust runs across the col between Foinaven and Meall Horn. The peaks of Ben More Assynt and Conival lie within a particularly wide area of the Thrust Zone, and here the sequence of gneiss, Torridonian sandstone and quartzite has been forced on top of the underlying quartzites and limestones along the line of the Ben More Thrust.

Moving southwards from Assynt, the Moine Thrust Zone crosses Loch Broom to run just east of An Teallach and through the remote Letterewe and Fisherfield forests. Thrusts have again brought older rocks on top of younger here, so that on the eastern slopes of Mullach Coire Mhic Fhearchair Lewisian gneisses have been thrust up on top of Cambrian quartzites. Further south, the Thrust Zone continues across the eastern slopes of Beinn Eighe and into the Coulin Forest. In the view south from Liathach, the Coulin peaks seem to be 'striped' by alternations of red Torridonian sandstone and white quartzite.

Northern Highlands

The great mountainous expanse east of the Moine Thrust and north of the Great Glen also forms a more or less geologically distinct block. The area extending from Ben Hope and Ben Loyal to the wilds of Knoydart, and including Glen Affric and Glen Shiel, is almost all underlain by one massive unit of rocks known as the Moines. These are metamorphosed sedimentary rocks that tend to form scattered outcrops on rounded, often peat-covered hills, contrasting with the sandstone and quartzite crags and screes to the west of the Moine Thrust. Indeed, *moine* means bog in Gaelic – a truly appropriate name.

Most of the Moine rocks in this area are psammites and schists, which are both widely distributed – indeed the two rock types are often interlayered on a scale ranging from tens of metres to several kilometres. In general, though, schists are more common in the south-west of the area, particularly around Morvern and Knoydart, while psammites are more common towards the north. These rocks were originally formed between about 1,000 and 870 million years ago, when sand and mud were gradually laid down on the floor of a great ocean off the margin of an ancient continent. However, it is difficult to unravel the history of these rocks after they were deposited. On many of the mountains in the region, there may seem to be very little variation in the rocks underfoot, but careful study of their mineral content has allowed us to work out something of their history.

It is now thought that these rocks were deformed and metamorphosed in not one, but two mountain building events. The first event, called the Knoydartian Orogeny after the area where it was first recognised, occurred around 800 million years ago. The second event was the Caledonian Orogeny, some 430 million years ago, when England and Scandinavia collided with Scotland. During this event, the Moine rocks were deformed and metamorphosed again in the core of the mountains, and were forced westwards almost 100 kilometres along the Moine Thrust to their present position. The evidence of these events can be seen in many places in the Northern Highlands. In some places such as Kintail and Glen Affric, it is possible to see a strong set of what appear to be parallel layers in the rock. This layering structure, or cleavage, was formed as the rocks were compressed and metamorphosed. The angle of this cleavage varies, but it is particularly clearly seen where the layers are near-vertical, as on the Forcan Ridge. In some places, the rocks buckled under the strain, and the layering is folded and twisted into complex patterns. Metamorphic minerals such as red garnet crystals are common in the Moine rocks, and were formed when rocks that were originally mudstones were placed under high temperatures and pressures. In many places they are associated with large 'books' of sheet-like mica crystals.

Although most of the Moine mountains consist of fairly similar rocks, there are some that have unusual features. In some places, it is possible to see slivers of the gneiss that underlies the Moine rocks at depth. These are similar to the Lewisian gneisses away to the west, but are typically highly deformed, and the Fannaichs are perhaps the best mountain area in which to see such exposures. On other mountains, the Moine rocks show local variations. Ben Klibreck, for instance, is characterised by abundant quartz-rich granite bodies lying within schists that are rich in red garnets. The Moine rocks here have been buried so deeply that small pockets of the rock began to melt. The melt would have collected within cracks in the surrounding rock, before cooling and crystallising again to form pods and layers of granite.

Not all the mountains within this area are composed of Moine rocks, and there are also some igneous rocks which were formed at various stages of geological history. The most spectacular body of igneous rock is that forming Ben Loyal. This is a great mass of syenite, a coarse grained rock similar to granite but more alkaline – that is, having a higher potassium and sodium content. It consists largely of crystals of the mineral feldspar that are up to 1cm across, along with some quartz. The Ben Loyal syenite formed in the waning stages of the Caledonian orogeny, when magma from deep within the Earth was intruded into the Moine rocks shortly after they were moved. Other igneous rocks are scattered across the area, although in many places they occupy lower ground. The Corbett of Carn Chuinneag, in Easter Ross, is formed of a granite that shows evidence of deformation during a mountain building event and is believed to have formed around 600 million years ago. Undeformed granites, considered to have formed about 400 million years ago, are also found in a few places, notably the Strontian area.

Central and Southern Highlands

Two major fractures in the Earth's crust, the Great Glen Fault and the Highland Boundary Fault, define the limits of a third area that is geologically distinct, and which encompasses most of the Central and Southern Highlands. The Great Glen Fault forms the straight line of Scotland's longest glen, which extends from Inverness down to Fort William. The Highland Boundary Fault runs from Stonehaven on the east coast down to Loch Lomond and the Mull of Kintyre, and is less distinctive on a map but unmissable on the ground. This fault forms the threshold between upland and lowland that is crossed at some point on every journey into the Highlands from the south, and is marked by decisive changes in topography north of Balloch on the A82 and close to Dunkeld on the A9.

The Central and Southern Highlands contain Scotland's highest mountains and have widely varied geology. The main rocks of this area are the Dalradian metamorphosed sedimentary rocks, but there is also a range of igneous rocks, from the granites of the Cairngorms to the lavas of Ben Nevis.

The Dalradian rocks are much more diverse than the Moine rocks to the north. The oldest Dalradian rocks are found in the northern part of this area, forming the high, broad plateaux of the Drumochter hills, the Monadh Liath, Ben Alder and the hills around Rannoch Moor. These are mainly psammites, quartz-rich metamorphosed sandstones that often have a layered appearance. Rock outcrops tend to be sparse on these hills, with the exception of some corrie walls, as in many places the rocks are covered by thick glacial deposits resulting from the Ice Age (Chapter 3). Further south and west, the Dalradian rocks become much more varied, with many different layers including sandstones, mudstones and limestones, all of which have undergone metamorphism. The harder rocks form the mountains, while the softer metamorphosed limestones and slates are typically found in the valleys and on lower ground.

The Grey Corries and the Mamores are characterised by abundant metamorphosed quartzites that are interlayered with schists. These quartzites cap many of the hills, and the craggy north-eastern face of Stob Ban in the Mamores includes spectacular exposures that have been contorted into large folds. The distinctive

Looking north-east across the metamorphosed quartzites of the Grey Corries to Stob Coire Claurigh. These Dalradian quartzites are interspersed with schists and are significantly older than those of the North-west Highlands

peak of Schiehallion is also capped by quartzite, but lower down on its northern slopes are outcrops of a characteristic rock layer known as the Schiehallion Boulder Bed. This contains a variety of pebbles and boulders set within a metamorphosed mudstone. The pebbles and boulders are thought to have dropped from melting ice towards the end of a major Ice Age that occurred over 600 million years ago. This Boulder Bed is correlated with similar deposits that are exposed towards the west coast and on Islay, and probably formed at the same time as other ancient glacial deposits around the world.

The hills around Glen Lyon and Ben Lawers are largely composed of mica schists, which are locally rich in calcium and create famous havens for alpine plants, while the southernmost peaks such as Ben Ledi and Ben Chonzie are predominantly formed from gritty metamorphosed sandstones. These schists and psammites form a number of popular climbing crags, including Craig a' Barns, The Cobbler and Ben An, with narrow flakes and ledges developed along the cleavage of the rocks. Many of the Dalradian rocks are folded into complex shapes that record the continental collision around 470 million years ago, and garnet crystals, which are common within the mica-schists, would also have formed at this time.

Although the Dalradian rocks make up much of the Central and Southern Highlands, the areas that are of most interest to mountaineers are underlain by igneous rocks. A glance at the geological map of Scotland will show that it is covered by irregular red blobs, corresponding to large masses of granite that were formed around 400 million years ago. Perhaps the best known is that of the Cairngorms, which covers over 350km² from Ben Avon to Glen Feshie, and is composed almost entirely of coarse-grained pink granite. The individual crystals of different minerals can be clearly seen in any fresh piece of Cairngorm granite

The west face of Aonach Dubh showing the distinct transition between the vegetated andesite and cleaner rhyolite of the Glen Coe caldera

and include grey, rounded quartz crystals, rectangular crystals of pink and white feldspars and flakes of black biotite mica. In the past, many areas of the Cairngorms, particularly the trough of Loch Avon, have been quarried for 'Cairngorm' crystals. These are crystals of smoky quartz that grew very slowly into cavities within the granite, and were consequently able to develop well-formed crystal shapes. The Cairngorm granite is coarse and fairly homogeneous, but is split by conspicuous joints. These fractures result from the combined effects of contraction as the magma cooled, and subsequent expansion of the granite as the weight of overlying rock was eroded away. Over millions of years and with the aid of glaciation, the rock has spalled away along these joints, resulting in the characteristic blocky architecture of the tors and crags of the Cairngorms.

Lochnagar is composed of another very similar granite mass that lies a short distance to the south east of the Cairngorms, and other such intrusions are scattered across the Grampians, including Bennachie, Ben Rinnes, the eastern Monadh Liath and the isolated Munro of Beinn Dearg, above Blair Atholl. This general area also includes intrusions of related but chemically different igneous rocks known as diorites, which can be seen in Glen Tilt and Glen Doll.

Another cluster of large masses of granite and associated igneous rocks lies further to the west and forms many fine hills. Much of Rannoch Moor is underlain by granite, which can be seen on some of the hills around Loch Ossian. For mountaineers, however, the most significant of these features is the Etive Complex, a massive body of igneous rock that extends from the head of Glen Coe to Ben Cruachan, underlying many of the Glen Etive hills such as Ben Starav. The Etive

Complex contains a variety of different types of igneous rock, including granite, diorite and many intermediate forms. In many places the granite contains large white or pink rectangular crystals of feldspar over a centimetre in size.

The Etive Complex forms a partial ring around one of the most important features of Scottish geology for the mountaineer; the Glen Coe Volcanic Complex. Intrusion of large granites such as the Etive Complex heated up the water in the surrounding rocks, and this hot water circulated through fractures in the crust, dissolving and redepositing various elements; the Cononish gold deposit, in the glen below Ben Lui, formed at this time.

Glen Coe represents a spectacular remnant of an ancient volcano, and is the classic example of a process known as caldera subsidence. The geological heart of Glen Coe is a roughly elliptical outcrop of volcanic rocks extending from Aonach Dubh, the westernmost of the Three Sisters, to Meall a' Bhuiridh. These are surrounded by Dalradian rocks that occur, for example, on the Pap of Glencoe. When the Glen Coe volcano began to erupt around 400 million years ago, the earliest magmas formed were thick, viscous andesites. These were not erupted at the surface and instead, the magmas flowed into mud on the floors of shallow lakes, heating and baking it. Sheets of purplish-coloured andesite, separated by thin layers of reddened mud, can be clearly seen today on the lower slopes of Aonach Dubh, and can be studied during the ascent into Coire nam Beith.

At a later stage, the type of volcanic activity changed as groundwater percolated downwards into the magma chamber, heating up to produce steam. Huge

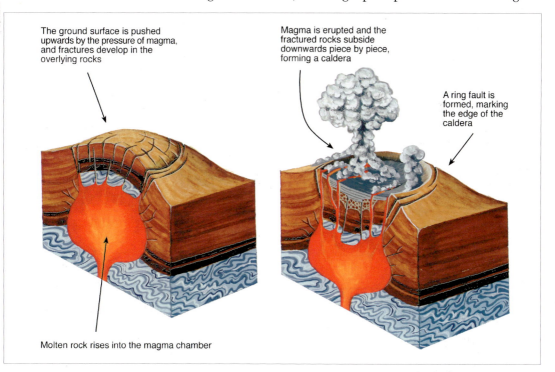

The ground surface is pushed upwards by the pressure of magma, and fractures develop in the overlying rocks

Magma is erupted and the fractured rocks subside downwards piece by piece, forming a caldera

A ring fault is formed, marking the edge of the caldera

Molten rock rises into the magma chamber

A simplified diagram illustrating caldera subsidence, which is recorded by the present-day geology of former volcanoes such as Ben Nevis and Rum. At Glen Coe, recent studies have shown that the process of caldera formation was much more complex than this, with several stages of eruption and subsidence explosive eruptions began to occur, possibly resembling the 1980 eruption of Mount St Helens in the Western USA. These produced a type of silica-rich magma called rhyolite, which was erupted in great lava fountains and then spread out across the area. These rhyolites form most of the higher cliffs and crags of Glen Coe and provide some of the most popular climbing, including the classic routes on Rannoch Wall. The most instructive view of these volcanic rocks is from the Clachaig Inn, where a clear distinction can be seen between the vegetated andesite lower on Aonach Dubh and clean crags of rhyolite above.

As the eruptions continued, the centre of the volcano began to subside, forming a large crater or caldera. Rock falls occurred around the edges of the caldera and are recorded by distinctive rocks known as breccias, which can be seen in various places including Coire nan Lochan. Searingly hot ash clouds, or pyroclastic flows, raced across the caldera floor and have been preserved today as rocks called ignimbrites, which are particularly well seen on the north-eastern face of Stob nan Cabhar, on Buachaille Etive Beag. Above these rocks, the high peaks of Bidean nam Bian are composed of greyish andesites. Although the eruptions probably produced many more volcanic rocks, these have been eroded away.

As magma was removed from below the volcano by eruption, the volcanic rocks within the caldera sank downwards piece by piece into the magma chamber so that they were actually below the level of the surrounding land surface. This explains why the volcanic rocks at Glen Coe have been preserved today and have not been eroded away. The rocks of Glen Coe are surrounded by a major fracture known as the Main Ring Fault, which indicates where the caldera would once have been. The Main Ring Fault runs across the southern slopes of the Aonach Eagach, round the western side of Bidean nam Bian and down to Glen Etive, where it disappears beneath granites of the Etive Complex. The eastern end of the 'notched ridge' of the Aonach Eagach is composed of volcanic rocks, but the western part is of Dalradian schist. Many of the notches have formed where dykes, mostly of andesite, cut through the ridge and have been weathered away more easily than the surrounding rock.

Britain's highest mountain has many similarities with Glen Coe, not only in its attraction for mountaineers, but also in its geology. The upper part of Ben Nevis, including the spectacular north-east face, is also composed of volcanic rocks that were preserved because of caldera subsidence. New surveys of this face are taking place at the time of writing, and complex sequences of rhyolite, andesite and breccia have been described, although there will certainly be more detail to come. The rhyolite and andesite were formed as erupted lavas, whilst the breccias formed when blocks of volcanic rock and ash were ejected from the volcano and landed in lakes or rivers on the caldera floor. Rocks of this type are particularly well seen, for example, on the upper sections of some routes on Carn Dearg Buttress. Although the summit block of Ben Nevis is composed of extrusive volcanic rocks, its lower slopes and the nearby ridges of Carn Mor Dearg and Aonach Mor are underlain by granite. The granite weathers to form much more rounded, less craggy slopes, thus creating the contrasting scenery seen on the upper and lower parts of Ben Nevis. The granites are attractively exposed in the Allt a' Mhuillin, where their large crystals are beautifully seen on water washed surfaces.

Southern Scotland

The hills to the south of the Highland Boundary Fault fall into two broadly distinct groups, with volcanic remnants around the Central Belt contrasting with the

The greywackes and black shales of the Southern Uplands are well exposed in the deep gash of Hartfell Score on the flanks of Hart Fell above Moffat

mainly sedimentary mass of the Southern Uplands.

The most spectacular remains of the volcanic eruptions of 400 million years ago can be seen at Ben Nevis and Glen Coe, but volcanic rocks of this age also form the Ochils and Sidlaws. These hills are composed of a thick pile of mainly andesitic lavas that were erupted from volcanic vents, the remains of which are now probably hidden beneath younger rocks to the south. The spectacular scarp face of the Ochils above the Hillfoots towns corresponds to the Ochil Fault, which marks a boundary with softer sedimentary rocks that have been eroded away, leaving the Ochils standing proud.

Many of the other hills around the Central Belt, including the Pentland Hills and Tinto, are formed of similar igneous rocks of the same age. One of the more striking rocks of the Pentlands is the Carnethy Porphyry, a lava that contains very large crystals of white feldspar. Volcanic rocks of this age also underlie other significant British mountains, including most of the Lake District and Snowdonia. However, some Central Belt hills, including the Lomonds, Campsies and Kilpatricks, reflect more recent volcanic activity, dating from about 350 million years ago. The dominant rocks here are typically basaltic, with higher iron and magnesium contents than most of the rocks of the Ochils, and are generally darker in colour and less varied. The Lomonds are underlain by the Midland Valley Sill, a thick sheet of dolerite that intruded along subterranean lines of weakness and forms some of the Central Belt's popular climbing venues.

To the south, the Southern Uplands have fairly unvaried geology. They are largely composed of coarse-grained sandstones known as greywackes, which were formed when submarine avalanches of sand and rock fragments swept down the margins of the ancient Laurentian continental shelf, between about 420 and 460 million years ago. Thin layers of ash and lava occur within these rocks, indicating that there was also volcanic activity in the ocean at that time. When England and Scotland collided, these sedimentary rocks were bulldozed between the continents, compressed and piled up. The layers of greywacke are now steeply inclined in most places and have been intensely folded in some areas. The greywackes form thick units that are separated by thin layers of black shale, which contain a variety of fossils that have been used to date the rocks accurately. These studies have revealed that a series of thrusts piled older rocks in the north-west of the Southern Uplands onto younger rocks in the south-east, although the exact way in which this happened is still the subject of debate.

One of the more geologically unusual features of the Southern Uplands occurs around Leadhills and Wanlockhead, on the north-west flanks of the Lowther Hills. Here, the greywackes are cut across by abundant veins, each about a metre wide, which consist chiefly of quartz and carbonate minerals but also contain some ore minerals, mainly galena (lead ore). These veins were probably formed around 350 million years ago, as fluids carrying dissolved metals from deeper levels flowed along cracks and faults. On reaching an impermeable barrier, such as a shale layer, the dissolved elements were deposited to form the ore minerals. These veins represent the largest lead-zinc deposit in Scotland, and were extensively mined in the 19th century.

In south-west Scotland, the sandstones are cut by three large masses of granite, around 400 million years old, which form the hills of Mulwharchar near The Merrick, Criffel and Cairnsmore of Fleet. These intrusions contain several types of granite of slightly different composition, which form zones within the rock mass. While some types form low ridges such as Mulwharchar itself, others have been eroded away to form low and boggy adjacent ground. Some of the higher hills in this area, including the Merrick itself, are actually formed of sedimentary rocks that were baked and hardened by the intrusion of the granites.

The Inner Hebrides

The youngest rocks in Scotland are also among the most interesting for mountaineers. The volcanic foundations of Arran, Mull, Ardnamurchan, Rum and Skye were formed 55-60 million years ago during the Palaeogene period, and belong to the geological zone known as the British Palaeogene Volcanic Province. The rocks of this zone extend well beyond Scotland, including Lundy Island in the Bristol Channel and the lavas of Antrim, which are most famous for the Giant's Causeway.

There are three main groups of rocks within this province: intrusive rocks, which can in turn be sub-divided largely into granites and gabbros, and extrusive rocks, which are largely basaltic lavas. These three groups of rocks typically form very different landscapes. The granites tend to be pale in colour, grey or reddish, and commonly form more rounded hills, or break into smooth slabs like those on Cir Mhor on Arran. The gabbros are darker in colour and form the jagged Cuillin peaks. The basalts tend to form a subdued, 'stepped' topography that is best developed on parts of Mull.

The high mountains of Arran, around Glen Sannox and Glen Rosa, are formed of a mass of granite made up of large crystals of quartz and feldspar with some flakes of black biotite mica. Erosion along joints has led to slabs of granite spalling away to leave smooth surfaces behind, creating a characteristic rock architecture resembling that of the Cairngorms. The resulting slabs and cracks provide much of the climbing that attracts mountaineers to Arran today. The shape of these

Flat layers of gabbro, resulting from changes in the composition of the magma, give the distinct layering to the summit section of Askival on Rum

mountains has also been strongly influenced by the presence of later basaltic dykes cutting across the granite, which have generally weathered away to form gullies. These dykes are generally of dark grey to black colour and can easily be seen crossing the paler granite outcrops.

Further north, Mull displays a widely varied geology, with all three groups of igneous rocks represented across the island. The oldest of these are the lavas, which are well exposed on the northern and western parts of the island and would have flowed out from a central volcano, destroying virtually everything in their path. In places, however, fossil trees are preserved, entombed in the lava flows, and one of the most famous is MacCulloch's Tree, on the Ardmeanach peninsula on the west coast.

Around the coast, the lavas form flat-lying layers that reflect a characteristic pattern of erosion. The top of each lava flow broke up as it was exposed to the air and cooled rapidly. These shattered flow tops, or boles, were then covered by new lava, but remained as lines of weakness within the lava pile. After volcanism had ceased, the flow tops were more easily eroded than the main parts of the lava piles, but as they eroded back under the influence of wind, water and glacial ice, the harder rock above would eventually have collapsed. This process has produced the characteristic 'stepped' topography seen on Mull's west coast, and on basalt landscapes elsewhere in the world, in which each flat step represents an eroded flow top. The pile of lavas on Mull is very thick and the island's highest peak and only Munro, Ben More, is entirely composed of these rocks. East of Ben More, these lavas are cut by younger intrusive rocks including granites and gabbros.

The islands of Skye and Rum have very similar geology, and both have a jagged Cuillin and a range of more rounded Red Hills. The mountains of both islands are mainly composed of intrusive igneous rocks formed in deep magma chambers. The Cuillin of both Rum and Skye are largely made up of coarse-grained gabbros,

Looking across Glen Sligachan from Bla Bheinn. The rounded granite of the Red Hills in the foreground, contrasts with the jagged gabbro peaks of the main Cuillin ridge behind. The sharp intrusive contact between the two is clearly seen on the Druim Hain ridge, centre left

while the Red Hills of both islands are underlain by granite.

In some locations, the Skye and Rum gabbros form distinct layers of different colour and texture, which result from variation in the amounts of their constituent minerals – feldspar, olivine, and pyroxene. These layers developed during the cooling process as solid crystals began to form, settling through the magma to accumulate on the solid rock below. New magma was periodically introduced, changing the overall chemical composition of the molten liquid mass in the magma chamber and, in turn, the types of crystals forming. The resulting layers can be seen in various parts of the Skye Cuillin, including some of the higher corries above Glen Brittle and on the Druim Hain ridge between Coruisk and Srath na Creitheach, where almost black bands rich in pyroxene are interspersed with paler layers containing more feldspar. In many places on the shores of Loch Coruisk, the layers have been distorted and folded by currents that flowed through the magma chamber.

Both the Skye and Rum Cuillin also contain a number of other rocks that influence their character to varying degrees. In some parts of both ranges, and particularly above Loch Coire a' Ghrunnda on Skye, there are outcrops of rocks known as peridotites, that are similar to gabbros but are almost entirely made up of olivine. This mineral is very soft and these rocks have only avoided being weathered away completely because they contain a certain proportion of hard feldspar. Similar bands of peridotite can be seen on the summits of Hallival and Trallval on Rum, where these soft layers are exploited as nesting sites by Manx shearwaters. By contrast, some of the highest peaks on Skye, including Sgurr Alasdair and Sgurr Dearg, are made up of volcanic breccia, comprising fragments of gabbro and extrusive igneous rock firmly cemented together by fine-grained material from within the volcano. These breccias were probably formed by some of the last ever eruptions to occur on Skye.

The jagged form of the Skye Cuillin is largely due to later rocks which form dykes and sills that cross-cut the gabbro. These intrusions appear as sheets of fine-grained grey rock, mostly basalt, which are up to a few metres wide. Many of the sills are actually 'cone-sheets' shaped rather like an inverted cone hundreds of metres across, and form gently dipping but often slippery ledges such as Collie's Ledge. They are particularly well displayed in Coire a' Ghrunnda, where they can be traced across the great boiler-plates of gabbro and up the cliffs at the side of the coire. These sheets of basalt would once have been feeder pipes that carried magma to the surface to be erupted. Once volcanic activity ceased, the magma cooled and solidified rapidly in these cracks, and subsequent erosion has exposed these rocks to view.

Because the dykes and sills are fine-grained, they tend to fracture more easily than the gabbros, and have consequently been eroded away in many places, forming the notches that give the Cuillin ridge its serrated nature. In some places, however, the dykes and sills are actually more resistant than the surrounding rocks, and a particularly good example is the Inaccessible Pinnacle, formed from a single dyke that stood proud as the rocks around it were weathered away. Although the majority of the dykes and sills are basalt, some are more silica-rich and akin to granite, and the Great Stone Shoot of Sgurr Alasdair is eroded along an intrusion of this type. The composition of these magmas may be due to their having melted and consumed older, silica-rich rocks through which they ascended.

Bla Bheinn is a geological outlier of the Skye Cuillin and its summit and upper slopes are also composed of gabbro, although much of the ascent from Loch Slapin is over extrusive basaltic lavas. The gabbros of Bla Bheinn would originally have been connected to the main Cuillin ridge but were subsequently cut across by younger rocks, forming in a new magma chamber at depth. The new magmas were of the silica-rich type, cooling to form the granites which underlie the Red Hills and much of the low ground between Bla Bheinn and the central Cuillin. The view southwards down Glen Sligachan reveals a clear line between pink granites and near-black gabbros in the Cuillin foothills.

Palaeogene igneous rocks also occur on Ardnamurchan and the western part of this peninsula consists of three overlapping 'centres' or major bodies of igneous rock, each of which is roughly circular in shape. The oldest, most easterly centre consists largely of volcanic breccias that are cut across by sills and cone-sheets similar to those seen on Skye. The two younger centres consist chiefly of gabbros, with each separate intrusion having a characteristic ring shape. The most recent of these forms a prominent circle of low, craggy hills that is strikingly obvious in aerial photos, and indeed on the Ordnance Survey map. By contrast, the nearby 'holy mountain' of Ben Hiant consists of a large intrusion of dolerite, a finer-grained equivalent of gabbro.

The rocks of the Inner Hebrides represent the most recent event in Scotland's history during which rocks were formed in significant quantity. Since then, Scotland's varied geology has been exploited, shaped and scoured by a variety of natural processes including, most significantly, the glaciers that covered much of the country at intervals during the last 2.5 million years. It is this interplay between geology and other forces of nature that has created the spectacular mountains of modern-day Scotland.

The slow disintegration of rock releases its constituent minerals, which can greatly influence the nutrient content of soils, leading to highly visible differences in mountain vegetation, wildlife and land use. These effects are considered in the chapters that follow.

Schist

Schists are the most common rocks across much of the central and western Highlands. They are of variable grain-size and usually appear grey, but often sparkle in the sun because of the presence of flakes of mica. On closer examination, typical schists are largely composed of grains of grey or white quartz and shiny flakes of black or grey mica, sometimes with crystals of black amphibole or red garnet. The latter vary from less than 1mm up to 1cm in size and often stand proud of the rock as red or rust-coloured projections.

Tom Prentice

mudstone or shale

Schists are formed by the metamorphism of sedimentary rocks that contain abundant flakes of clay. These clays are broken down under high temperatures and pressures, and replaced by sheet-like mica crystals with their flat surfaces perpendicular to the main pressure on the rock. The alignment of these sheets gives the rock a very fine layering, or schistosity, and cliffs of this rock are usually characterised by abundant cracks and narrow flakes, although exposed surfaces that are parallel to the layering may be very smooth. These layers are often folded into highly visible contorted patterns, which result from changes in the direction of the pressure acting on the rock.

Psammite

metamorphed sedimentary rock

Psammites form many of the hills north of the Great Glen, including the ridges of Kintail and Glen Affric. These rocks are of variable grain size and tend to be grey in colour (darker than quartzite). They are largely composed of quartz, but also contain relatively small amounts of other minerals such as feldspar and mica. Psammites are formed by the same processes as schists and the two rock

Noel Williams

types intergrade, forming outcrops of similar general character, so that clear distinction is not always possible. Because of their lower mica content, psammites tend to be less well-layered than schists, with a weaker schistosity, and are of less sparkly appearance.

Most psammites in Scotland were originally formed as sandy sediments on the margins of an ancient ocean, and were metamorphosed during continental collision and mountain building. The difference between schists and psammites lies in the proportion of sand to mud in the original sediments: mud-rich rocks are metamorphosed to form schists, while sand-rich rocks give rise to psammites. Some psammites, as shown here, display cross-bedding; preserved ripples in the sand.

Gneiss

Gneisses are coarse-grained rocks with large crystals that can be seen with the naked eye, and a characteristic striped appearance known as gneissic banding. From a distance, the weathered surfaces of outcrops generally appear grey to white, but on closer inspection these rocks are typically characterised by alternating dark green to black bands, largely composed of amphibole or pyroxene crys-

Kathryn Goodenough

tals, and pale pink to white bands of quartz and feldspar. Gneisses are formed when granites or other rocks are metamorphosed at relatively high temperatures and pressures, and in common with other rocks of similar origin, the layers are often conspicuously folded and contorted. Other minerals, such as red garnet crystals, are also present in some gneisses.

Gneiss is largely confined to the north-west of Scotland, including the Outer Hebrides, Wester Ross and Sutherland. However, these are the most widely occurring rocks across much of this area, and are very likely to be encountered. Lewisian gneiss forms some significant crags, including the Lewis sea-cliffs, Sheigra, Carnmore and the cliffs in the Gairloch area, and their roughness to the touch is accompanied by excellent frictional properties.

Sandstone

Sandstones are sedimentary rocks that vary in colour from brick red to yellow, grey or green, and are largely made up of rounded grains of quartz that can usually be distinguished with the naked eye. The most important examples of these rocks in the Scottish hills are the reddish Torridonian sandstones, which are coarse-grained and rough to the touch, with an abundance of small, rounded

Tom Prentice

pebbles in many places. Torridonian sandstones weather to highly characteristic rounded shapes and are punctuated by fairly regular vertical and horizontal breaks, resulting in a sculpted appearance. These rocks are extensive in the north-west and form many well known mountains, including Suilven, An Teallach, Stac Pollaidh and the Applecross hills.

Sandstones are formed by the slow accumulation of layers of sand, which are cemented by minerals deposited from fluids that percolate between the grains. Torridonian sandstones were laid down in seasonal rivers and owe their reddish hue to tiny fragments of iron ore, which have rusted because they were exposed to air when deposited. Such tints are widespread among sandstones formed under such conditions, while sandstones that were deposited in the sea are commonly grey to brown in colour.

Quartzite

Quartzites are very pure sandstones made up almost entirely of quartz grains. They are typically white or pale grey, and fresh surfaces have a 'sugary' appearance not unlike that of Kendal Mint Cake. Quartz is very hard and these rocks can be differentiated from rocks of similar appearance, including marbles, because quartzites are not easily scratched with a penknife. Quartzites typically form smooth slabby outcrops, mobile screes and summit blockfields composed of angular boulders which, by

virtue of their fine surface texture, are slippery when wet. They are perhaps most prominent in north-west Scotland, forming the white, rocky summits of numerous mountains including Foinaven and Beinn Eighe. They also occur in the Central Highlands, capping many tops in the Mamores and Grey Corries. The latter quartzites have undergone metamorphism, but this has barely affected their appearance as quartz is virtually pure silica, and no new minerals have been able to form.

The Scottish quartzites were deposited in the intertidal zone as beach sands. The Cambrian quartzites of the north-west were laid down on an ancient coastline hundreds of kilometres long, and similar rocks can be found today in western America and Greenland.

Greywacke

In Scotland, greywackes are almost exclusively found in the Southern Uplands and typically form rounded hills, including many major summits such as Broad Law and White Coomb. These rocks are unusual sandstones that contain many tiny, angular fragments of the rocks from which the sediments were formed. They are generally grey to brown in colour and clearly layered, with a coarse-grained, gritty appearance when seen close up. The angular shape of the fragments is important in definitively identifying these

rocks, but is often hard to discern with the naked eye as these are generally no more than a millimetre or two across, and greywackes can otherwise appear similar to other sandstones.

Although pebbles and rock fragments occur in the majority of sandstones, these have generally been rolled about by wind or water, becoming rounded at the edges. The presence of angular fragments indicates that these sediments were laid down very rapidly, and the greywackes of the Southern Uplands were deposited by submarine avalanches. Greywackes were previously known as 'whin' by quarrymen because of the abundance of gorse on these hills, although this name and characteristic have also been associated with dolerite.

Mudstone

Mudstones are fine-grained sedimentary rocks in which the constituent grains cannot be seen with the naked eye. They can be variable in colour, from red and purple to grey, green and brown. Close inspection reveals that they are generally finely layered. A variety of fossils can often be found in these rocks and may be detected on careful examination. Mudstones are fairly soft and easily eroded and are conse-

Kathryn Goodenough

quently rather localised in the Scottish mountains, tending to occur as thin layers within other sedimentary rocks such as the Torridonian sandstones, or on lower ground. This includes a number of sites in the North-west Highlands and deposits of Jurassic age along the eastern Trotternish and Strathaird peninsulas of Skye.

Mudstones are formed by the slow deposition of mud, largely in lakes or on the seafloor. In places they preserve features of these environments, such as ripples or desiccation cracks that formed on the bed of a dried-out lake. The main importance of mudstones in mountain areas is as the precursors for metamorphic rocks such as schists or slates.

Limestone

Limestones are pale grey to cream coloured sedimentary rocks that are typically fine grained, and are made up of calcium or magnesium carbonate. They are soft and are easily scratched with a penknife. Limestones are slowly dissolved by rainwater, often hollowing out small pockets or dissecting the rock into sculpted, semi-detached blocks. These rocks are uncommon in the Scottish hills and are only important in the north-west, par-

Tom Prentice

ticularly in Durness and Assynt, providing extensive cave networks around Inchnadamph. Limestones also occur very locally amid the Dalradian rocks of the Central Highlands. Limestone areas provide relatively rich grazing and can often be identified at long range by the presence of lush, green grassland, contrasting strongly with the rough wet heaths, with heather and purple moor grass, that are typical of the north-west.

Limestone is formed by the slow accumulation of calcium carbonate on the seabed, and its presence thus indicates an area that once lay beneath the sea. If the limestones are later metamorphosed at high temperatures, they form marbles, often with spectacular patterns and colours. In Scotland, true marbles are only found in a few places, including Ledmore, below Ben More Assynt, and Torrin on Skye.

Andesite

Andesites are commonly fine-grained, so that their individual constituent crystals cannot be distinguished with the naked eye. In places, however, they contain larger crystals, often of pink feldspar. These rocks are relatively smooth to the touch and are often purplish-grey in colour, but may also show less distinctive shades of dark grey or brown. Andesites have a limited but highly significant distribution in the Scottish mountains, forming the summit of Ben Nevis and the lower slopes of Bidean nam Bian. Andesites also occur in the Ochils and Pentland Hills.

These rocks take their name from their type area in the Andes and are typically formed by eruption from volcanoes, although they may also be derived from magmas that are intruded just below the Earth's surface. Some andesites contain vesicles, rounded holes in the rock formed when gas bubbles were trapped in the lava as it cooled. In places the vesicles have been filled with silica that has been deposited from fluids flowing through the cooling lava pile, forming banded agates that are generally purple or green in colour. These are easily seen in parts of the Ochils, and larger examples are sometimes collected and polished for ornamental purposes.

Rhyolite

Rhyolites are relatively smooth, fine-grained igneous rocks that are more silica-rich than andesites and paler in colour, generally ranging from pink to grey. In common with andesites, however, rhyolites may contain large crystals, most commonly of white or pink feldspars, set within the finer material. Rhyolites are hard and resistant to erosion, typically forming clean, unveg-

etated outcrops. These have a very distinctive angular weathering pattern, forming sheer faces punctuated by sharp-edged ledges, providing an abundance of small but positive holds. These rocks are rare in most of Scotland but important in Glen Coe, where pink-tinged banded rhyolites form many of the upper parts of the mountains including the spectacular faces of Buachaille Etive Mor and the upper crags of the Three Sisters. Rocks of this general type also form the major climbing crags of Snowdonia and the Lake District.

Rhyolites are formed by eruption from volcanoes and are derived from magmas of high silica content. These magmas have the same chemical compositions as those that form granites, and the considerable difference in appearance between these rocks is essentially due to the very rapid cooling process by which rhyolites are formed.

Tuff, breccia and ignimbrite

Tuffs, breccias and ignimbrites are made up of many shards of rock in a mass of fine-grained volcanic material. In tuffs and breccias, these are visible as angular fragments, whereas in ignimbrites the fragments have been compressed and flattened to give the appearance of fine banding. The distinction between tuffs and breccias is based on the size of the shards. Breccias are chiefly composed of large volcanic fragments that are typically several centimetres or more across, whereas in tuffs the fragments are smaller. These rocks are very variable in colour and pattern, and the tints in a single piece of rock can vary from green and grey to pink and purple. In Scotland, they are best developed on the Glen Coe hills, although tuffs can also be seen on the mountains of Rum and elsewhere in the Inner Hebrides.

Breccia

These rocks are the products of explosive volcanic eruptions in which ash and rock fragments are thrown out of a volcano. Tuffs and breccias are formed when the volcanic products settle passively, while ignimbrites are formed by pyroclastic flows, immensely hot and fast-moving clouds of eruptive material comprising ash and rock debris.

Granite

Granites are easily recognisable rough, coarse-grained igneous rocks, with individual crystals that are generally a couple of millimetres or more across and clearly visible, particularly on less weathered surfaces. Granites are largely made up of grey quartz and rectangular crystals of feldspar, which vary in colour from white to pink (respectively known as plagioclase feldspar and potassium feldspar). This in turn results in corresponding differences in the overall colour of the rock. Most granites

Nick Kempe

also contain darker minerals such as amphibole, which typically forms stubby black crystals, or biotite mica, which forms black flakes that glint in the sun. Many large bodies of granite include other coarse-grained igneous rocks of similar general appearance, such as diorites, which contain more amphibole and less feldspar and tend to appear greyer. The hardness of granite is attributable to the solid, interlocking pattern of its constituent crystals.

Natural outcrops assume a highly characteristic overall appearance, tending to form rounded blocks separated by frequent horizontal and vertical breaks. Scotland's largest single mass of granite is in the Cairngorms, but these rocks also occur in other significant mountain areas including Arran and the peaks around Glen Etive.

Gabbro

Gabbros are coarse-grained igneous rocks that contain greater proportions of dark minerals than granite, and are typically grey, brown or black in colour. Gabbros are primarily composed of white, rectangular feldspar crystals, green to black crystals of pyroxene, and orange-brown olivines, and it is common to see these minerals concentrated in layers of different colours. Gabbro is exceptionally rough to the touch, indeed almost prickly, because the feldspar crystals are resistant to erosion and stand proud of the

Kathryn Goodenough

rock surface. This rock is the main constituent of the Black Cuillin of Skye and has acquired legendary status among climbers because of these frictional properties. Gabbro is also important on Rum, Mull and Ardnamurchan, but is less common elsewhere in Scotland.

Gabbros are formed in a similar way to granites, through the cooling of magma deep beneath the Earth's surface. The difference between gabbro and granite is due to the variation in chemical composition of the original magma. Minerals such as olivine and pyroxene typically have high contents of iron or magnesium, and can only form from magmas that are rich in these elements, while the magmas that form granites and rhyolites contain a much higher proportion of silicon.

Peridotite

Peridotites are igneous rocks that are almost entirely composed of the iron and magnesium-rich mineral olivine. Although olivine is a bright grass-green when fresh, it weathers to an orange-brown colour, giving these rocks an extremely distinctive hue which is obvious even from a distance. Peridotites are commonly seen as layers in gabbro, for instance on the Rum and Skye Cuillin, where their brown colour contrasts strongly with the harder adjacent rock. In places the peridotites can contain a reasonably high content of feldspar, resulting in an 'egg box' appearance with networks of hard white feldspar standing proud of softer areas of brown olivine, which can be well seen at the head of Coire a' Ghrunnda on Skye. In common with gabbro, peridotite is very rough

Noel Williams

to the touch, with frictional properties that are welcoming to climbers.

The peridotite layers seen in the Skye and Rum Cuillin were formed from gabbro magma in the early stages of cooling, as olivine crystals began to form before any other minerals. These were relatively dense and sank to the floor of the magma chamber where they accumulated to form peridotite. As the magma continued to cool, feldspar and pyroxene crystals began to form, creating gabbro.

Basalt

Basalts are grey or brown volcanic rocks that are smooth, fine-grained and slippery when wet. They contain the same minerals as gabbro and dolerite, but the crystals cannot be seen with the naked eye. However, as with other volcanic rocks, they may contain larger crystals, typically white feldspars, within the fine-grained body of the rock. Basalts are usually derived from magma erupted from volcanoes, but also occur in sills and dykes that have intruded just beneath the surface. These rocks are most abundant on Skye, Mull and lower hills close to the Central Belt, such as the Campsie Fells, but also form occasional small intrusions elsewhere, sometimes

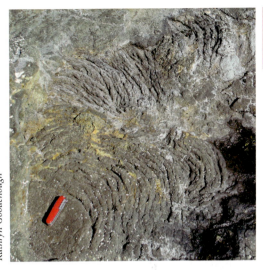

Kathryn Goodenough

amid sedimentary or metamorphic rocks. Basalt intrusions are common in the Skye Cuillin and can easily be identified as bands of distinct colour and much smoother texture amid the surrounding gabbro. Outcropping basalts may show varying degrees of columnar jointing, as famously seen around Fingal's Cave on Staffa.

Many basalts contain vesicles formed by gas bubbles trapped in the lava during cooling, and these may be filled by minerals deposited from fluids flowing through the hot lava, with superb examples occurring at Talisker Bay on Skye.

Dolerite

Dolerites are igneous rocks that are made up of the same minerals as gabbros, but they are less coarse-grained, and some eye straining is required to pick out the individual crystals. They are brown to grey in colour, often with flecks of white feldspar. Many dolerites are characterised by 'onion-skin' weathering, with thin layers of rock spalling off from a central, rounded core, and these rocks can show something of the columnar structure associated with basalts. The main development of dolerite in Scotland is in the Central Belt, forming various important crags including the Hawkcraig and Auchinstarry Quarry, but dolerites also form many of the sills and dykes that cut across the gabbros of Skye, Rum and Mull.

Dolerites are derived from the same magmas that form gabbros and basalts, and are of broadly intermediate grain size. Gabbros are formed when magma cools very slowly at considerable depth,

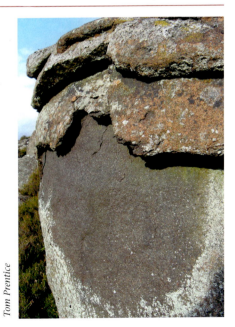

Tom Prentice

but dolerites are formed when the magma is intruded into cracks which are closer to the surface – often only a few hundred metres down. Basalts, by contrast, are formed from magma intruded very close to the surface or, more usually, erupted, and the three rocks thus reflect a corresponding range of cooling rates.

Shaping the Landscape

John Gordon

The glacially sculpted granite cliffs of Creag an Dubh Loch continue to be modified by postglacial rockfalls, which add to the large scree cone below the central gully (see p74)

Introduction

The diversity of Scotland's mountains is quite remarkable for such a small country. Compare the massive grandeur of the Cairngorms, the long, sweeping ridges of Lochaber and Kintail, and the jagged skyline of the Cuillin, described by Sorley MacLean as an "exact and serrated blue rampart". Why are these areas so different? What forces have shaped the rocks and landforms?

The great variety of our mountain landscape owes much to the interactions between their geological foundations and the processes of weathering and erosion by frost, ice, water and wind, acting over many millions of years. The most dramatic single influence has been that of the Ice Age glaciations, which have left a particularly distinctive legacy in our present mountain landscapes. This bold imprint was highlighted in 1901 by the great Scottish geologist, Sir Archibald Geikie, who observed that the records of the Ice Age "are so abundant, so clear, and so indisputable…Everywhere the trail of the ice meets our eye".

This chapter brings the geological story of Scotland's mountains up to the present day and includes the shaping of the pre-glacial landscape, the changes produced by the Ice Age glaciers and the processes that continue to alter the hills today. To help appreciate this story, it is useful to introduce some of the geomorphological processes that have been of particular importance during this period.

Weathering

Rock at or near the Earth's surface slowly disintegrates through a combination of physical and chemical processes that are collectively known as 'weathering'. These processes underlie many of the changes that are currently shaping Scotland's mountains, and they have operated with varying intensity at different times in the past.

The most important physical weathering process is frost action, associated with the freezing of water and the growth of ice in fractures in the rock. This process has resulted in a widespread cover of debris on summits and upper slopes, which varies in character according to the underlying geology. Some relatively resistant rocks, such as quartzite, break down into blockfields composed of large, angular boulders, with little fine material. Granites and Torridonian sandstones, by contrast, usually weather by granular disintegration, producing a surface cover of stones and coarse sand. This has relatively little cohesion and the finer material is winnowed out by the wind, leaving behind a gravelly residue. Finer-grained rocks, such as schists, break down into a mixture of stones, sand and silt.

Frost weathering is facilitated by pre-existing lines of weakness in the rock, and has contributed to the characteristic architecture of different types of rock outcrop in the uplands. This is most obvious in rocks that are split by more or less regular joints, such as granite and Torridonian sandstone. Frost weathering is also largely responsible for the rockfall debris that forms numerous scree slopes below exposed rockfaces in corries and along the flanks of glens. In *A Man in Assynt*, Norman MacCaig eloquently encapsulated this process:

> "And frost
> thrusts his hands in cracks and, clenching his fist,
> bursts open the sandstone plates,
> the armour of Suilven:
> he bleeds stones down chutes and screes,
> smelling of gunpowder."

Chemical weathering involves the alteration of minerals containing silica, such as micas and feldspars, which break down naturally under favourable conditions to produce clay minerals and other products, destroying the interlocking crystal structure of the rock. Clay minerals swell on contact with water and this process creates further physical stresses in the rock. Chemical weathering is most rapid under hot, humid climatic conditions, which have prevailed in Scotland at various times in the past. Under such conditions, it can result in considerable thicknesses of decomposed rock, sometimes exceeding 30m in depth. Chemical weathering continues, somewhat more slowly, in our present climate.

Glacial processes

Glaciers are moving bodies of ice, and form in areas where more snow accumulates in winter than melts in summer. Over time, the snow is transformed into ice, which deforms and flows downhill to lower altitudes, where it melts. In the upper reaches of a glacier, there is consequently net accumulation of snow, with net melting at lower levels, and the boundary between the two areas is known as the 'equilibrium line'.

The presence or absence of water at the bed plays a crucial role in how a glacier flows, the processes of erosion and deposition, and the landforms that result, and depends on the temperature of the bottom layers of ice. A glacier is said to be

Modern corrie and valley glaciers with end moraines, Kebnekaise, northern Sweden

'cold-based' if the temperature at the base is below the melting point, which is actually less than $0°$ C due to the pressure of overlying ice. Under these conditions, the glacier does not slide over its bed, but moves largely by slow internal deformation of the ice. Conversely, if the basal ice layer is at the pressure melting point, the glacier is said to be 'warm-based', and slides over its bed, or an underlying layer of deforming sediment, assisted by the lubricating effects of meltwater. Cold-based glaciers generally occur today in polar and continental areas, where temperatures and precipitation are very low, whereas warm-based glaciers tend to occur in oceanic areas where temperatures and precipitation are higher. Warm-based conditions are also likely to develop where the glacier bed is steeply sloping, or the overlying ice is very thick. Warm-based and cold-based areas can therefore occur contiguously in a single glacier where there is a change in the underlying topography or the thickness of the ice.

Glaciers occur in many shapes and sizes, but it is convenient to distinguish two broad types that formerly existed in Scotland. The first includes large, dome-shaped ice sheets and ice caps like those in Greenland and Antarctica, which are very thick and can bury entire mountain ranges. The second includes bodies of ice that are confined by the surrounding topography, forming valley and corrie glaciers like those in the Alps, or more complex networks of interconnected ice-fields and valley glaciers like those in the St Elias Mountains of Alaska or Patagonia. Ice sheets contain areas of relatively fast flowing warm-based ice, known as 'ice streams', which drain their interiors. These may be flowing at speeds of 2km a year or more, while the intervening cold-based ice may only move a few tens of metres per year. Ice caps are smaller than ice sheets and are likewise drained by outlet glaciers, which tend to be warm-based and to follow the underlying valley patterns.

Glaciers erode their beds through a combination of processes. Rock particles embedded in the base of the ice scratch and groove the underlying bedrock, with an action like an enormous file, a process known as 'abrasion'. The flow of the glacier may also crush or fracture the underlying rock and accentuate existing weaknesses. If water is present at the glacier bed, fluctuations in the water pressure inside any joints can further reduce the strength of the rock. The fractured material is then plucked away by the ice. Warm-based glaciers are therefore much more effective agents of erosion than cold-based glaciers. Estimates of current erosion rates range from 0.01mm/year for cold-based polar glaciers to 1–10cm/year for large, fast moving, warm-based glaciers in oceanic areas like south-east Alaska. Small glaciers such as those in the Alps typically erode at intermediate rates of around 1mm/year. This contrast between the different types of glacier has played an important part in creating Scotland's diverse mountain landscapes.

Glaciers transport and deposit considerable amounts of rock debris that is frozen into the basal layers of the ice, or dragged along underneath. The debris comprises boulders and stones together with rock that has been ground down to sand and silt, and is either smeared onto the underlying ground or dropped when the ice melts. This type of deposit is called 'till', a word of Scottish derivation used to describe a coarse, stony soil, and is plastered over the floors and lower slopes of most glens. Till may be shaped into a variety of landforms, including streamlined mounds which develop beneath the ice, and various types of moraine that are dumped or bulldozed at the glacier margins. Where glaciers flow in valleys with cliffs along their edges, rockfalls also contribute debris to the glacier surface. Some of this may find its way to the glacier bed, but much of this material is carried at or near the surface, so that the glacier acts like a conveyor belt. Depending on its thickness, this surface debris slows the melting of the underlying ice, creating particularly chaotic surface topography.

Melting glaciers release vast quantities of water that flows in rivers along the glacier margins, beneath the ice in ice-walled tunnels and meltwater channels eroded into the underlying bedrock, and down valley away from the glacier fronts. Such meltwater rivers transport large amounts of rock debris. This is then laid down as a variety of so-called 'glacifluvial' deposits, sometimes beneath the ice or as thick accumulations of sand and gravel, known as 'outwash plains', in front of the glacier snouts. Although these processes are no longer active in Scotland, their traces are clearly visible in many upland glens and straths.

Periglacial processes

The mountain landscape also carries the hallmarks of a variety of cold-climate 'periglacial' processes that involve the action of frost, ice and wind on the soil and rocks. These processes were most active in periods of restricted glaciation in areas beyond the glaciers, but continue today on the higher Scottish mountains.

Cold climatic conditions result in relatively rapid accumulation of frost-weathered rock debris on mountain slopes and summits. This debris may be sorted by frost heaving, which occurs more readily in finer-grained soils, resulting in various types of patterned ground. Weathered debris can also move downhill, often for surprising distances, under the influence of two distinct processes. On slopes, material heaved upwards by winter freezing resettles on melting in the spring, resulting in a progressive downhill movement known as 'frost creep'. Weathered debris of certain consistencies also flows slowly downhill when saturated with water following the melting of ice lenses in the soil, a process known as

Braiding and meandering, as exhibited here by the River Feshie in the Cairngorms before recent pinewood regeneration, are characteristic of a highly dynamic gravel-bed river

'gelifluction'. These two processes are collectively referred to as 'solifluction', and have produced a range of characteristic landforms on many Scottish mountains.

Today, the periglacial environment of the Scottish mountains is characterised by wet and windy conditions rather than extreme cold, and this is reflected in the landforms and patterns of erosion found on exposed slopes and summits.

River processes

Rivers gradually transport rock debris from their catchments to the sea. Whereas water travels from source to sea in a matter of days or even hours, sediment moves downstream much more slowly and erratically, and is repeatedly transported and stored for varying lengths of time in the riverbed, along the channel margins or as river terraces. In a 'textbook' river, most sediment originates in the upland parts of the catchment and is deposited in the lowland reaches. However, few rivers in Scotland conform to this idealised model because of the combined effects of glaciation and geology. Instead, they tend to show a great deal of variability along their courses, and steep rocky sections alternate with gentler reaches of lower gradient, which is where most sediment deposition occurs.

Channels that are cut into bedrock are relatively stable and are often confined in gorges, with waterfalls, potholes and plunge pools. These often run along faults or other lines of weakness in the underlying rock. By contrast, stretches of river where sediment is deposited, known as 'alluvial' reaches, run over beds of sand and gravel. These materials tend to be transported and redeposited during spates, and are spread across the full width of the area that the river occupies in such conditions. This expanse of sediment is known as a 'floodplain'.

Alluvial river channels become more or less meandering over time because accumulations of sand and gravel, known as 'bars', encourage the development of a sinuous flow pattern. Erosion is greatest on the outside of each bend, while bars build up on the inside of each bend, and these effects combine to accentuate the meandering course of the river. River channels of this type usually develop on floodplains with low gradients. Where gradients are steeper, and there is an abundant supply of sediment from banks that are easily eroded, rivers can become 'braided', with shifting networks of interconnected channels separated by gravel bars. Some rivers show characteristics of both meandering and braiding and are termed 'wandering gravel-bed rivers'.

Rivers tend to build up their floodplains during periods of abundant sediment supply, which occurs, for example, when their upper catchments are occupied by glaciers. If the amount of sediment then decreases or the discharge of water increases, the river cuts down into its floodplain, forming a new one at a lower level, and the former floodplain is left abandoned at a higher level as a river terrace. These commonly formed along the flanks of glens during and after the melting of the last glaciers, as rivers eroded downwards into glacial outwash plains.

The history of the mountain landscape

The rocks that form the Scottish hills are of great antiquity and the processes through which they were created, in particular those of the Caledonian orogeny 430 million years ago (see p29), laid the foundations of today's mountain landscapes. The high Caledonian mountain chain was extensively eroded and by the start of the Palaeogene, 65 million years ago, Scotland was an area of relatively low relief close to sea level. About 60 million years ago, the opening of the North Atlantic Ocean, and the intense volcanic activity that gave birth to the rocks of Skye, Rum and Arran, was accompanied and followed by repeated episodes of uplift and erosion of the Scottish landmass during the Palaeogene, Neogene and into the early Quaternary. Parts of the land surface were raised by 1km or more, with some tilting to the east. This uplift brought Scotland's mountains to roughly their present-day height above sea level.

The tilting of the landmass to the east resulted in the development of the main watershed near, and roughly parallel to, the west coast, with short, steep rivers draining to the west and longer ones to the east. This pattern persists today. These rivers dissected the upland landscape, particularly in the west, tending to follow natural drainage lines created by the existing surface relief. In the North-west Highlands, the orientation of glens was influenced by north-west to south-east faulting in the underlying Lewisian rocks. Much of the landscape south-east of the Great Glen, by contrast, has a south-west to north-east grain that is directly inherited from the Caledonian orogeny. By the onset of glaciation, the broad outlines of Scotland's mountains, and the intervening network of glens and straths, were therefore in place. This pre-glacial relief had a significant influence on the development of the Ice Age glaciers and the resulting glacial landforms.

The Quaternary Period, or Ice Age, began about 2.6 million years ago, and was associated with the intensification of a long-term cooling trend that commenced during the Palaeogene. The Ice Age was not one long unbroken period of glaciation, but was interrupted by many short intervals, known as interglacials, when the climate was similar to that of the present day.

During the early part of the Ice Age, from about 2.6 to 0.75 million years ago, relatively small mountain glaciers and icefields formed repeatedly in the Scottish Highlands. At intervals thereafter, a succession of vast ice sheets enveloped the

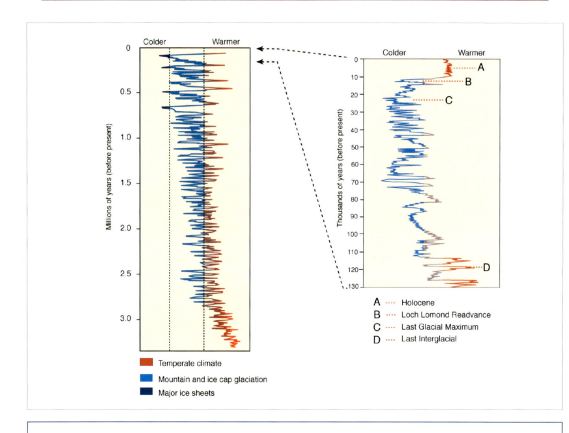

Climate records for the North Atlantic area over the last 3 million years (left) and the last 130,000 years (right). These reconstructions are based on measurements of oxygen isotopes in deep sea cores (left) and the Greenland ice sheet (right), and demonstrate the dramatic variations in climate during the Ice Age. The left hand diagram includes an indication of the likely presence of glaciers in Scotland, which has been repeatedly covered by ice sheets during the last 750,000 years.

whole country. These extended out across the floor of the North Sea, which was then dry land owing to the volume of water locked up in the globally expanding glaciers, and merged with ice spreading westwards from Scandinavia. In the west, the ice spilled across the continental shelf to terminate near its edge, beyond the Outer Hebrides. At other times, the mountains were again occupied by less extensive corrie glaciers and icefields. The scenery of Scotland's mountains has therefore been sculpted over the course of many phases of glaciation.

The last of the great ice sheets built up after about 35,000 years ago and reached its maximum extent about 26,000 years ago. It may then have retreated for a short time before advancing again around 22,000 years ago. At its maximum, the ice sheets probably buried even the highest summits. The main area of ice accumulation lay in the West Highlands, with an ice shed (analogous to a watershed) extending from Sutherland to the Clyde. Local ice centres also formed on the islands of Skye, Mull and the Outer Hebrides, their outflows merging with mainland ice flowing west and north-west.

The period from about 17,000–11,700 years ago was one of intense environmental change. The glaciers retreated, with some local readvances, and vegetation began to re-establish on the unstable, stony soils. Around 14,700 years ago, the climate warmed extremely rapidly from full glacial conditions to temperatures similar to those of today. However, the Ice Age had a sting in its tail. By about 12,900 years ago, the climate was again cooling, and glaciers once more expanded in the Highlands. This most recent glacial event is known as the Loch Lomond Readvance, after the area in which its traces were first identified. The largest ice-field built up in the West Highlands, extending from Wester Ross to Loch Lomond, with smaller icefields on Skye and Mull and numerous small corrie and valley glaciers elsewhere. There was a very strong climatic gradient from west to east, so that only small glaciers formed in the Cairngorms compared with the large icefield 50km to the west. Glacier equilibrium lines correspondingly rose from about 300m on Mull to over 1000m in the Cairngorms, reflecting snow-bearing winds from the south-west. Mean July temperatures in western Scotland were some 6-7° C lower than at present, and permafrost probably extended down to sea level.

Around 11,700 years ago, the climate warmed rapidly again and the last glaciers disappeared from Scotland. Their legacy was, however, stamped on the Scottish hills which would, by this time, have physically resembled the familiar landscapes of today. The climate warming marked the beginning of the present interglacial, known as the 'Holocene'. The landscape continued to change as a direct result of the shift to non-glacial conditions. Rockfalls and landslides modified unstable slopes, while upland rivers, relieved of their sediment burden from the glaciers, began to cut down into their flood-plains. Low-growing vegetation re-colonised the mineral soils and was soon followed by the return of trees to the glens.

Periglacial processes have continued to shape the mountain slopes and summits during the Holocene, although under windy and wet, rather than intensely cold, climatic conditions. Indeed, the mountain landscape

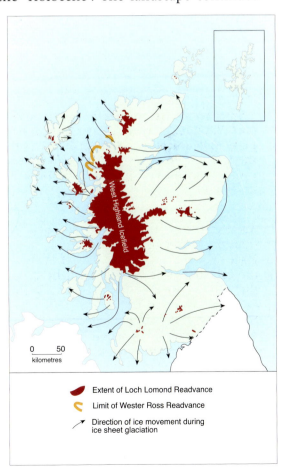

Directions of ice flow during the last major ice sheet glaciation, reconstructed using striations and the movement of erratics. The extent of the Loch Lomond Readvance glaciers (12,900-11,700 years ago), is based on their associated end moraines and other evidence. A well-defined end moraine extending from Coigach to Applecross records an earlier regional readvance of the ice around 15,000 years ago, known as the Wester Ross Readvance.

West Highland Icefield

0   50
kilometres

Extent of Loch Lomond Readvance

Limit of Wester Ross Readvance

Direction of ice movement during ice sheet glaciation

The Cairngorms are a classic landscape of selective glacial erosion. Remnants of ancient plateau surfaces with tors and shallow valleys are truncated by the glacially eroded cliffs at the head of Loch Avon

appears to have become more dynamic during the last few hundred years, with more frequent landslips and river channel changes, and more intense soil erosion and periglacial activity. This has been linked to an increased frequency of storms or flood events associated with the Little Ice Age of the 16th to 19th centuries. It is possible, however, that these effects may have been enhanced, directly or indirectly, by human activity such as forest clearance or overgrazing.

The evidence of pre-glacial events, and of glacial and periglacial processes, is etched on the mountain landscape in a variety of characteristic landforms. Many of these are evident on the ground and some from 1:50,000 maps.

Pre-glacial landforms

The overall topography and drainage pattern of the Scottish hills reflect the geological structure and the processes of uplift, tilting, weathering and erosion of the landscape prior to the Ice Age. This inheritance underlies the contrast between the deeply dissected Western Highlands and the extensive plateaux of the east, although it has been accentuated by glacial erosion.

Traces of the pre-glacial landscape have survived in a number of areas. During the Palaeogene and Neogene, the climate was relatively warmer and more humid than today, resulting in chemical weathering and disintergration of the bedrock. The weathered land surface was periodically uplifted, tilted and eroded, forming gently sloping plateaux at different altitudes. The remnants of these ancient land surfaces or 'palaeosurfaces' can be seen in the general similarity of summit levels across the Highlands, and were noted by Geikie in 1901, drawing attention to what he called the 'table-land', and the 'long level line of the Highland hill-tops'. In reality, the degree of uplift varied across Scotland, and several surfaces were formed at different levels at different times, rather than a single, vast plateau.

These palaeosurfaces are particularly well preserved in the Grampian Highlands, where subsequent glacial erosion was relatively localised. The view north-west from Lochnagar shows the landscape rising towards the Cairngorms in a series of level surfaces and steps, culminating in the rolling summits of Beinn a' Bhuird and Ben Avon. Similar expanses of ancient plateaux can be seen from the west Drumochter hills, looking north to the Monadh Liath and east towards the Gaick, with the land surface rising to around 800–900m. Other examples to the east of the Cairngorms and south of the Dee rise to about 800m, and the latter is clearly visible from the Munros above Glen Clova. The former mantles of weathered rock that covered these surfaces have been largely stripped away, but some local pockets have survived in the Cairngorms and the Gaick. In Coire Raibert in the Cairngorms, for example, there is an exposure of granite that has disaggregated into a granular mass that can be crumbled in the hand. Similar pockets of rotten granite occur alongside some of the burns draining the Moine Mhor, the high plateau at the head of Gleann Einich.

Many summits in the Cairngorms are crowned by tors that rise abruptly from the surrounding terrain. Tors have been formed by long-term differential weathering of the bedrock and erosion of the weathered material. The present tors were often thought to be remnants of the pre-glacial landscape. However, the development of a new dating technique has enabled estimates of when the tops of the tors were first exposed to the atmosphere. The method is based on measurements of the abundance of certain radioactive nuclides in the surface layers of the rock, which is related to the time that the rock surfaces have been affected by cosmic rays. This technique now indicates that the oldest surviving tors today are likely to have been first exposed within the last million years or so and hence have evolved during the Quaternary. The survival of these old tors through several glacial cycles suggests that the summit plateaux were, in general, not heavily eroded by the glaciers, although in places some tors have been moulded by glacier ice and others have been partially or totally destroyed, leaving behind a scattering of boulders.

The tors of Beinn Mheadhoin, Bynack More and Ben Avon are particularly spectacular, and rise up to 25m above the adjacent ground at the Barns of Bynack and Clach Bun Rudhtair. Some of the tors on Ben Avon, notably Clach Bhan, are pock-marked by remarkable weathering pits some 2m across. According to tradition, the lady of Fingal bathed in one of the water-filled cavities, and until the mid-19th century there was a custom for pregnant women to visit Clach Bhan and sit in one of the potholes, in the belief that it would lead to an easy labour.

In the first edition of the SMC guide to the Cairngorms in 1928, Sir Henry Alexander noted that the granite has often "weathered into horizontal slabs, so well defined and so regular as to give the impression of titanic masonry". This layering, known as 'sheet jointing', is usually parallel to the adjacent plateau surface, and formed through the unloading and expansion of the granite in pre-glacial times, as the overlying rock was eroded away. Similar layering can also be seen near the tops of the headwalls of some Cairngorm corries.

Although the West Highland landscape has been more deeply dissected than in the east, there are still remarkable similarities in the heights of the summits in many areas, which may indicate uplift and dissection of older land surfaces. In other parts of the Highlands, the landscape has become so fragmented that only isolated peaks remain. Some mountains of this type, such as Schiehallion, are clearly formed from more resistant rocks than those of surrounding areas. In other places where the rocks are of more or less uniform hardness, such isolated peaks are thought to reflect dissection and gradual inward erosion of a larger mountain mass. For example, the spectacular and unique residual mountains north of Ullapool, which rise abruptly above the ice-scoured Lewisian basement, represent the last remnants of what was once a vast cover of Torridonian sandstone. Differential pre-glacial weathering has also created some large basins set among the mountains, such as Rannoch Moor.

For the most part, traces of the pre-glacial landscape are confined to the large-scale topography of the mountains, and the detailed form of the hills and glens has largely been determined by subsequent glaciation.

Glacial landforms

The effects of glaciation occur so extensively that they can sometimes be difficult to grasp, particularly because the glaciers themselves have now disappeared. This was not lost on John Muir, whose description in *The Yosemite* could equally have applied to Scotland:

"...glaciers, back in their white solitudes, work apart from men, exerting their tremendous energies in silence and darkness. Outspread, spirit-like, they brood above the predestined landscapes, work on unwearied through immeasureable ages, until, in the fullness of time, the mountains and valleys are brought forth, channels furrowed for rivers, basins made for lakes... then they shrink and vanish like summer clouds."

Glacial erosion has formed several characteristic types of mountain landscape that vary across the country. In broad terms, the intensity of erosion was greatest in the west and least in the south and east. This pattern is explained by a combination of several factors. As noted earlier, higher snowfall in the west favoured the development of extensive ice cover in this part of Scotland. The pre-existing landscape in the west was also more intensively dissected, with steeper glens and more potential sites for corrie development. These circumstances would have favoured the development of thick, fast-flowing warm-based glaciers, which were able to scour the bedrock extensively and excavate deep troughs, rock basins and breached watersheds. Widespread scouring of the bedrock by warm-based ice sheets is referred to as 'areal scouring', and has created the rugged and largely low-lying 'cnoc and lochan' terrain of Sutherland and parts of the Outer Hebrides. Broadly similar landscapes also occur in other parts of western Scotland, including the Galloway Hills east of The Merrick. The depth of erosion has probably been relatively limited, but the action of the ice has emphasised the irregularities in the underlying bedrock. The landscapes of parts of Knoydart and Ardgour also feature ice-scoured and roughened surfaces extending right up to the summits. Elsewhere in the west, the landscape has been predominantly shaped by mountain glaciation, creating the heavily dissected 'alpine' forms, with numerous corries and arêtes, that are so characteristic of Lochaber and the Cuillin of Skye.

By contrast, mountain landscapes further east reflect more 'selective' glacial erosion, as it was only in the glens and straths that the ice was sufficiently thick and fast flowing for warm-based conditions to develop. These were consequently deepened by powerful ice streams, while adjacent watersheds and plateaux

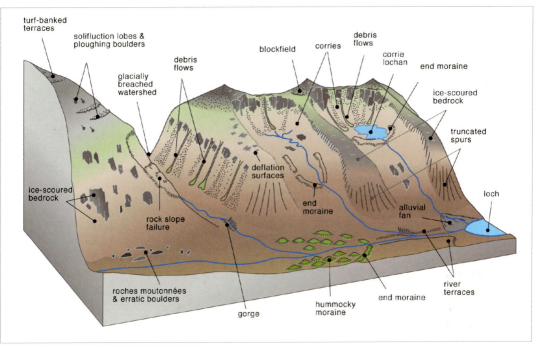

turf-banked terraces

solifluction lobes & ploughing boulders

blockfield

corries

debris flows

corrie lochan

end moraine

debris flows

glacially breached watershed

ice-scoured bedrock

truncated spurs

ice-scoured bedrock

deflation surfaces

loch

rock slope failure

end moraine

alluvial fan

roches moutonnées & erratic boulders

gorge

hummocky moraine

end moraine

river terraces

Mountain landforms in the Western Highlands (top) and Eastern Highlands (bottom). These diagrams are schematic and not all of these features necessarily occur on any one hill

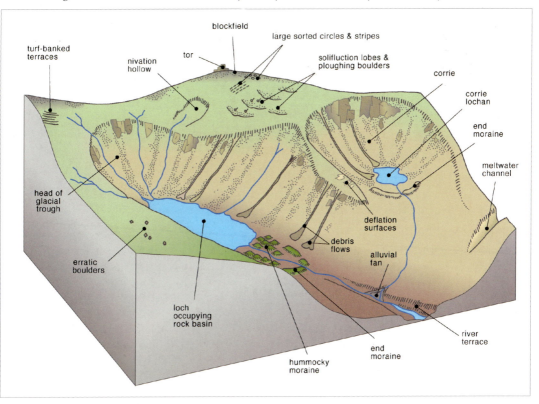

blockfield

large sorted circles & stripes

turf-banked terraces

nivation hollow

tor

solifluction lobes & ploughing boulders

corrie

corrie lochan

end moraine

meltwater channel

head of glacial trough

deflation surfaces

debris flows

alluvial fan

erratic boulders

loch occupying rock basin

river terrace

hummocky moraine

end moraine

The Lairig Ghru is a spectacular glacial breach cutting through the plateaux of the central Cairngorms. The former 'east ridge' of the Devil's Point, left, has been shaved off by glacial erosion, forming a truncated spur

remained little modified under cold-based ice. This relatively benign ice cover helps to explain the survival of some older features, such as tors and deeply weathered bedrock, in and around the Cairngorms. In these hills, the landforms of glacial erosion are sharply juxtaposed with the extensive areas of largely pre-glacial plateau into which they are cut, and similar landscapes typify the Gaick, Glen Clova and Creag Meagaidh areas.

These diverse landscapes include a number of hallmark glacial landforms, which are particularly abundant in the Western Highlands.

Glacial troughs

Erosion by ice streams and valley glaciers has often excavated deep glacial troughs, and Glen Coe, Glen Avon and the Lairig Ghru are particularly good examples. In some areas, such as Lochaber and Arrochar, these merge to create a highly interconnected pattern of glens that isolate the main mountain massifs.

Glacial troughs are often described as 'U-shaped valleys', which is correct in some places, including parts of the Alps and Norway. Most Scottish examples, however, are really parabolic, and this is well seen in the classic view of the Lairig Gartain from the A82. They are usually greatly deepened in comparison with normal river valleys and often have rock basins excavated in their floors. These have sometimes been filled with fluvial deposits and appear relatively flat, but many have since become occupied by lochs, which can be very deep. Well known examples include Lochs Lomond, Ness and Morar, which are respectively 190m, 239m and 310m in depth. In some instances, the lower reaches of glacial troughs have been flooded by the sea, creating the spectacular fjord-like sea lochs, such as Loch Hourn and Loch Nevis, that occur along much of the west coast.

The excavation of these troughs straightened out the pre-existing glens, and the ends of spurs or ridges that extended into the original valleys were frequently cut off. The resulting truncated spurs are very common, the Devil's Point being a classic example, but these features

0   50
kilometres

▮ Rock Basins

The density of glacially excavated rock basins is greatest in the north and west of Scotland, reflecting more intense glacial erosion there. The basins are aligned in the direction of ice flow and typically follow lines of geological weakness exploited by the glaciers.

are also well seen in Glen Coe and the Angus glens, for example in the view down Glen Esk from Mount Keen. Where the amount of erosion and downcutting in the main glens exceeded that in tributary glens or corries, these were left perched as hanging valleys. Waterfalls often pour over the resulting steps, and the almost Himalayan ambience of upper Glen Nevis owes much to the spectacular cascade above Steall flats.

The glaciers often created new glens by carving through the pre-glacial watersheds, and there are numerous examples of such 'glacial breaches', particularly in the north and west. In the North-west Highlands, the ice shed lay to the east of the pre-existing

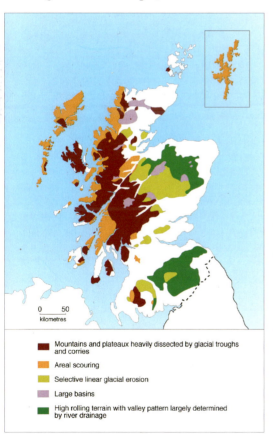

0   50
kilometres

▮ Mountains and plateaux heavily dissected by glacial troughs and corries

▮ Areal scouring

▮ Selective linear glacial erosion

▮ Large basins

▮ High rolling terrain with valley pattern largely determined by river drainage

Varying patterns of glacial erosion in the Scottish uplands.

watershed, and a series of glens were cut through it. These often now provide important transport routes, for example to Ullapool, Kinlochewe and Shiel Bridge. Rannoch Moor was a major ice accumulation area and the surrounding glens and lochs have a very striking radial pattern, which reflects the outward movement of ice streams from this centre. Many of these ice streams also cut through the previous watersheds, for example at Glen Coe, Loch Treig, Strath Ossian and Loch Ericht. To the east, the Lairig Ghru and Lairig an Laoigh are spectacular glacial breaches in the west-east watershed of the Cairngorms, and were probably cut by glaciers spilling northwards when their outflow to the south was blocked by ice along the Dee.

Watershed breaching has altered the courses of some rivers. The headwaters of the River Feshie formerly flowed east to the Dee but now turn sharply west to join the Spey, in an abrupt dog-leg that is conspicuous on the 1:50,000 map. Similarly at Inchrory in the eastern Cairngorms, the River Avon was formerly the headwater of the Don, but now flows north through a glacial breach to join the Spey.

Corries

Corries are well known features of many Scottish hills and typically have a steep headwall and gently sloping floor, sometimes containing a rock basin and small loch. Their appearance from above suggests a scallop removed from the mountain by a giant biscuit cutter. Although they have been buried and perhaps modified by ice sheets, their distinctive forms largely developed during periods of more restricted glaciation, when they carried small mountain glaciers or fed into larger valley glaciers. Their steep upper headwalls were shaped by intense frost weathering and rockfall, while their lower headwalls and floors reflect erosion beneath the ice. The rates of erosion by comparable modern glaciers suggest that some corries may have required half a million years to reach their present size, indicating that their formation has spanned several glacial periods.

Corries occur at lower altitudes and are more frequently encountered in the Western and Northern Highlands, due to higher snowfall there during periods of mountain glaciation, and range from near sea level on Hoy to over 1100m in the Cairngorms. They also typically, but not exclusively, face north through to east, since redistribution of snowfall by the prevailing south-westerly winds, and greater shading, would have favoured the development of glaciers on these slopes. Some of the most spectacular and atmospheric corries are hewn from Torridonian sandstone in the North-west Highlands, notably Coire Mhic Fhearchair and the great corries of Beinn Bhan. Where the walls of adjacent corries were eroded back and intersect, they form narrow, sharp-crested ridges, exemplified to perfection by the Carn Mor Dearg arete and almost any part of the Skye Cuillin.

Ice-moulded bedrock

Where the bedrock is exposed on the lower slopes and floors of glacial troughs and corries, it can clearly be seen to have been shaped by the passage of the glaciers. The abundance and architecture of these outcrops reflects the local geology, the intensity of erosion and the extent of overlying glacial deposits, but a number of characteristic features can often be identified. These include 'striations' produced by the abrasion of rock debris beneath the glaciers, and streamlined rock knolls moulded by ice movement. Both of these glacial trademarks can often be seen on the same piece of rock. Distinctively shaped, asymmetric rocky knolls known as 'roches moutonnees' are also quite frequent, and vary from small rock

Beinn Dearg Mor from An Teallach. A large end moraine, marking the limits of a Loch Lomond Readvance glacier, forms an arc across the ice-scoured slopes below the corrie

features a metre or so high to quite substantial hills.

Moraines and erratics

As a counterpoint to features created by erosion, the glens and lower slopes are covered with a variety of glacial deposits, which are often shaped into recognisable forms. The most spectacular of these are the end and lateral moraines that mark the limits of Loch Lomond Readvance glaciers. These can be seen in many locations, including the corries of An Teallach and the Cuillin, above Glen Brittle, and along the eastern flanks of Ben Hope. There are also fine examples of boulder moraines in several Cairngorms corries, including Coire Bhrochain, Coire an t-Sneachda and Coire nan Clach, the 'corrie of the stones', on Beinn a' Bhuird. Small Loch Lomond Readvance glaciers deposited end moraines at Tauchers and Loch Dungeon in the Galloway Hills, and moraines of the same age can be seen further east at Loch Skeen above the Grey Mare's Tail.

The former presence of Loch Lomond Readvance glaciers is often indicated by areas of 'hummocky moraine', perhaps most famously exemplified by the 'Corrie of the Hundred Hills', Coire a' Cheud-chnoic, in Glen Torridon. This curious landscape is far from unique, and similar arrays of hummocks can be seen in numerous places, including Sligachan on Skye, Rannoch Moor and the Drumochter Pass. Smaller groups of moraines are dotted around many glens.

Glaciers also frequently deposited large boulders and smaller fragments of rock which were transported some distance from their sources, and which are known as 'erratics'. These are often composed of different rocks to those on which they now rest. For example, granite erratics from Rannoch Moor are scattered over the

The Parallel Roads of Glen Roy are the shorelines of a series of ice-dammed lakes that formed during the Loch Lomond Readvance

Dalradian rocks of the Drumochter Hills, extending right up to the summits, and in Galloway, blocks of Loch Doon granite occur on the greywacke summit ridge of The Merrick. Sometimes, distinct 'boulder trains' can be traced away from source areas, and a trail of Torridonian sandstone boulders leads westwards from Canisp and Suilven across the lower, ice-scoured landscape of Lewisian gneiss.

Meltwater features

Torrents of glacial meltwater also helped to shape the mountain landscape. Short-lived but powerful rivers flowing beneath the glaciers often eroded channels in the underlying topography. Because the water followed pressure gradients determined by the ice, rather than gravity, these channels often cut across spurs or along slopes, and sometimes even run uphill. A good example is the Chalamain Gap, which is now a convenient route into the Lairig Ghru from Glen More. Networks of meltwater channels often formed major drainage systems and can be seen, for example, along the lower slopes of the Lammermuirs, the northern flanks of the Cairngorms and the southern flanks of the Ochils. The erosive action of meltwater was not confined to the surface of the land, and contributed to the formation of the cave systems in the Cambrian limestone at Inchnadamph, in Assynt.

As the glaciers retreated, powerful braided rivers built up extensive outwash plains of sand and gravel in front of the glacier snouts. These deposits sometimes buried areas of glacier ice, which subsequently melted to leave undulating landscapes of mounds, known as 'kames', and depressions known as 'kettle holes'. Some of these hollows now contain quite substantial water bodies, such as Loch Morlich. The outwash plains were subsequently incised by the rivers to form terraces, which are common along the margins of a great many glens, notably including Glen Feshie. Where Loch Lomond Readvance glaciers terminated at sea level along the west coast, large outwash plains were built out into the sea, forming underwater deposits known as deltas. Good examples are the flat-topped terraces at Corran, Ballachulish and Loch Eil, which were formed as the glacier in Loch Linnhe retreated.

During the retreat of the last ice sheet and the subsequent Loch Lomond Readvance, glacier-dammed lakes existed in a number of glens. The most famous of these is Glen Roy, which has three prominent shorelines, or 'parallel roads', running around its upper reaches. These were formed by changes in the level of the lakes, whose sudden drainage released vast floods underneath the ice into Glen Spean, through the Spean gorge into the Great Glen, and ultimately into the sea at the site of Inverness. Meltwater rivers sometimes transported large volumes of sediment into such lakes to form deltas. Particularly fine examples occur at Achnasheen, in Gleann Einich and at the north end of the Lairig Ghru, where the former deltas, now dissected by later river erosion, can be clearly seen as large flat-topped terraces. At Fersit, a delta built outwards into an ice-dammed lake in Glean Spean, partially covering the icefront. The thawing of the buried ice is now recorded by a hummocky kame and kettle landscape.

Periglacial landforms

The higher parts of Scottish hills display a striking array of periglacial landforms. Frost weathering over long periods of time has produced a layer of rock debris on the higher summits, which ranges from coarse blocks to stony silt according to the local geology (see p82). On some summits, this debris has a clear lower limit, or 'trimline', below which the bedrock is ice-scoured. On the north flank of An Teallach, there is a sharp contrast between ice-scoured bedrock with scattered erratic boulders on Meall Garbh, and frost-weathered debris on the plateau above at 700m, while in Knoydart, the summit of Ladhar Bheinn is covered by frost-weathered debris above 940m with ice-scoured bedrock below. The summits and upper slopes of the Trotternish ridge are covered in frost-weathered debris, block-fields and solifluction features, while intervening cols have ice-scoured bedrock and roches moutonnées. Similar patterns of landforms occur on hills such as Ben More Assynt and Conival, and Clisham and Uisgnaval Mor on Harris. Such trimlines were formerly thought to mark the upper surface of the last ice sheet, suggesting that the summits of these mountains rose above the ice as nunataks. However, erratics on the surface of summit blockfields in the North-west Highlands have now been dated to the time of the last ice sheet, indicating that it covered most if not all of the mountain tops. The trimlines are now thought to mark a temperature boundary within the ice sheet. On the slopes above, cold-based ice remained frozen to the underlying surface and left it largely unmodified. On the slopes below, the frost-weathered debris was removed and the bedrock scoured and moulded by the passage of warm-based ice.

Other processes have shaped the frost-weathered summit debris into a variety of features. Seasonal freezing and thawing can rearrange the debris into recognisable patterns of coarse and fine material, forming sorted circles on flat or low-angled ground and sorted stripes on steeper terrain. The formation of ice in the

Prostrate heather formed into wind stripes at an altitude of 560m on the northern flanks of An Teallach, below the subsidiary top of Mac is Mathair (behind). The prevailing wind blows from right to left

surface layers heaves the soil upwards into a dome shape and a combination of processes tends to move small stones towards the surface. When they reach the surface, these stones creep sideways to the margins of the dome of finer-grained sediments.

Large, inactive sorted circles occur on a number of summits, and can be seen on Ben Macdui, Beinn Fhuarain to the north of Conival, and Sron an t-Saighdeir in the Western Hills of Rum. These are a legacy of cold but non-glacial intervals during the Ice Age. Smaller features remain active on many mountains today, and are by no means confined to the highest ground. One of Scotland's best examples of active sorted stripes occurs on Tinto hill in the Southern Uplands, and recent experiments have demonstrated that they can reform, after disturbance, within a single season. Non-sorted frost features are sometimes seen on more vegetated ground, which can be heaved up into low mounds, elongating on steeper slopes into ridges and furrows aligned downhill. These are particularly well developed on Ben Wyvis and Glas Maol. Excavation has revealed that the underlying soil layers follow the irregularities of the surface topography with no sign of disruption, so these features are probably inactive.

On many slopes and summits, rock debris has crept downhill under the influence of solifluction to form sheets and lobes. This process was particularly active at the time of the Loch Lomond Readvance, but continues today. Solifluction features are widespread and are particularly extensive on the Fannaichs and Ben

Wyvis. Where weathering of the bedrock has produced very coarse debris, for example in the Cairngorms and on Lochnagar, Creag Meagaidh and Mount Keen, large 'boulder lobes' are common. Such features probably formed at the time of the Loch Lomond Readvance and are now inactive. Higher slopes are also frequently dotted with so-called 'ploughing boulders'. These are often active and creep a little further downhill in the spring, when the soil is saturated with meltwater. These easily recognisable features are most common on the schists of the Western, Central and Northern Highlands, because the fine silty debris derived from these rocks more readily traps water, encouraging ice formation in winter.

Long-lived snowbeds can leave their mark on the underlying ground by a variety of processes, including increased frost weathering and enhanced solifluction and erosion resulting from the abundance of meltwater. This combination of processes can accentuate natural snow-holding pockets to form shallow scoops, which are usually lined with various types of vegetation associated with prolonged snow-lie (see p106). Once again, the Cairngorms provide excellent examples, such as Ciste Mhearaid, about 1km north-east of the summit of Cairn Gorm, and the large scoop just north of Stob Coire Etchachan, both of which are clearly apparent on 1:50,000 maps.

The finer detail of many summit landscapes is shaped by the wind, which can strip vegetation and finer soil from exposed brows, cols and ridges, to leave bare 'deflation surfaces'. Fine, wind-blown sandy material is correspondingly deposited in sheltered lee sites. Large areas of such features are particularly prominent on some Torridonian sandstone mountains in the north-west, reflecting the particular conjunction of geology and wind exposure on these hills. Deflation is highly dynamic and buried soil layers in the sand indicate that there have been periods of stability, which allowed vegetation to develop, between periods of erosion. A variety of forms of wind-patterned vegetation also occur on exposed mountain slopes, including alternating stripes of vegetation and bare surfaces. On steeper slopes, solifluction and the effects of wind exposure on the vegetation can create miniature terraces running uphill like a staircase or trending obliquely across the slope.

During and following the melting of the glaciers, corrie headwalls and other crags continued to disintegrate through rockfall, producing the screes that are now so ubiquitous in the hills. Many scree slopes accumulated on ice-free ground at the time of the Loch Lomond Readvance. These are generally large and inactive compared with screes that formed later during the Holocene, which often continue to accumulate today through intermittent rockfall. This generally

Terraces (left) and solifluction lobes (right), Sgurr Mor, Fannaichs

occurs on a small scale, but larger rockfalls can modify well-known climbs, as with the classic 'Parallel B' on Lochnagar in 1995 and 2000 and 'The Giant' on Creag an Dubh Loch in 2001.

A few scree slopes that accumulated during the Loch Lomond Readvance record the presence of long-lived snowbanks. Debris sliding and rolling down the surface of hard snow formed ridges that run across the fall line at the base of the slopes. These features, known as 'protalus ramparts', occur at around a dozen locations in Scotland, typically forming arc-shaped ridges up to a few hundred metres long and less than 10m high on their outer sides. Several occur in the Cairngorms, including one at the foot of the Devil's Point in Glen Ghuibhsachain, while others can be found on Creag Meagaidh and An Teallach.

A number of other processes continue to reshape the deposits of till, scree and other rock debris on hill slopes. Snow avalanches carry loose material downhill, which is often apparent in spring as 'fresh', angular rock fragments covering vegetation or perched on boulders at the base of scree slopes. In a few locations, including the Lairig Ghru, upper Glen Luibeg and Coire na Ciste on Ben Nevis, repeated avalanches along particular lines have produced tongues of boulders spreading across the adjacent glen and corrie floors.

Very heavy rain during summer convective storms, or prolonged frontal rainfall, can also unleash landslides composed of fast-moving slurries of rock detritus, which are known as 'debris flows'. These are very common, their tracks scarring many hill slopes, and there is some evidence that their frequency has increased in the last few centuries. Such incidents can also block roads, including the A83 south of the 'Rest and Be Thankful' and the A82 in Glen Coe, but can be much more destructive. Debris flows obliterated the settlement of Achtriochtan, a short distance east of Clachaig, during the 18th century. An intense rainstorm in summer 2002 produced a spectacular debris flow below Aladdin's Couloir in Coire an t-Sneachda, in the Cairngorms. In some places, for example in Glen Coe, repeated flows from the same source areas have built up large cones of debris on the slopes below.

Rock slope failure

A range of landforms results from the downslope movement of large masses of bedrock. Landslides of this type are collectively termed 'rock slope failures'. Glacially steepened mountainsides often became unstable when the ice melted, because the glaciers tended to buttress the cliff faces. When this support was removed, the release of stress in the bedrock sometimes resulted in the opening of deep-seated fractures, often with spectacular effect. Most rock slope failures are believed to have occurred soon after deglaciation, but the response has occasionally been delayed, and some are thought to be of more recent origin. Over 600 such rock slope failures are known in the Highlands and Islands, with 140 exceeding 0.25km^2 in area. They occur on all kinds of bedrock, but the largest clusters are in the western ranges around Glen Affric, Kintail and Knoydart, in the Mamores and Grey Corries, and in the Southern Highlands. These are generally modest in scale, however, in comparison with catastrophic events in Scandinavia, the Alps and higher mountain ranges of the world.

In a few cases, rock slope failure has led to the collapse of whole sections of mountainside, producing spreads of large boulders on the slopes and glen floors below. Particularly good examples occur in the Lost Valley in Glen Coe and on Beinn Alligin. In the latter case, a large part of the rock face collapsed below the

Rock slope failure on Mullach na Dheiragain, north of Glen Affric

ice-steepened summit of Sgurr Mhor, leaving a scar that can be seen from the south shore of Loch Torridon and forming a tongue of bouldery debris extending over 1km down Coire Toll a' Mhadaidh Mor. Application of a technique which allows the dating of rock surfaces suggests that this spectacular event occurred around 4,000 years ago. This would clearly have been a bad time to camp in this corrie, but the bouldery debris resulting from these slope failures can provide excellent sites for 'howffs', such as the Shelter Stone. In a few places, including the eastern flanks of the Trotternish Ridge on Skye, and parts of Raasay and Mull, thick beds of lava have failed over weaker sedimentary rocks, leading to large-scale landslides. Weathering of the slipped blocks of lava has produced dramatic rock pinnacles at The Storr and Quiraing.

The results of slope failure have usually been less spectacular, however, with the detached mass only slipping or creeping a short distance, or even remaining largely in place. The largest and best example in Scotland is on the southern slopes of Beinn Fhada, above Gleann Lichd, where rock slope deformation features extend over a distance of 2.5km. Here, the upper and middle slopes are crossed by a remarkable series of asymmetric ridges several hundreds of metres long and up to 10m high. These run approximately parallel with the contours, with their steeper slopes facing uphill, and are known as 'antiscarps'. Near the top of the slope, at the junction with the plateau, a scarp slope 90m high indicates where the deformed mass has moved downhill, but the base of the slope shows no evidence of displacement out into the glen. The whole hillside has deformed downslope under the effects of gravity, but rather than failing catastrophically, it

Alluvial deposition at the head of Loch Etive; Stob Dubh, centre, and Buachaille Etive Mor, left

has bulged out, with the compressional stresses being taken up by the formation of the antiscarps.

The long mountain ridges on either side of Glen Shiel have also been modified by rock slope failures, which have created notches and narrow ridges at Saileag and Aonach Meadhoin, and have split the ridge of Sgurr na Ciste Duibhe. Here, a large failed area includes open fissures and antiscarps, and a debris lobe descends to the Shiel gorge. In the Southern Highlands, notable examples occur on Beinn an Lochain and Ben Donich in Arrochar, and Benvane in the Trossachs. The summit of The Cobbler owes its very distinctive form to these processes, and its ridge is split by fissures associated with a rock mass that has partially slipped away on the south side. Rock slope failures are scarcer in the Eastern Highlands, but good examples occur in the Gaick Pass and at Corrie Brandy in Glen Clova. The traces of rock slope failure are of more than passing interest to climbers and hill-walkers, and the deeply fissured ground of slope deformations is a potential hazard for the unwary, particularly when snow-covered.

Rock slope failures are thought to have occurred on slopes weakened by fracturing as a result of stress release from the unloading of the ice sheet during deglaciation. It has been suggested that they were triggered by earthquakes associated with uplift of the land and fault movements within a few millennia following deglaciation. The slope failure on Sgurr na Ciste Duibhe coincides with the Glenshiel Fault, which might have been reactivated seismically, and the local mountain name of Aonach air Chrith, the 'ridge of trembling', may hint at folk memories of earthquakes.

River landforms

Glaciation has not only determined the form of Scotland's glens and corries, but has also influenced the detailed courses of the rivers that drain them. Erosion of glacial deposits and the downstream movement of sediment has continued during the Holocene and various active river features can be seen in the glens.

There are some general contrasts between the rivers that drain west and east from the main watershed. The pattern of pre-glacial uplift, and more intensive glacial erosion, means that westerly-draining rivers have relatively short, steep courses. In some instances, these have been lengthened by glacial breaching, and rivers such as the Coe and Shiel now have relatively low-angled upper reaches, then descend rapidly to the west in rocky gorges down on to the flatter floors of the glacial troughs. The steep rocky courses of western rivers, along with relatively high precipitation, give rise to so-called 'flashy' flow regimes. Such rivers are characterised by fast responses and short periods of great activity, when floods can dramatically alter the positions of channels and bars, interspersed with longer periods of relative inactivity. Rivers draining to the east, such as the Dee, Spey and Tay, are generally longer, larger and more powerful.

Against this background, Scotland's mountain rivers display some common features. The upper tributaries of Highland rivers typically include sections cut into bedrock with gorges and waterfalls, interspersed with steep reaches that have bouldery beds. These represent a legacy of accumulated glacial debris that was left behind as finer material was transported downstream. The streams may only shift these boulders during extreme floods, but these can produce dramatic effects. The Allt Mor, for example, swept away part of the Cairngorm ski access road during a flash flood in August 1978. Attempting to cross such rivers in spate, when boulders are moving along the bed, can be particularly hazardous.

Downstream, lower gradient alluvial reaches alternate with steeper rock sections, reflecting bedrock outcrops and patterns of glacial erosion. Glacial deposits and river terraces along the glen margins provide abundant sources of sediment, and the alluvial reaches of the main glens and straths are typically occupied by wandering gravel-bed rivers, which occasionally shift to different courses, leaving abandoned channels on their floodplains. These rivers are generally meandering in the manner of the Derry Burn, but occasionally they split into 'braided channels' superbly illustrated by the River Feshie. Lochs act as sediment sinks and their upstream ends are gradually filled in to form deltas, which are often particularly obvious when looking down from neighbouring ridges. Loch an t-Seilich in Glen Tromie provides one of many examples.

Sediment is deposited at river confluences where steep tributary streams enter a main glen, accumulating to form more or less triangular-shaped spreads of water-worn debris known as 'alluvial fans'. These sometimes have a modern active fan set into an older, larger fan surface, which can be furrowed by abandoned river channels. Numerous good examples occur in the Highlands, including glens Coe, Lichd and Shiel. Some of the best are in Glen Feshie, where the Allt Lorgaidh and Allt Garbhlach join the main glen.

These, then, are the processes that have shaped the mountain landscape in Scotland, now highly valued as part of our geoheritage. As well as influencing the form of the land surface, the diversity of rock types, landforms and surface deposits has played an important role in providing the mosaics of habitats available for plants and animals. The development of vegetation also contributes to soil formation through the gradual accumulation of organic plant material, although this process can be very slow at higher altitudes. The resulting soils vary according to geology, climate and topography, and these factors are visibly imprinted on the vegetation that now cloaks the mountains of Scotland.

Striated rock surfaces

These are rock surfaces that have been abraded by glaciers, and can often be seen on exposed slabby outcrops on the lower slopes and floors of glens and corries. The rock surfaces frequently have a smooth or polished appearance and are commonly marked by parallel scratches and grooves (or 'striations'), which were produced by rock fragments embedded in the basal layer of the ice. These are sometimes accompanied by crescent-shaped gouges or 'chattermarks', which are up to a few centimetres across and occur in lines up to a metre long. These were created when boulders in the ice impacted sharply with the underlying bedrock and were dragged across its surface.

Striations and chattermarks in ice-scoured quartzite

Noel Williams

Striated bedrock can be seen throughout the Scottish hills, although the characteristic marks are generally poorly preserved on granite. Not surprisingly, they are also better seen on less weathered rock surfaces. Particularly good examples occur on ice-smoothed gabbro at Loch Coruisk and in the Cuillin corries, and on the Torridonian sandstones of Applecross and Torridon. The orientations of striations have been used to help reconstruct the former directions of flow of the glaciers.

Streamlined bedrock and roches moutonnées

Glacial abrasion frequently formed streamlined knolls of bedrock that are elongated in the direction of former ice movement, and whose surfaces are typically smoothed and striated on all sides. These features are common throughout the hills, but particularly good examples occur in the corries of the Cuillin and at Loch

Roche moutonnée south of Lochailort

John Gordon

Coruisk. For obvious reasons, these landforms are sometimes referred to as 'whalebacks'.

In contrast, roches moutonnées are asymmetric bedrock forms that are smoothed and streamlined on the up-glacier side but end much more steeply and abruptly on the down-glacier side, where weakened rock has been plucked away by the ice. They vary enormously in size, ranging from rock knolls a metre high to hills a few hundred metres in height. Good and conspicuous examples of small roches moutonnées occur around Polldubh in Glen Nevis, in the Cuillin of Skye and on Rum. Larger features of this type occur on both sides of the River Dee between Braemar and Balmoral, and in Strathspey south of Aviemore, including the 428m hill of Ord Ban above Loch an Eilean. The name is derived from a supposed resemblance to 18th century wigs that were slicked down with mutton fat.

Erratics

Erratics are glacially transported rocks that have been deposited some distance from their source outcrops. The most conspicuous of these are boulders dotted across the ground surface, but they also occur as smaller rock fragments incorporated in deposits of till. Erratics are a common feature of glens and straths in mountain areas, and are not infrequent on upper slopes and summits in the Central and Eastern Highlands. Any big, isolated boulder that is not in the fall line of a crag or scree slope is likely to be of this origin, but several other features can provide

Granite boulder below The Cobbler (mica schist)

further confirmation. The rock type of the boulder is often different from the local bedrock and many such boulders are 'perched', sometimes delicately poised on smaller rock fragments, and resting on bare, ice-scoured rock surfaces. Erratics also tend to be slightly rounded off, in contrast to the more sharply angular form typical of rockfall debris.

Erratics are particularly abundant in the West and North-west Highlands, and Torridonian sandstone and Cambrian quartzite erratics are widespread in Torridon and Assynt. The dispersion of erratics from known geological sources has been used, in conjunction with striations on the bedrock, to reconstruct the direction of former ice movement.

Glacial and meltwater deposits

Sediments deposited by glaciers (till) or meltwater (glacifluvial deposits) cover the floors and lower slopes of most glens and straths. These deposits are usually concealed by vegetation, but are sometimes revealed along eroded riverbanks and landslips, or beside bulldozed tracks.

Till typically consists of a jumbled mixture of stones and boulders in a matrix of sand, silt and sometimes clay. 'Lodgement' till is plastered onto the underlying surface when the glacier is no longer able to drag the debris forward. It is usually highly compacted and contains sub-angular shaped stones. The latter are often aligned in the direction of ice flow and have striated surfaces. 'Melt-out' till is deposited by melting out of debris directly from the ice. It is generally coarser, less compacted and has fewer striated stones.

Meltwater deposits, by contrast, consist of sand and gravel that have been washed and

Lodgement till

sorted into layers according to size, and individual stones are more rounded than in till. The two main types of deposit are usually easier to identify when they are associated with landforms which are obviously of glacial or fluvial origin; glacial sediments form moraines, while meltwater sediments are found in outwash terraces and fans.

79

End and lateral moraines

End and lateral moraines develop along the fronts and edges of glaciers, and sometimes consist of a single ridge of variable height, but more usually a series of ridges or mounds, formed from till and other debris deposited by the ice. End moraines typically extend in an arc across the floor of a glen or corrie and merge with lateral moraines. Sometimes, several moraines are arranged concentrically.

Loch Lomond Readvance end moraine between Loch Glascarnoch and Loch a' Gharbhrain (left)

Nick Kempe

Good examples occur at the bottom end of Glen Torridon and the head of Loch Glascarnoch. The massive rampart of the latter is clearly visible from the Dirrie More road south of Ullapool. Many others are tucked away in the hills and will be encountered during approaches via glens and corries.

Some moraines are formed from coarse debris and occur as low boulder ridges, or as spreads of boulders which end more or less abruptly at the former positions of glacier snouts. Good examples occur in a number of corries in the Cairngorms and in the corrie of Lochan a' Chnapaich, to the south of Eididh nan Clach Geala in the Beinn Dearg group. Most moraines in the Highlands were formed by Loch Lomond Readvance glaciers.

Hummocky moraine

The descriptive term 'hummocky moraine' is applied to a distinctive form of moraine that is typically, but not exclusively, associated with Loch Lomond Readvance glaciers. It has the appearance of a chaotic array of mounds and ridges when seen on the ground. The mounds are variable in height, ranging from a few metres to tens of metres, and clusters of larger moraines

Hummocky moraine below White Coomb, Moffat Dale

Andy Dugmore

can be arduous and frustrating to traverse. When moraines of this type are viewed from above, they are often seen to be aligned in parallel rows.

There are several explanations for the origin of these distinctive landforms. Where the hummocks are aligned in rows at an angle to the axis of a glen, they indicate the sequential ice margin positions of retreating glaciers. In other cases, where the hummocks are aligned parallel to the axis of a glen, they may have formed beneath the glaciers by deformation of underlying till. Some more irregular forms may reflect the melting of glaciers whose surfaces were covered by a variable blanket of rock debris. Depending on its thickness, this would have insulated the ice below, inhibiting melting and creating a chaotic hummocky relief.

Meltwater channels

A variety of channels and gorges are associated with the release of vast quantities of meltwater by the receding glaciers. In some cases, the water cut channels and gorges along pre-existing drainage routes. Corrieshalloch Gorge is a particularly spectacular example, but any larger gorge in the hills that is now occupied by a river is likely to have originated in this way.

Other meltwater channels were cut in places that now carry little or no drainage, and have been left high and dry. The flow of water was sometimes directed along the edges of the glaciers, and the former courses of these rivers can now be seen as dry channels running across hillsides parallel to the former ice margins, and bearing no relation to normal river courses. A number of meltwater channels can also be seen cutting across spurs, particularly in the Eastern Highlands. These tend to have a characteristic appearance in which shallow cols are deeply and abruptly incised by straight,

Meltwater channel between Glen Lui and Glen Quoich, Cairngorms

steep-sided notches, such as Clais Fhearnaig between Glen Lui and Glen Quoich. Many of these distinctive features can be picked out on 1:50,000 maps as well as on the ground.

River terraces

The floors and flanks of glens and straths frequently contain flat-topped terraces that drop abruptly to the level of the present river – which consequently appears to flow along a large incut trench. These terraces generally consist of sand and gravel deposited by rivers during the latter stages of the last glaciation, when

River terraces, Glen Roy

large quantities of sediment were available from melting glaciers and from unstable, unvegetated slopes. The tops of the higher terraces thus often mark the outwash plains of former glacial rivers, and sometimes contain traces of abandoned braided river channels. The rivers subsequently cut down into these deposits and formed new floodplains.

Small terraces sometimes run along the sides of glens well away from, and unrelated to, the existing rivers. These 'kame terraces' were deposited by meltwater rivers running between a glacier and the valley side, and are sometimes associated with meltwater channels. Large, flat-topped terraces can also be produced where deltas that accumulated in ice-dammed lakes were incised by the postglacial rivers. These delta terraces are much less widespread and tend to be broader, but with limited lateral extent along the glen sides. They often 'block' the mouths of glens, where lakes were dammed by different glaciers (see p71).

Blockfields

Some summits and upper slopes have an extensive cover of interlocking boulders that form level or gently sloping blockfields bare of soil and vegetation. These can be hazardous to cross particularly when wet or snow-covered. They form in situ in massive and well jointed bedrock as the freezing of water in joints and along bedding planes splits apart the rock. Good examples occur on the Cambrian quartzite summits in the North-west Highlands, such as Ben More Assynt, Conival and Canisp; on the Dalradian quartzites of Schiehallion and the Mamores; on some granite summits in the Cairngorms, such as Derry Cairngorm and Cairn Toul, and the Red Cuillin; and on the microgranite of Sron an t-Saighdeir on Rum. On other rock types, such as micaceous schist, granite and sandstone, the blocks are more commonly incorporated in a matrix of finer material produced by granular disintegration of the bedrock. Surface exposure dating of erratics lying on blockfields in the North-west Highlands indicates that the blockfields there formed before the last glaciation, surviving this period under a protective cover of cold-based ice.

Blockfield on the summit of Ben More Assynt

John Gordon

Solifluction sheets and lobes

Solifluction, the slow downhill movement of frost-weathered debris resulting from seasonal freezing and thawing and melting of ice lenses, has produced a range of distinctive landforms which are well seen in the photo of Sgurr Mor Fannaich (see p73). These may include turf-banked terraces (opposite) or larger solifluction sheets several tens of metres across. The latter appear from a distance as more or less uniform areas of stony

Boulder lobes, Lurcher's Gully, Cairngorms

John Gordon

or vegetated ground and tend to be more obvious where they terminate downslope in a low step, about a metre or less high, which often has an irregular lobe-like form. Where weathering has produced particularly coarse debris, for example on Cairngorm granite, the lower edges of the sheets form conspicuous boulder lobes with fronts that may be over 3m high. Larger features of this type are now inactive, but many smaller vegetated lobes remain active today. The latter can usually be distinguished by their steep fronts.

Solifluction features are common throughout the Scottish hills, but are particularly apparent on most upper slopes of the Cairngorms, the Fannaichs and Ben Wyvis. Some of the best examples of boulder lobes occur on the central Cairngorms, Lochnagar and Creag Meagaidh.

Ploughing boulders

Ploughing boulders have moved downslope faster than the soil in which they are partly embedded, leaving a furrow in their wake and pushing up a mound or ridge of soil in front, like a 'bow wave'. These boulders are typically 0.5–2m across and are easily recognised by the trenches on their uphill sides, which can be two metres or more in length.

John Gordon

Ploughing boulders are common on many mountains in the Highlands, and are particularly characteristic of the fine, silty soils derived from weathering of schists. They can also be seen in the Southern Uplands, but are less common on granites and Torridonian sandstones. Good examples occur on Ben More (Crianlarich) and neighbouring hills, and on the Fannaichs and west Drumochter hills.

Ploughing boulders on higher slopes are often active, and measured rates of movement range from a few millimetres to a few centimetres per year. Excavations have revealed the formation of ice 'lenses' under the boulders in winter, and when these melt in spring, the boulders slide downhill on the saturated soil. The shelter of the hollows behind the blocks may help the vegetation to keep pace, and there is generally no bare ground to betray this movement.

Turf-banked terraces

On fairly steep upper slopes, the interaction of solifluction and the effects of wind on vegetation growth can create cascades of flat-topped terraces that resemble a staircase. Each tread is typically a few metres from front to back, but they can extend for much greater distances across the slope, and are particularly visible at long range under a light cover of

Mark Wrightham

Turf-banked terraces associated with active solifluction, Strathfarrar

snow. They may take a variety of forms and sometimes run obliquely across the slope, indicating a strong effect of wind on the vegetation. Exactly how they form is uncertain, but the vegetation may play a role by 'damming' the downhill movement of debris. Terraces with steep, bulging fronts indicate active solifluction, whereas lower-angled features are static. The latter may grade into wind-patterned vegetation (see p84).

The environment at ground level, in particular exposure to wind, may change dramatically across individual terraces and may be reflected by gradations in the vegetation, which can change significantly within a few feet. These can resemble transitions seen on a much larger scale with increasing exposure on upper hill slopes. The steep risers may be carpeted, for example, by wind-trimmed dwarf shrub heath, which gives way to bare ground or *Racomitrium* on the treads.

Sorted circles and stripes

On many upper slopes and summits, frost action has sorted stony surface debris into distinct patterns. Small sorted circles are active on unvegetated ground on many mountains. These typically appear as net-like patterns of stones with a 'mesh' about 10–20cm in diameter and finer material in the centre. When the ground is snow free in winter, the centres of the 'circles' are often domed upwards by several centimetres, due to frost heave and needle ice formation. Much larger

Sorted stripes

Mark Wrightham

inactive sorted circles can be seen on a few hills (see p72) and are probably at least 11,700 years old. These can be up to several metres across and are edged by stones and boulders over 15cm in size. The finer centres of these features are often covered in vegetation.

On steeper slopes there is a transition from sorted circles to sorted stripes, with alternating bands of stones and finer debris. Inactive forms typically consist of stones and boulders more than 15cm across in strips several metres apart, with the intervening material usually vegetated. Smaller active forms occur on unvegetated ground, and experiments have shown that individual stones can move as much as 0.4m downhill during a single winter.

Deflation surfaces and wind-patterned vegetation

Deflation surfaces and erosion scars produced by the action of wind are common on exposed sites such as bealachs, ridge crests and plateau rims. These generally appear as areas of bare ground where the vegetation cover has been broken and the finer soil removed, leaving a residue of coarse gravel and larger stones. Remnants of the former ground surface sometimes occur as 'islands' of soil and vegetation. The eroded finer material is deposited

Deflation surface

John Gordon

in lee areas as sheets of sand, which easily take the imprint of a boot and are every bit as unstable as they appear. Particularly extensive deflation surfaces and wind-blown sand deposits occur on some Torridonian sandstone hills, including An Teallach, Ben Mor Coigach and Cul Mor, but similar features can be seen in the Cairngorms and elsewhere.

On low-angled ground, wind action also creates patterned vegetation, typically consisting of wavy stripes of prostrate heather or crowberry alternating with bare ground (see p72). The vegetation may alternatively appear as small crescents on otherwise bare surfaces. These are particularly common in the Cairngorms, and good examples occur on the northern spurs of Beinn a' Bhuird and Ben Avon, and on Sròn an Aonaich on Cairn Gorm.

Debris flows

Debris flow tracks are common in the Highlands, occurring as long, narrow gashes on scree slopes and hillsides. Recently active features appear as freshly eroded scars running straight downhill on scree, or as bare gullies on otherwise vegetated slopes. Older tracks tend to be wholly or partially vegetated, and appear as gullies that are usually fairly shallow, with relatively little sign of regular drainage. Debris flows variously originate in rock gullies or bowl-shaped hollows on open slopes, and rounded, lobed tongues of debris usually occur at the base of the slope. Repeated flows can build up large cone-shaped accumulations of material, for example in Glen Etive and below the Chancellor on the Aonach Eagach.

In many parts of the Highlands, including Glen Coe, the Blackmount and the Bridge of Orchy hills, largely inactive debris flow tracks seam many hillsides, creating a distinctive parallel-furrowed appearance which is particularly obvious on the otherwise uniform sides of long glacial troughs, especially in low light. Because debris flows are triggered by infrequent

John Gordon

Debris flow, Coire an t-Sneachda, Cairngorms

bouts of heavy rainfall, many such features can appear at more or less the same time. Many debris flows in the Cairngorms date from intense summer rainstorms in 1956 and 1978.

Rock slope failures

Rock slope failure sometimes results in catastrophic rockfalls, creating obvious accumulations of angular debris that may include very large blocks. A much more common outcome in the Scottish Highlands, however, is the less spectacular deformation of slopes as huge bodies of rock

Tom Prentice

Mullach Coire a' Chuir, 'Summit of the Snow Hollow', Cowal

shift a short distance downhill. This process can create a wide range of visible features.

Larger failures can extend for over a kilometre and are visible from a distance. These may have distinct source cavities appearing as shallow hollows in the hillside, with uneven or bulging ground below where the slumped mass has come to rest. They may also be identified by the presence of one or more parallel ridges running across slopes, with steep uphill faces (or antiscarps) up to 10m high, or by other noticeably unusual features such as double summit ridges and split ridges. At close quarters, it is often possible to see open tension fractures in the bedrock on slopes and ridges, which range from a few centimetres to many metres wide and deep, and are not necessarily associated with visible traces in the slope below. Such features are particularly common in the Western and Southern Highlands.

Scotland's Mountain Environment

Cnoc-and-lochan topography

Cnoc-and-lochan topography or terrain comprises rocky knolls and irregular depressions, the latter often filled by small lochs. It is a product of areal scouring by warm-based ice sheets. The irregular form of the landscape closely reflects the pattern of fracture zones, faults and dykes in the bedrock which produced an irregular depth of pre-glacial weathering. Despite their appearance, landscapes of areal scouring have

Cnoc-and-lochan terrain on Lewisian gneiss south of Suilven, Assynt

Tom Prentice

not been heavily modified by glacial erosion. Rather, the ice sheets extensively scraped and scoured the terrain, removing the variable cover of pre-existing soil and weathered bedrock and selectively eroding areas of weaker bedrock. Such landscapes, with their distinctive mosaics of rocky knolls and lochans, are characteristic of the Lewisian gneiss of North-west Scotland and parts of the Outer Hebrides, but also occur elsewhere in western Scotland (e.g. in the Galloway Hills east of The Merrick). In Wester Ross and Sutherland, the Torridonian sandstone mountains contrast sharply with the cnoc and lochan topography of lower ground, which is formed on an ancient exhumed platform of Lewisian gneiss. Elsewhere, areal scouring is commonly represented by ice-roughened terrain of bare rocky knolls that in places extends up to the summits (e.g. Luinne Bheinn and Meall Bhuidhe in Knoydart).

Kame and kettle topography

Glacial meltwater rivers transported large volumes of sand and gravel that were deposited under and around the melting ice. Where these rivers flowed along the ice margins, kame terraces formed between the ice and the adjacent valley sides. Where the rivers flowed in tunnels under the ice, sinuous ridges of sand and gravel, known as 'eskers', now indicate their former subglacial courses. Where the rivers flowed out from the glacier

Kame and kettle topography, east of Ryvoan, Cairngorms

John Gordon

fronts, large outwash plains with braided channels accumulated downvalley.

Sometimes the sand and gravel buried areas of glacier ice, or bodies of ice became cut off from the active icefronts. Subsequent melting of the buried ice produced a hummocky landscape of kames (mounds) and loch-filled kettle holes (hollows). Good examples of kame and kettle topography occur in upper Strath Spey between Boat of Garten and Kincraig, with kettle hole lochs at Loch Garten, Loch Mallachie, Loch Vaa and Loch Alvie. Often meltwater channels, eskers, kames, kettle holes and outwash deposits occur together, for example in Glen Feshie and along the northern flanks of the Cairngorms extending eastwards to Abernethy, and in Glen Clova and Glen Shee.

LANDFORMS

Nivation hollows

Nivation hollows are shallow depressions or small stream valley heads that have been enlarged through the processes of weathering and erosion associated with late-lying snowbeds. Both active and inactive examples occur in the Highlands. While the precise role of present-day processes such as frost weathering is unclear, signs of erosion associated with snow melt include the presence of rills and washed sand deposits on the floors and at the fronts of some hollows. Good examples of nivation hollows occur in the Cairngorms, notably at Ciste Mhearaid and Coire Domhain, on the eastern

Nivation hollow, Ciste Mhearaid, Cairngorms

flanks of the summit plateau of Ben Wyvis and on the upper slopes of Coire nan Tota on An Teallach. Nivation hollows provide important habitats for plants that favour long snow-lie. The deep accumulations of snow can also be attractive sites for winter mountaineers for the construction of snow holes on otherwise exposed slopes and wind-swept plateaux. During the Little Ice Age, travellers in the Cairngorms noted late-lying snow in the mountains, and it is likely that many more snowbeds survived throughout the year than today. Snow may even have covered the Cairngorm plateau for decades at a time. Visiting Ciste Mhearaid in September 1801, Mrs Sarah Murray noted that the snowbed never melted.

Tors

Tors are upstanding masses of rock rising abruptly above the surface of a plateau or ridge. Where they form the summit of a hill, for the hillwalker they can add some scrambling interest to the last few metres of ascent. They are best developed on the granites of the Cairn-

Summit tor on Ben Avon

gorms (notably on Ben Avon and Beinn Mheadhoin) and neighbouring areas (e.g. Lochnagar, Broad Cairn, Ben Rinnes, Bennachie and Clachnaben), but also occur on the syenite of Ben Loyal, on the granite hills of north Arran and on the conglomerates of Morven, Maiden Pap and Smean in Caithness. Variations in the density of steeply dipping joints in the rock resulted in differential chemical and frost weathering of the bedrock over long periods of time during the Quaternary. Areas of more densely fractured rock were heavily decomposed underground, leaving intervening, less densely jointed areas relatively intact. As the weathered rock was repeatedly stripped away by solifluction and other processes, the more intact masses of rock were exposed as upstanding tors. Many of the Cairngorm tors also display sheet jointing broadly parallel to the adjacent ground surface.

Vegetation Cover

Mark Wrightham

Life on the edge: stunted Scots pine marks the limit of tree growth on Creag Fhiaclach above Strathspey

Introduction

Why should mountaineers care about vegetation? Geological processes exert a greater influence on the upland landscape, for there would otherwise be no hills. Vegetation, however, is the palette from which the mountains are coloured, and underpins all the wildlife with which they are populated. Hill vegetation also provides a direct readout of local environmental conditions and past human activity. It seems only natural that we should be attuned to these signals, which are nothing less than the pulse of these places that matter so much.

Even the most unassuming plants enrich hill days in some small way. On the Leac Mhor of Garbh Bheinn, W.H.Murray recalled that: "while searching for a handhold the eye would alight on a blade of grass peeping from a crack, and see the amazing grace of its fluting, the fresh brightness of its green against the rock; and although the joy was that of one second the memory lived on".

Upland vegetation reflects a range of environmental influences which can vary across entire regions, across individual mountains or within a couple of paces across a summit ridge. Large scale variation is visible from a considerable distance, and the patchworks of plant communities on a hillside can often be decoded from the summit, bothy or pub across the glen. It is worth bearing in mind, however, that small changes in the balance of species, or their state of growth, can make the same type of vegetation vary in appearance between different hills and times of year.

In order to identify the key factors that determine what grows where, it is useful to understand some ecological principles.

Climate, geology and soils

Perhaps the most important general influence is the temperate oceanic climate of Scotland. Our mountain vegetation includes many distinctive plants which are suited to high winds and rainfall, high atmospheric humidity, cool summers and mild winters. Against this overall background, however, there are significant climatic differences between hills in the extremely oceanic west and north-west, and those which lie further south and east, and these contrasts are reflected by their vegetation.

Geology also exerts a strong influence, as the chemical composition of the underlying rock affects the acidity and nutrient content of soils. Most of our mountains are composed of rocks with a high silica content, including gneiss, sandstone, quartzite, granite and most of the Moine metamorphic rocks of the Central Highlands. The associated soils are relatively acid and low in sodium, potassium, magnesium and calcium, favouring plants that are adapted to these austere conditions. By contrast, basalt, dolerite, gabbro, limestone and calcareous schist give rise to less acid soils which are enriched, to varying degrees, with these nutrients. The availability of calcium is of particular importance and these plant-friendly soils support a wider range of species.

Altitude

Scottish mountain vegetation shows marked changes with altitude which are shared, to some degree, with mountains throughout the world. The most important landmark in this environmental gradient is the limit of tree growth, or tree-line. This biological limit is not completely understood, but the mean temperature during the growing season may be critical. Trees seem to be disadvantaged under colder conditions, partly because the growing shoot tips are fully exposed to the elements and closely reflect the temperature of the surrounding air. Lower, denser vegetation, by contrast, can maintain significantly warmer conditions around the all-important growing tissues. This effect is compounded by our oceanic climate, as high winds can depress shoot growth by dessication, physical damage and, under wet conditions, by windchill.

The treeline is therefore of generally low altitude in Scotland, by comparison with other mountains at similar latitudes. The exact position of this limit varies, however, across the country. The particularly wet and windy western summers result in a treeline that is usually between 200m and 450m above sea level, but can be even lower in exposed parts of the far north-west. On more eastern hills, the tree line occurs at around 500–650m, although stunted trees can be found in sheltered sanctuaries at higher levels. Other types of upland vegetation show similar effects, occurring at lower levels in the 'hyperoceanic' north-west.

The Scottish uplands have relatively little native tree and shrub cover, so the tree line is usually invisible on the ground. This limit nonetheless marks a very real ecological watershed. On drier ground below this level, low vegetation with dwarf shrubs and grasses often results from human management, and would be replaced by woodland if grazing and burning were to decrease. Above this limit lies the alpine zone, where low-growing vegetation naturally predominates. The Central and Eastern Highlands have more extensive alpine zones than western hills despite the higher tree line, because of their plateau-like forms.

Eroded peat on Ben Halton above Glen Artney, Southern Highlands. Vegetation on the haggs is cut off from the underlying rock debris and mineral nutrients, but the thinner eroded peat in the foreground has been colonised by straw-coloured mat grass. Similar patterns can be seen on eroded peat areas throughout the Scottish hills

Snow

Snow-lie increases with altitude and is greatly influenced by the form and aspect of slopes and summits. Snow cover creates a sheltered underworld in which vegetation enjoys some protection from freezing, drying and scouring spindrift. The underlying soil is also slightly enriched with mineral and organic nutrients, which accumulate in the snowpack as wind-driven rock and plant debris and are dumped on the ground by the spring thaw. These benefits are, however, gained at a price, as snow cover reduces the effective growing season, leaving a shorter time window for the critical parts of plant life cycles. Distinct types of vegetation tend to occur where snow is more persistent.

Drainage

Not surprisingly, water movement has a strong influence on Scotland's mountain vegetation. Steep slopes drain freely, resulting in well-aerated soils that support active invertebrate and microbial populations. This soil ecosystem breaks down dead plant material and recycles nutrients, increasing soil fertility. In many parts of the Highlands, however, high rainfall offsets this benefit by leaching out calcium and other nutrients, which are washed downwards and redeposited beyond the reach of plant roots, or carried away in draining waters. This process reinforces the predominance of acid and nutrient-deficient soils in our uplands, often in places which would otherwise be relatively congenial to plants.

In less well-drained areas, permanently waterlogged plant remains accumulate to form peat. This can reach a depth of up to 10m on broad straths and bealachs, although depths of 1–2m are more typical, often with signs of erosion. The peat mass can grow at up to 2mm/year under favourable conditions, isolating the surface vegetation from the underlying bedrock and from associated nutrients such as calcium, sodium and potassium. The raised peat surface is also isolated from water movement through adjacent soils and draws its entire water content from rainfall, which is naturally slightly acidic. This combination of circumstances ensures that these soils are consistently wet, acid and nutrient deficient, with a number of correspondingly specialised plants.

Areas that receive drainage are known as flushes, and present a marked contrast. These habitats have largely distinct vegetation which reflects various factors including the height of the water table, the intensity of water flow and the nature of the underlying ground, which may range from sodden peat to shifting gravel. The most important influence, however, is the chemical composition of the irrigating water. Nutrients that are leached by the movement of water through surrounding soils become concentrated in drainage lines, and many of the plants in these habitats closely reflect this enrichment. The availability of calcium is the most important single factor, as in drier soils, and more or less directly reflects the local geology. As with drier habitats, flushes therefore form a spectrum from the relatively acid to the more calcareous.

The relationship between topography and drainage is often complicated by the subversive effects of unseen glacial deposits, which are extremely common in upland glens. These vary from fine, clayey and impervious to coarse, bouldery and free-draining, and sometimes account for unexpectedly dry expanses of heather moorland on valley floors, or improbable bogs perched on surprisingly steep slopes.

Land management

The effects of human activity are overlaid upon all of these factors and extend right onto the summits of many Munros and Corbetts, although they are usually more obvious on lower slopes. The level of grazing by large herbivores is almost entirely determined by land management and is the most pervasive human imprint on the hills. Red deer are widespread, and in the absence of natural predators, their populations are largely, though not exclusively, determined by the annual cull. Sheep or cattle have also grazed some areas for centuries, or indeed millennia, their numbers ebbing and flowing according to social, economic and political imperatives.

Sheep and other large herbivores are blessed with surprisingly discerning palates and do not simply munch indiscriminately across the hillsides. All else being equal, the nutrient content of vegetation reflects that of the underlying soil and is greatest over nutrient-rich rock, where enriched water drains from above, or where improved drainage aerates and energises the soil ecosystem. Herbivores preferentially target these areas to varying degrees, in a finely-honed evolutionary strategy to derive maximum benefit from hill grazings which are generally rather poor. Nobody really knows how they do this and it may be that richer grazing simply tastes better.

Preferential grazing results in characteristic changes to upland vegetation. Tree seedlings are the first to go, being both nutritious and inherently exposed to large herbivores, and sustained grazing gradually eliminates woodland by preventing natural regeneration. Heather and other dwarf shrubs are also vulnerable because they grow 'from the front', with their actively dividing tissues at the shoot tips. These vital areas are readily nipped off, and although heather can withstand the loss of up to 40% of each year's growth, more severe defoliation initiates a gradual decline. Grasses and sedges, by contrast, are supremely adapted to resist grazing, as their dividing tissues are tucked away close to ground level and new leaves are fed upwards like printouts from a supermarket till.

Areas which are heavily grazed for long periods thus shift from the dark hues of dwarf shrubs to the fresh green or bleached white of grassland. In some areas, the prevalence of richer rocks has resulted in a historic concentration of pastoral agriculture, so that entire hills are carpeted by grassland. Elsewhere, patchworks of grass and heather occur on a smaller scale, often betraying subtle variations in the nutrient content of the underlying bedrock or glacial deposits which result in differential grazing. Similar effects can often be seen along drainage lines, which stand out as broad green lawns or sinuous ribbons. Grassland may also pick out better aerated soils on steeper slopes and vegetated scree.

Fire can encourage vigorous growth of heather and certain grasses, and has long been used to provide improved grazing for sheep or grouse. Deliberate burning, or muirburn, has often amplified the effects of grazing, and these activities combine to maintain grassland or heather moorland over much lower ground which might otherwise carry woodland. Much of our former woodland has also been gradually removed by unsustainable harvesting for firewood and for the construction of everything from wooden spoons to the masts of warships, further increasing the extent of open ground. The net loss of woodland has not, however, been a remorseless one-way process, and tree cover has probably waxed and waned in line with different historic phases of land use. Beneath the ancient pinewoods of Abernethy lie the remains of Neolithic cultivation.

Scotland's vegetation history

The vegetation of the Scottish mountains is relatively young. Sparse semi-fossilised pollen records of 15,000 years ago suggest a very limited vegetation which would have been confined to ice-free areas, often on unstable debris deposited by glaciers or meltwater. The retreat of the ice sheets 11,500 years ago allowed plants to fully colonise the denuded landscape, and today's hill vegetation reflects the combination of natural processes and human activity since that time.

The early post-glacial period was marked by the spread of tundra vegetation, including dwarf shrub heaths with abundant crowberry. Similar types of vegetation are still common in the alpine zone but their pre-eminence was curtailed, at lower altitudes, by the later expansion of woodland. This process was driven by northward migration of tree species from mainland Europe and culminated in maximal forest development roughly 7,000–8,000 years ago. This so-called Great Wood of Caledon is often portrayed as a continuous forest blanket across the glens and lower slopes, but was probably interspersed with heath and bog vegetation, at least in wetter or more exposed areas. The climate seems to have deteriorated between 4,500 and 6,000 years ago, although the detailed sequence of events is both complex and unclear. This environmental shift reduced the natural range of woodland and encouraged the accumulation of blanket peat in many areas. A further climatic deterioration occurred around 2,500 years ago, and the broad climatic context was now established for the upland vegetation of today.

These climatic trends have been interwoven with the impacts of human activity. The outcome is often characterised as a process of continuous degradation, which has been most acute in recent centuries. This perception owes much to the pioneering ecologist Sir Frank Fraser Darling, whose resonant description of

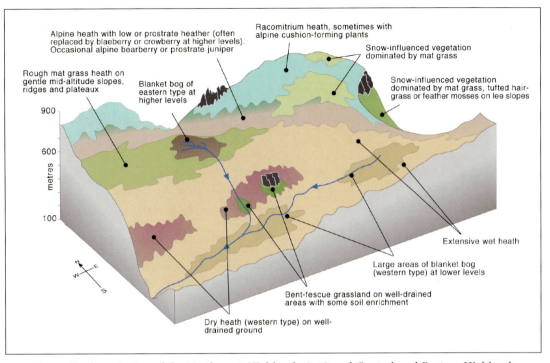

Generalised vegetation of the North-west Highlands (top) and Central and Eastern Highlands (bottom). These patterns are often blurred or obscured in more intensively grazed areas, including the Southern Highlands and Southern Uplands. Scattered woodlands occur at lower altitudes and small flushes are widespread

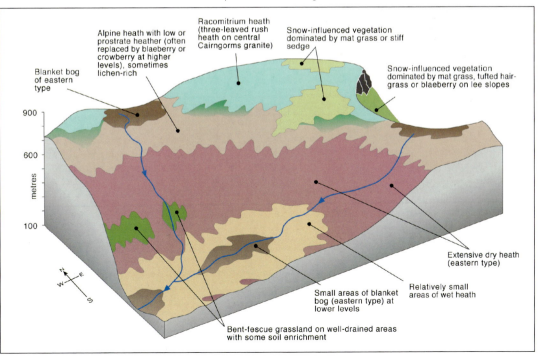

the Highlands as a 'wet desert' has done much to influence emerging conservation policy and practice over the last 50 years. Human imprints have probably, however, been much more complex and variable than this generalisation would suggest. Although often modified by management, much heath and bog vegetation at lower altitudes may be largely natural, particularly on wetter and more exposed sites and towards the north-west. The visible effects of land management on hill vegetation are explored in more detail below.

Glens and lower slopes

The vegetation of glens and lower slopes broadly consists of woodland, grassland and heather moorland, taking the latter to include any plant communities in which heather plays a significant role. Seepage areas, with various types of flush vegetation, run through all of these habitats.

Heather moorland

Throughout the Scottish uplands, and particularly in the west, poorly-drained ground is occupied by blanket bog. This type of vegetation is associated with deep peat, and may pick out small troughs in hummocky moraine or cover the floors of broad straths, reaching its apogee on the immense flows of Caithness and Sutherland. At low altitudes in the west, blanket bogs are dominated by variable mixtures of heather, cross-leaved heath, deer grass and purple moor grass, or *Molinia*. Their key characteristics, however, are an abundance of colourful *Sphagnum* mosses and the nodding heads of cotton grasses. Blanket bog also occurs in comparable situations in the drier Central and Eastern Highlands, although suitable conditions are much less extensive. Dwarf shrubs are much more abundant in these bogs and include cowberry, bearberry and cloudberry, which have distinct arctic tendencies and thrive on the colder, drier climate.

Sphagnum mosses greatly influence the appearance and ecology of blanket bogs. These plants are intolerant of dry conditions and their stems and leaves contain networks of large, hollow cells which draw up water and retain it around the growing shoot tips. These cells confer a sponge-like character, which is very obvious if saturated plants are squeezed. An abundance of *Sphagnum* therefore accentuates soil waterlogging, maintaining oxygen-starved conditions which stifle the soil ecosystem. This in turn inhibits the breakdown of plant remains, which gradually accumulate to form peat. The carnivorous round-leaved sundew is another curious hallmark of lower level blanket bogs. Trapping insects provides supplementary nitrogen and phosphorus in this nutrient-deficient habitat, but requires complex leaves that are a considerable metabolic burden to maintain. In common with many other carnivorous plants, sundews therefore favour open, well-lit sites where competition is reduced, including patches of bare peat and the tops of *Sphagnum* colonies.

Deep, sodden and impoverished peat will only support low-growing plants and is not generally colonised by woodland. Although often modified by human use and abuse, blanket bog is therefore essentially natural, and would undoubtedly attract more attention if it shared the popular appeal of native woodland. Scotland is a major centre for this underappreciated habitat, with 10% of the global total.

In the west and north-west, gentle slopes below about 500m are usually covered by more shallow peaty soils. This type of terrain often accounts for most of the land surface and is carpeted by great tracts of wet heath, which is almost universal from Lochaber to the Reay Forest. This is essentially a slightly drier blanket

Extensive wet heath below Beinn Eighe. Heather forms a mixed cover with abundant purple moor grass, deer grass and the dead flower spikes of bog asphodel

bog, with a similar abundance of heather, cross-leaved heath, deer grass and purple moor grass. *Sphagnum* mosses are quite common, but less so than in blanket bog, and the most abundant is the beautiful crimson *Sphagnum capillifolium* which can tolerate a lower water table than most of its relatives. Deer grass and purple moor grass are often the most obvious species and colour entire glens and lower hill slopes, particularly in summer, when the rampant growth of *Molinia* conceals intermingled dwarf shrubs. The green of summer gives way to rich autumnal oranges and browns, finally passing to the bleached white of dead *Molinia*, which persists through the winter and spring, entangled with the heather. Similar vegetation can be found on lower ground in the Central and Eastern Highlands, but is less extensive than in the west.

A characteristic group of small flowering plants is also scattered through both blanket bog and wet heath. These include lousewort, heath milkwort, devil's bit scabious and tormentil, which appears with unflagging consistency in many types of upland vegetation. The vivid golden-yellow spikes of bog asphodel illuminate these landscapes in July and August.

On more freely-drained areas in the west, including moraine tops and the steepening sidewalls of glens, blanket bog and wet heath give way to dry heath. Drier acid soils favour heather, which thickens into the rank tangles that provide 'Thank God' holds on many Scottish belay ledges. The ascendency of heather and decline of deer grass and purple moor grass are obvious from afar as a visible darkening, and the steep slopes of Beinn a' Chrulaiste, behind the Kingshouse Hotel, provide a prominent example. At lower levels in the west, bell heather is the only

Dry heath, with more or less continuous heather cover, on the approach to Geal-charn Mor, Speyside. Patchwork muirburn can be seen on the slopes opposite

dwarf shrub that can hold its own against the more common 'ling' heather in this type of vegetation. At higher levels hereabouts, and on cooler northerly aspects, bell heather is gradually replaced by the fresh green shoots of blaeberry. On moving uphill, the heather carpet is also increasingly punctuated by glossy mats of crowberry, whose name graces the famous ridge on Buachaille Etive Mor.

In a few high, wild sanctuaries in the north-west, the combination of a northerly aspect, long heather and coarse boulders creates exceptionally humid conditions below the dwarf shrub canopy. On the steep slopes of hills such as Liathach and Beinn Alligin, these places harbour the enigmatic 'mixed northern hepatic mat', an intricate liverwort community that is confined to these extremely oceanic parts and has few international parallels. This has considerable cachet in conservation circles, combining the compelling elements of rarity and remoteness in settings which are never less than spectacular. The upright orange-brown shoots of the liverwort *Herbertus aduncus* subspecies *hutchinsiae* form dense mats, creating an even more humid microenvironment in which more than 15 other liverworts can flourish, erupting through this carpet in a rainbow tangle which extends from lush greens to vivid purple.

Dry heath with rampant heather is the most abundant vegetation of lower altitudes in the Central and Eastern Highlands, and extends much further onto poorly-drained ground which, in the west, would be covered by open, grassy wet heath. This dark, vigorous and uniform heather carpet is strongly characteristic of glens and straths around Drumochter and the Cairngorms. As in more eastern blanket bogs, heather is joined by dwarf shrubs with northern or arctic affinities, including blaeberry, cowberry and, particularly towards higher levels, crowberry and bearberry. The western bell heather is still around, but is restricted to lower altitudes, usually on more or less south-facing slopes.

Burning is a long-established tradition across much of the Highlands. In western areas, the aim is often to encourage the regeneration of *Molinia*, which responds with a flush of new growth that is relatively palatable to sheep. Fires are often poorly controlled, not least because of the frequent shortage of labour on upland farms, and tend to sweep across large tracts of moorland until they burn out or reach some natural barrier. Many areas of blanket bog have also been drained in the past to try and improve their grazing value, and the legacy of this back-breaking labour can sometimes be seen from adjacent ridges as lines, grids or herring-bone patterns. Much heather moorland in the Central and Eastern Highlands is rotationally burnt in small strips to encourage new growth of heather, most commonly for the benefit of red grouse. The resulting angular patchworks are prominent features of the hill landscape, especially when picked out by a dusting of snow. Temporary removal of the heather canopy creates a brief opportunity for other dwarf shrubs which exist in its shadow, and burnt strips can be highlighted by the fresh green of blaeberry or, in sheltered south-facing spots, the bright purple of flowering bell heather.

Grassland

Sustained grazing encourages the spread of grasses at the expense of dwarf shrubs, and different species benefit under different circumstances. On wetter western moorland, grazing, burning and draining conspire to entrench *Molinia* and deer

Sheep vote with their feet on the Luss Hills. Grazing has encouraged the widespread development of coarse grassland with mat grass and heath rush, and on the best-drained sites, relatively rich, bright green bent-fescue grassland. The latter areas are preferentially grazed, as seen above

grass, creating very uniform vegetation in which these often seem to be the only visible plants. On slightly better-drained ground, persistent heavy grazing encourages the spread of small, wiry tussocks of mat grass, which is also very common in the Scottish hills. The most freely-drained sites, which would otherwise be occupied by dry heath, can develop relatively lush green grasslands dominated by common bent and sheep's fescue. Bent-fescue grasslands are the most productive rough grazings in the uplands and are very attractive to sheep, frequently appearing as closely-cropped lawns. Such grasslands can cover large areas, such as the steep slopes below Ossian's Cave in Glen Coe, but suitable soils are at a premium in the sodden north-west. Here, bent-fescue grassland is confined to the very best sites, including vegetated scree fans and steep aprons below rock outcrops.

The Dalradian metamorphic rocks of the Southern Highlands and softer sediments of the Southern Uplands are often calcium-rich, and combine with the more amenable climate of these areas to provide relatively productive grazings. This factor, along with proximity to lowland markets, has encouraged a historic concentration of grazing by domestic livestock, most recently sheep, which is reflected by the extensive grassy vegetation of glens and lower slopes.

Better-drained slopes hereabouts can readily develop bent-fescue grasslands, which are relatively acid or calcareous according to the underlying rocks. Grasslands of the latter type can support incredibly rich mixtures of small herbs, with over 30 species per square metre. This diversity is sustained by light grazing and trampling by hooves, which maintain a short and relatively open grass cover in which more bulky and competitive species are unable to gain a decisive edge. This type of calcareous grassland occurs on numerous 'Dalradian' hills including Ben Lui, Ben More and the Lawers and Caenlochan ranges, and is readily identified by the tiny, scented shoots of wild thyme and the multi-lobed leaves of common ladies' mantle.

On less well-drained soils in the Southern Highlands and Southern Uplands, grazing and burning have encouraged the spread of coarse grasses and rushes. The slopes of many hills are dominated by great expanses of rough grassland with bulky tussocks of *Molinia* and, at higher levels, wiry clumps of mat grass and glossy tufts of heath rush. These grasslands often merge seamlessly with alpine mat grass heaths in which the abundance of this species is largely natural. Although most common in the south, extensive tracts of rough grassland can also be seen in some more northerly ranges, including the hills in and around Glen Shiel.

The lower reaches of heavily-grazed hills can also carry great tracts of bracken which are well seen, for example, on the Glen Lochay slopes of Meall Ghaordie. The expansion of this fern has been encouraged by fluctuating sheep stocking, which is characteristic of economically marginal hill farms, as the plant requires periodic relief from grazing in order to spread. Subsequent reintroduction of sheep merely entrenches bracken cover, as these animals do not graze or trample dense areas of mature fronds. Bracken favours slightly richer soils and is sensitive to frost, which can readily damage its root system. These characteristics restrict the plant to relatively low altitudes, and result in characteristic distribution patterns which are particularly visible in autumn. Ideal conditions are frequently provided by the 'armpits' at the foot of slopes, where soil and associated nutrients accumulate by downwash, and these sites are usually the first to be colonised by the fern. On wetter slopes and valley floors, however, the high water table confines bracken to drier ground such as the tops of moraines.

Beinn Chabhair above Glen Falloch in summer. Historic grazing, and perhaps burning, is reflected by the prevailingly grassy vegetation. The boulder is capped by a rowan sapling and dry heath, indicating the potential vegetation of well-drained sites, although very different conditions prevail on the ground nearby

The abundance of bracken is a distinctly mixed blessing. On the one hand, this fern undoubtedly enriches the landscape, burning a rich russet in the low autumn sun. On the other hand, vigorous bracken excludes most other plants and provides an ideal habitat for sheep ticks, which latch onto hillwalkers and animals alike. Bracken is a well-established feature of these hills and may be commemorated in the name of Meall Corranaich, west of Ben Lawers, which is sometimes translated as 'round hill of the bracken corrie'.

Woodland

Climate change and human management have greatly reduced the extent of native woodland compared to its post-glacial peak 7,000 to 8,000 years ago. Native trees are now largely confined to better-drained sites, and crags and gorges beyond the reach of sheep and deer. Birches are by far the most widespread and characteristic, particularly in the west and north-west. In these areas the predominant species is downy birch, which is particularly tolerant of wet and exposed habitats, but this tree is accompanied, in more easterly parts, by silver birch. In *The Living Mountain*, Nan Shepherd captured the essence of these woods on crystalline winter days. "In a low sun", she wrote, "the spun silk floss of their twigs seems to be created out of light". Local residents have often taken a more pragmatic view. In his *Encyclopaedia of Trees and Shrubs*, published in 1842, G.C.Loudon states that: "The Highlanders of Scotland make everything of (birch); they build their houses, make their beds and chairs, tables, dishes and spoons; construct their mills, make their carts, ploughs, gates and fences and even

*Native oak-birch woodland beside Loch Lomond. The abundance of oak in many
south-western woods is probably related to historic management to provide timber, bark for
tanning and charcoal for smelting*

manufacture ropes of it. The branches are employed as fuel in the distillation of
whisky and the spray is used for smoking hams and herrings".

Scots pine is particularly competitive on sharply-drained, leached and acid
soils, and is most common in the Central and Eastern Highlands, with scattered
pockets further west. Much has been written about the venerable pinewoods of
the Cairngorms, whose resinous atmosphere seems to freeze the passage of time,
and Strathspey and Deeside contain 60% of the Scottish total. The dark pine
canopy is usually interspersed with birch, which sometimes reflects slight soil
enrichment, for example by seepage from above.

The prevailing acidity of pinewood soils is reflected by the distinctive
vegetation which develops underneath. The most rampant species is usually the
feather moss *Hylocomium splendens*, which often forms thick, luxuriant blankets
intermingled with cowberry and blaeberry. Somewhere in the Tolkienian depths
of these forests, the more fortunate may stumble on rarities whose limited
Scottish populations reflect the distribution of the habitat itself. These include the
twisted white flower spikes of creeping lady's tresses, a pinewood orchid, and the
delicate twinflower whose paired flowering heads resemble a Victorian lamp
standard. These pinewoods are a Scottish outpost of the boreal taiga, the great belt
of pine and spruce forest that encircles the Arctic.

Both Scots pine and birch tend to form patches of uniform age, a trait which
reflects their mode of reproduction. Different tree species adopt contrasting
strategies to maximise seed establishment. The familiar oak exemplifies one
extreme, producing bulky acorns which contain substantial nutrient reserves. This

adaptation allows seeds to germinate in relatively unfavourable sites, including tall vegetation where there is fierce competition for light and soil nutrients. The benefits of this approach are gained at the expense of mobility, as cumbersome seeds do not travel so readily over large distances. Pine and birch, by contrast, produce vast amounts of relatively mobile seed with minimal on-board nutrient reserves, which can be widely dispersed by the wind. This lightweight 'Alpine-style' approach means that these trees cannot usually become established in tall vegetation or existing woodland, but can opportunistically seed in large numbers onto suitably open sites, including ground exposed by fire or physical disturbance. Pine and birchwoods are not therefore static, and time-lapse photography extending over several centuries would reveal pulses of woodland oscillating around the upland landscape like the lights of the aurora borealis.

Various other trees grace particular parts of the uplands. Sessile oak forms magnificent woods in the South-west Highlands, including Morar and Sunart, while ash forms scattered woods on more calcareous soils. A number of smaller, less competitive trees grow below the woodland canopy, as small patches of scrub or as scattered individuals. These include eared willow, which is quite widespread, and juniper, which is more prominent in the east. The blazing berries of rowan are a common sight throughout the Scottish hills and this bird-sown tree often forms lone sentinels, or belays, on crags or erratic boulders.

Commercial conifer plantations are widespread in the Scottish uplands and are now much more extensive than native woodland. In most areas, these are dominated by Sitka spruce, a North American import which thrives on poor, wet soils. The ubiquitous Sitka is often accompanied and occasionally replaced by larch or lodgepole pine. The uniform composition and intrusive, angular design of many such plantations reflects an outmoded forestry policy which attracted considerable public criticism during the 1980s. Current policy places greater emphasis on native trees, either alone or in conjunction with these commercial species. These changes have been accompanied by improved standards of design and there are now opportunities to address these issues as plantations are felled and restructured at the end of their first 50 year rotation.

Fragments of treeline scrub persist in a few locations, hinting at the altitudinal limit for woodland in various parts of the uplands. Low ground below such hills as Foinaven and Ben Hope carries stunted downy birch, barely 2m high, which is close to its climatic limit at an altitude of around 200m. On the sheltered eastern flanks of Beinn Bhan above Ballachulish, dwarfed downy birch and eared willow dwindle away at 450 – 500m above sea level. Further east, a rare remnant of treeline Scots pine scrub survives at Creag Fhiaclach, north-west of Sgor Gaoithe. Between 550m and 600m lies a belt of increasingly suppressed pine whose stout trunks are often twisted into organ pipe coils, with many mature trees reaching less than 1.5m. These isolated fragments offer a tantalising glimpse of the way Scotland's hills might appear if the imprint of grazing was less pronounced. Deliberate or incidental reductions in grazing pressure have begun to encourage the development of sub-alpine pine scrub in other areas, including the slopes below the Northern Corries of Cairn Gorm.

Flushes

Seepage areas can play host to a large and distinct variety of plants. Relatively acid flushes predominate across most of the Scottish uplands. At lower altitudes, in places which combine deep peat with strong water flow, *Molinia* can rise to the fore, sometimes forming vigorous tussocks that exclude most other species. This type of vegetation can also be seen along 'flats' beside larger burns, which receive bursts of nutrients when submerged after heavy rainfall. On open hill slopes, acid flushes are more often announced by bright green *Sphagnum* mosses and the dark green 'bottlebrush' moss *Polytrichum commune*, sometimes interwoven with tall clumps of soft rush.

Where there is some calcium enrichment, these drainage lines assume a quite different appearance, with a predominance of sedges and, in many instances, a scattering of the unmistakeable insectivorous butterwort. These flushes also support a different range of mosses which are much less conspicuous than Sphagna, tending to form partially submerged purple-brown mats. These species can be intermingled with *Sphagnum* mosses around the main seepage line, indicating subtle changes in the chemistry of the irrigating water within a few centimetres. Various other plants occur in particular situations and open, gravelly flushes on more calcareous rocks are marked by the pale flowers of yellow saxifrage. Calcareous flushes are most common over Palaeogene volcanic rocks and Dalradian schists, but can also be seen quite widely amid large tracts of generally 'acidic' rocks. In these situations, they provide sensitive indicators of localised calcium-enrichment, reflecting variations in the composition of the bedrock, unseen basalt dykes or superficial deposits that have been transported from elsewhere by ice or water.

The alpine zone

The slopes and summits which stretch above the treeline are known as the alpine zone, and present a harsh environment in which only low vegetation can maintain a foothold. Exposed areas are frequently dominated by dwarf shrubs or woolly fringe moss (*Racomitrium lanuginosum*), but there is also much grassland where snow is more persistent, or where grazing has been more intense. Rock ledges and seepage areas often carry other types of vegetation which reflect irrigation, soil enrichment or relief from grazing.

Dwarf shrub vegetation

Heather is most competitive where snow-lie is relatively brief and is increasingly confined, with greater altitude, to wind-exposed slopes. In these situations, heather commonly forms dark, wind-trimmed carpets less than 10cm high, often accompanied by blaeberry or crowberry. This type of vegetation is quite common throughout the Highlands and is particularly extensive on the Drumochter Hills, Monadh Liath and Cairngorms, carpeting great expanses of their windswept flanks.

A number of distinctive plants can be found in or around wind-trimmed heather. Prostrate juniper clings to exposed ridges and slopes in the west and north-west, often where other vegetation thins out over unstable gravel. This shrub is extremely sensitive to burning and individual plants may be completely eliminated by a single fire. The scattered patches which occur on hills such as Beinn Eighe and Foinaven may therefore be residual fragments of a type of vegetation which was once much more widespread on their windward flanks. On gravelly ridge crests towards the north-west, prostrate heather is sometimes mingled with alpine bearberry. Although this dwarf shrub is fairly common in suitable habitats in this area, it was first discovered on the profoundly obscure summit of Ben Horn in eastern Sutherland, in 1767.

Lichens sometimes rise to prominence within prostrate heather, particularly in the Central and Eastern Highlands. The *Cladonias* are by far the most widespread and conspicuous, and may number up to ten species. In fractionally

Wind trimmed heather, crowberry and Cladonia lichens on the upper slopes of Meall Mor above Loch Glass

more sheltered locations such as east-facing summit slopes, these can thicken up to form a dense cover which exceeds that of heather. A small but exquisite *Cladonia* lawn can be found near the summit of A' Chailleach in the Monadh Liath, and is one of the subtle treasures concealed in these underrated hills. Much larger tracts of lichen-dominated tundra occur in the bitterly cold and very dry continental climates of arctic Scandinavia and Siberia, but these localised patches are the closest approximation that our climate will allow.

In very exposed locations the heather becomes extremely stunted, forming prostrate mats as the gnarled stems creep downwind. This type of vegetation often extends onto unstable wind-scoured and frost-shattered gravel, in which the minute pink flowers of creeping azalea add a splash of colour during June. In some areas, including the mobile granite gravel of the Cairngorms, prostrate heather forms stripes at right angles to the prevailing wind. The windward edge of each stripe is continually eroded and heather growth is only possible on the sheltered lee side. Various mosses find transient niches in this dynamic ecosystem, colonising and stabilising the gravel before the advancing heather front. Bearberry can sometimes also maintain a toehold by advancing ahead of the heather waves, as this dwarf shrub is better adapted to unstable terrain.

Small areas of alpine prostrate heather occur elsewhere in the UK and Scandinavia, but this type of vegetation is otherwise confined to Scotland, reflecting the combination of wind and humidity that so characterises our higher summits. The high and remote location of these heaths does not provide complete protection from human intervention and heavy grazing, as at lower levels, can eliminate heather cover. Burning can also cause net loss of heather in the alpine zone, in contrast to its effects at lower altitude, and this combination of factors has probably reduced the extent of this vegetation on many hills.

Broad, poorly drained bealachs and plateaux are frequently adorned by high level blanket bogs, which tend to contain mixtures of heather and arctic-alpine dwarf shrubs, in common with eastern blanket bogs at lower levels. Hare's tail cotton grass is prominent and may dominate, resulting in a 'grassy' appearance that is well seen, for example, on the Moine Bhealaidh above Glen Derry. The precise combination of climate and drainage often ensures that higher and more easterly blanket bogs are slightly drier than their western or lower level counterparts, and are more often eroded, in time producing the ramifying networks of haggs that are such a joy to traverse. The exact cause is still uncertain and this process may be largely natural.

Although there is much local variation, the stunted heather cover usually fades at around 650 to 700m in the west and north-west, and 850 to 1000m further east. A low cover of blaeberry and crowberry sometimes runs on uphill for a short distance, before the dominance of dwarf shrubs recedes altogether. On the most exposed brows and summits, a new ecological force now comes to the fore, as flattened carpets of woolly fringe moss form the remarkable plant community known as *Racomitrium* heath.

Racomitrium heath

Racomitrium lanuginosum is confined to mountains and tundra in cool, humid climates, but its abundance on our high summits rather belies this restricted global distribution. The moss is often overwhelmingly dominant and extends for many square kilometres across the plateaux of Creag Meagaidh, Ben Wyvis and the Drumochter hills, punctuated by little more than a scattering of stiff sedge.

In common with many other upland plants, *Racomitrium* does not grow optimally at high altitude, merely performing less badly than its potential competitors. This decisive edge can be traced to a number of adaptations. Rather ironically, dehydration is a major hazard for plants in parts of the alpine zone which have shallow, poorly-developed soils. Many mosses of drier habitats can tolerate occasional rain-free spells, but woolly fringe moss takes this to extremes and can recover after 12 months in the complete absence of water under laboratory conditions. Conversely, the moss can efficiently capitalise on periods of higher humidity by directly absorbing atmospheric moisture. Rainfall and other natural atmospheric deposition provide the plant with all of its nitrogen requirements and at least some mineral nutrients, such as potassium and calcium.

Where the underlying rocks are a little richer and, perhaps, the wind helps to open up the moss cover, a few characteristic plants may become established. These include pink-flowering thrift and moss campion, and the more inconspicuous mossy cyphel, which has diminutive and retiring yellow-green flowers. This effect becomes gradually more common on western ranges from around Kintail northwards, and all three plants are dotted through the summit moss-heath on Beinn Dearg, east of Ullapool. These species all grow as dense, compact cushions, a form which is adopted by many alpine plants and which offers a number of benefits. Each cushion acts like a greenhouse, creating a humid internal microclimate up to 20° C warmer than the bleak, wind-blasted exterior. This mode of growth may also increase the efficiency of nutrient recycling by trapping and retaining dead leaf material that would otherwise blow away. These plants provide havens for a wide variety of invertebrates, belying the lifeless appearance of thrift cushions under a thin veneer of February snow.

On a few hills in the west and north-west, *Racomitrium* heath is home to

Racomitrium heath with cushions of thrift in the left foreground on Sgurr a' Chaorachain, Loch Monar

extremely rare local specialities. Prostrate mats of the arctic-alpine shrub *Diapensia lapponica* persist on a small number of hills around Glenfinnan. This is an ancient relic of the early post-glacial vegetation of 11,000 years ago, and was only discovered in 1951. *Artemisia norvegica*, a high altitude relative of the daisy, ekes out a fragile existence on the summits of Cul Mor and the Beinn Dearg group, and nowhere else in Britain. This plant is by no means abundant in other mountain regions, and is otherwise confined to Norway and the Urals.

On many summits, particularly in the Southern Highlands and Southern Uplands, grazing has encouraged varying degrees of incursion by grasses, ranging from scattered shoots to almost complete cover. *Racomitrium* is not eaten by sheep, and this ecological shift largely reflects trampling by hooves and nitrogen enrichment from urine, which the plant cannot tolerate in excess. Aerial pollution results in increased deposition of nitrogen from the atmosphere and may have contributed to this effect. These influences have been more pronounced further south, and *Racomitrium* heath is more or less absent from the Lake District and Snowdonia. This process blurs the distinction between alpine plant communities and many hills in southern Scotland are clothed by uniform sweeps of grassy vegetation which extend right onto summit ridges.

On the upper slopes of some more calcareous hills, for example around Breadalbane, the grass cover is mingled with wild thyme, alpine ladies-mantle and, on the higher summits, moss campion. This type of alpine grassland is likely to reflect some degree of grazing, but it is unclear what sort of vegetation might have occurred in the absence of sheep, and *Racomitrium* may never have been extensive on these richer summits.

In common with other mosses, *Racomitrium* does not have true roots and depends on the combined strength of many weak attachments. The limitations of this mode of growth become apparent on the extremely unstable wind-blasted gravel fields of the Cairngorms and Lochnagar. Here, on very exposed terrain above 900m, *Racomitrium* is largely replaced by the even more specialised three-leaved rush, whose scattered tussocks dominate great expanses of otherwise almost barren plateaux.

The ecology of three-leaved rush was first teased out in 1938–39 during the 'Cambridge University Botanical Expedition to the Cairngorms', a title which tellingly evokes a bygone age. The plant forms tussocks which are anchored in the shifting gravel by dense and contorted tap roots. The older parts of this root system die off from the centre and the disintegrating tussocks often appear as circles or crescents up to 30cm in diameter, which provide a sheltered but transient sanctuary for mosses, lichens or the tiny least willow. Three-leaved rush also occurs in Scandinavia, the Alps and the Pyrenees, generally forming more continuous vegetation, and the precarious and threadbare 'rush heaths' of the Cairngorms have few close parallels elsewhere in Europe.

Vegetation influenced by snow-lie

On more sheltered ground at high altitudes, *Racomitrium* heath passes to a variety of plant communities which reflect, in varying degree, the influence of snow cover. The transition can be very gradual over rolling terrain, but can also be abrupt, for example where exposed ridges drop into cornice-rimmed corrie head-walls. Much snow-influenced vegetation is naturally grassy and different types can merge into one another, and into grassland on lower slopes which largely reflects grazing and burning. It is possible to identify a number of permutations which primarily reflect the duration of snow-lie and the angle of the underlying ground, although not all can be seen on every hill.

The most widespread and conspicuous vegetation of this type is dominated by wiry tussocks of mat grass and tends to occupy gentle slopes, plateaux, pockets and hollows. In contrast to lower altitudes, the ascendency of mat grass is entirely natural in these situations, and the species is most fiercely competitive where shallow peat overlies a source of mineral nutrients which is not too deep for the probing roots. These conditions are satisfied on many shallow upper slopes and summits, and subtle increases in shelter and snow retention, coupled with poor drainage, are enough to effect the switch from *Racomitrium* heath. Interweaving mosaics of these two plant communities can be seen on numerous summits, most obviously over gently rolling ground with both exposed brows and sheltered scoops.

Stiff sedge is scattered through this type of alpine grassland, but as snow cover becomes more prolonged on low-angled terrain, the sedge gains the upper hand to form almost homogeneous patches or lawns. This type of vegetation occurs throughout the Highlands, but is skewed towards central and eastern ranges, reflecting the extent of suitable snowfields. Stiff sedge lawns are particularly well seen around some broad plateaux, including the flat summit of Glas Maol.

Steeper snow-holding ground, including corrie headwalls and their corniced rims, is associated with distinct soil conditions which combine improved drainage with strong downward water movement and here, the ecological power balance tends to shift towards tussocks of tufted hair grass. These situations are also comparatively sheltered and humid, and this grass can face vigorous competition from feather mosses, which form an interwoven carpet between the tussocks or squeeze the grass out altogether. The resulting vegetation can therefore vary greatly in appearance, ranging from 'all grass' to 'all moss'. The latter form can be

Transitions between plant communities on the south-east flank of Sgurr nan Conbhairean, above Loch Cluanie. These are linked to subtle changes in drainage and shelter. Pale mat grass vegetation is replaced by darker Racomitrium heath on exposed slopes and brows to the top left, and on top of the solifluction lobe in the right foreground

quite strikingly beautiful, forming soft golden-green blankets which invite an extended coffee break. Not surprisingly, some survey data suggest that the grassy extreme is favoured in drier eastern ranges.

Relatively steep and sheltered ground, which is freely drained and comparatively dry, can also carry a further type of grassy vegetation which may be influenced by snow-lie. A slight prolongation of snow cover seems to be associated with the development of heaths in which the green stems and leaves of blaeberry are scattered through a mattress of grasses, including the soft, fine-leaved wavy-hair grass. This is very extensive on some hills in the Central and Southern Highlands, including Beinn Each and Stuc a' Chroin. On the Sow of Atholl, above the Drumochter Pass, this type of vegetation harbours the elusive blue or Menzies' heath. This dwarf shrub bears a passing resemblance to the ubiquitous crowberry and occurs on a handful of other hills in the Ben Alder Forest.

The most extreme snow-influenced vegetation is not surprisingly reserved for areas of relatively long snow-lie. Such vegetation is of varied appearance, but is generally dominated by patches or carpets of liverworts and mosses which grow as very small tufts. Chief among these is the moss *Kiaeria starkei*, which is very rare within the UK as a whole, but is scattered through the mountains of Europe, Asia, North America and Greenland.

Many higher slopes have areas of particularly unstable surface soil with a tendency to downhill slumping and solifluction. These can appear almost lifeless at first sight, with little obvious vegetation apart from scattered least willow and tufts of tiny mosses. Closer examination, however, often reveals that the surface

Snow-influenced vegetation below the cornice on Carn Ghlusaid. White tussocks of tufted hair grass are set in a thick carpet of feather mosses. Similar vegetation occurs on the steep north-facing slopes beyond, with paler mat grass vegetation on the gentle plateau above

is encased in a purple-grey crust that is puckered and cracked by the shifting of the underlying ground. This crust consists of an intricate mixture of minute liverworts which can only be seen with a hand lens, and not well even then. Suitable conditions sometimes occur on exposed deflation scars (see p84) as well as areas of long snow-lie, and the sharp-eyed can spot patches of this vegetation on many high slopes and ridges, including much of the summit of Aonach Beag, above Glen Nevis. This subtle but remarkable vegetation seems to be quite common on the silty summit debris produced by frost weathering of schists, and related plant communities occur in the Arctic tundra on ground that is churned by freezing and thawing.

The alpine heaths described above, dominated variously by heather, grasses, sedges and mosses, carpet most of the upper slopes and summits of the Highlands and Southern Uplands. A number of more localised habitats also enrich the Scottish hills, and perhaps the most obvious are cliff ledges and seepage areas.

Rock ledges

Broken rock outcrops are inaccessible to grazing animals and can harbour rank, chaotic cascades of woody and herbaceous plants. More acid rocks may support little more than the usual dwarf shrubs and vigorous tufts of great woodrush, whose leaves resemble an exceptionally large, coarse grass and are edged by sparse but oddly prominent hairs. The range of plants is much greater on more calcareous rocks, including the gabbros and basalts of Skye, the Dalradian schists of the Southern Highlands and enriched pockets elsewhere. Such outcrops may nurture lush hanging gardens with roseroot, moss campion, globeflower, mountain and water avens, and assorted saxifrages and ladies-mantles. For obvious reasons these sanctuaries are usually small, but occasional herb-rich meadows can develop where large shelves are isolated by crags. Coire na Poite, on Beinn Bhan, contains a ledge of this type which is enriched to an unusual degree for Torridonian sandstone. This discovery caused great excitement among the vanguard of Victorian botanists who no doubt proceeded, in the manner of their times, to plunder the site for their collecting tins. Scotland's rich heritage of 'traditional' gully climbs coincides with prime habitat for many cliff ledge plants, although this aesthetic quality is perhaps best appreciated with hindsight. In his classic account of the first ascent of Clachaig Gully, W.H.Murray wrote of the "riotous confusion" of alpine plants above the Great Cave Pitch, "amongst which I could name only the yellow saxifrage".

In a very few areas, dripping calcareous ledges play host to unusual low-growing alpine willows, which form extensive tracts of scrub in the mountains of Scandinavia but are much more restricted in Scotland. The least uncommon of these is downy willow, whose small leaves are covered in fine hairs that trap air and reduce moisture loss, an adaptation to alpine environments in which water supply can be interrupted for long periods by freezing. Downy willow can be accompanied by relatives which are rather more obscure, including the densely shaggy woolly willow. These combine to form a moderately extensive cover in various well-scattered locations, including a large ledge in Coire Sharroch, above Glen Clova. The male and female reproductive organs of willows occur on different plants, and cross-fertilisation between shrubs as far removed as Creag Meagaidh and the Ben Alder Forest is clearly improbable. The precarious state of alpine willow scrub has inspired numerous restoration projects which are beginning to reverse the decline in some places.

The surfaces of rock outcrops and debris can also provide a niche for mosses and lichens and, in turn, a hostile reception to smooth-soled rock boots. The same broad principles apply here as on soil surfaces, and different species occur on acid and calcareous rocks, exposed and sheltered surfaces, and where there is an irrigating water flow. Lichens which thrive on acid rocks are naturally the most widespread, and some of the more common species have practical use. The dark, curled lobes of *Umbilicaria* can be boiled to make 'rock tripe', a dubious delicacy which helped to sustain the first Franklin North-West Passage expedition (after they had eaten their boots).

An alpine spring on the upper slopes of Beinn a' Chaoruinn in the Cairngorms. The spring head in the foreground is marked by bright green Philonotis fontana and the purple liverwort Scapania undulata. These are replaced by pale purple Anthelia julacea with tussocks of tufted hair grass beyond the two prominent boulders, as the water flow weakens further away from the source

Alpine springs and flushes

The myriad springs and seepage areas of the alpine zone are in many ways similar to those of lower slopes, although purple moor grass and soft rush, which can both dominate at lower levels, fade away at these altitudes. Although *Sphagnum* mosses remain abundant in acid flushes, the overall range of species changes, and these habitats sometimes include distinctive specialists such as the large and elegant *Sphagnum lindbergii*, which is common in northern Russia and Scandinavia but absent from most European mountains.

A similar shift in composition occurs in calcareous flushes, with the occasional appearance of high altitude plants such as alpine bistort. This viviparous plant produces a curious flowering spike whose upper half is adorned by pinkish-white flowers, while the lower half consists of a stack of small purple bulbs that break off to form new plants. Such adaptations are common to a number of alpine species and help to bypass the uncertainties of sexual reproduction in demanding high altitude environments. Strongly calcareous rocks are infrequent at the very highest altitudes in Scotland, and associated seepages provide rare niches for esoteric species such as the rather retiring bristle sedge, whose only British population twitches in the wind on Ben Lawers.

Both acid and calcareous seepage lines often trace back to visible spring heads, which create splashes of intense colour against the soft tones of the high slopes. The most vivid displays occur in springs and streams where firm and often stony ground is washed by vigorous and relatively acid running water. Such areas often develop swollen masses of lush bright green and purple liverworts and mosses. The most characteristic of these is the moss *Philonotis fontana*, which forms intense lime green cushions that vaguely resemble a loosely-packed mass of narrow pipe cleaners, as the leaves are tiny in relation to the upright stems. The colour of this moss is so strident that springs can often be picked out from several hundred metres away. More calcareous spring heads are marked by deep, golden cushions of the beautiful feather-like moss *Palustriella commutata*, whose leaf tips are curled downwards like the claws of a sloth.

Where acidic, icy water dribbles more slowly over firm ground, a highly characteristic liverwort rises to prominence. *Anthelia julacea* provides a graphic demonstration of strength in numbers, as individual shoots roughly 0.5mm in diameter are packed into hard, dense grey-blue cushions which can support the weight of an average hillwalker. *Anthelia* cushions can extend for many square metres across low-angled hill slopes, punctuated by sporadic shoots of mat grass, tufted hair grass or bog asphodel.

Although common principles influence where plants are found, there is much variation, and the vegetation of every hill reflects the quirks of the local environment and past and present land use. This complex picture also shifts over time, and climate change will cause a decline in snow-bed communities and other specialised alpine plants. But small details of this shifting tableau capture the essence of the hills, as brilliant orange *Sphagnum* sparkles in an alpine spring or cotton grass flails in the wind on a high bealach.

The vegetation blanket is the foundation of the wider mountain ecosystem, providing essential food and shelter for upland invertebrates, birds and mammals. This relationship is arguably most intimate for invertebrates, whose complex life cycles are often strictly dependent on a single plant, and this little known facet of our upland wildlife is considered in the next chapter.

Birches (beithe) *Betula* species

Our native birches are readily identified by their familiar whitish bark,
but slightly more effort is required to
separate the two main species. The
clearest distinction can be seen at a
distance, as the branch tips of silver
birch (*B. pendula*) form delicate
hanging cascades which can faintly
suggest a crystal chandelier. This elegant form is prominent, for example,
in many birchwoods along the Spey,
which are well seen from the A9. At
closer quarters, the leaves of silver
birch are sharply pointed, with irreg-

Silver birch   *Downy birch*

ular and sometimes deeply-cut teeth. Downy birch (*B. pubescens*) is more common, especially in the west, and has more upright branch tips and rounded leaves with small, neat,
uniform teeth. Be warned, however, that these two nominal 'species' hybridise frequently,
and intermediate forms are very common.

Birches are well established in Highland tradition, appearing in mountain names such as
Tom Bheithe (birch hill) and Coire nam Beith (coire of the birch). In areas such as Deeside
where the old Scots tongue has been historically strong, these trees often appear as 'birk',
which is derived from the Norse 'bjork'. It is possible to make wine from birch sap, which
may represent a neglected business opportunity.

Oaks (darach) *Quercus* species

As with birch, the story of oak in Britain is
a tale of two species. The hardy sessile oak
(*Q. petraea*) is most widespread in the
north and west, while pedunculate oak (*Q.
robur*) occurs more towards the south and
east. The relative distributions of these
species are not however clear cut, partly
because of past planting, and either could
be encountered in the uplands – both
species are frequent, for example, in different parts of Skye. Oak forms extensive
woods in the South-west Highlands but is
increasingly confined to low south-facing
slopes further north, eventually dwindling
north of Assynt.

The two species are distinguished by
their leaves which, in the case of sessile
oak, taper at the base into a stalk around 10–20mm long. Pedunculate oak has much shorter-
stalked leaves which are more rounded at the base, forming small 'lobes' either side of the
stalk. The acorns are the opposite way round: virtually stalkless and sitting close to the twigs
on sessile oak, and long-stalked on pedunculate oak. In winter, the grey bark of both oaks
stands out amid the purple haze of surrounding birch. This bark becomes deeply fissured
with age, creating niches for a rich variety of invertebrates.

Rowan (caorann) *Sorbus aucuparia*

Rowan is extremely common throughout the Highlands, particularly in the north west. Lone individuals are often highly visible on crags, boulders or burnsides, but this tree also plays a supporting role in woodland dominated by pine or birch. The leaves are grouped into fronds which are typically 10–20cm long, with individual leaflets that are typically 3–6cm long. These are of classical, broadly oval 'leaf' shape, with tapering tips and an edging of well-defined teeth. Recognition is particularly straightforward around September, when these trees are reliably festooned with bright red berries.

Mark Wrightham

Rowan reaches higher altitudes than any other Scottish tree, and a stunted specimen has been reported at around 870m in the Rannoch area. A partial explanation for this hardihood is offered by experimental studies which show that the overwintering buds are extremely resistant to drying, perhaps allowing the tree to 'ride out' periods in which soil water is locked up as ice.

Rowan was often planted beside dwellings in the Highlands, as it was believed to confer protection against witchcraft. There is now dwindling evidence of this practice in Highland glens, as rowan seldom lives beyond 150 years and, poignantly, both tree and building have passed together into ruin.

Eared willow (seileach-cluasach) *Salix aurita*

Eared willow is common at lower levels in the Scottish uplands, forming scattered bushes or scrubby patches which rarely exceed 2m in height. The broad, faintly toothed leaves taper suddenly to small, pointed tips and are soft and deeply wrinkled, their woolly lower surfaces conferring a blue-grey hue that is visible at a distance. Identification can be confirmed by the presence of the 'ears', which are curious paired 'stipules', resembling miniature leaves, at the base of each leaf stalk.

Tom Prentice

On a few lonely crags or burnsides, the fortunate just might find solitary bushes of the rare arctic-alpine downy willow (*S. lapponum*), which are typically less than 1m high with more or less untoothed, elongated and downy leaves 1–2cm in length. Several other willows frequently form larger shrubs or small trees, usually in woodland, and chief among these are goat and grey willow (*S. caprea* and *S. cinerea*).

Willows have a certain notoriety among botanists for their frequent and promiscuous hybridisation. As with human relationships, the resulting pairings can often surprise those who are acquainted with both partners. Eared willow can occasionally hybridise with the much smaller creeping willow and, very rarely, with the diminutive alpine least willow (see p119).

113

Heather (fraoch)
Calluna vulgaris

The ubiquitous heather, or ling, is the most abundant dwarf shrub of the Scottish hills and can sometimes seem to be the only one. Prostrate, stunted forms at higher altitudes can appear strangely unfamiliar. Heather is differentiated from other Scottish dwarf shrubs by its tiny leaves, 1–2mm long, which hug the shoots and are almost indistinguishable at first glance. Small pinkish-purple flowers line the shoot tips in August–September.

Individual plants live for around 30 years, but usually lose vigour after about 15 years and die off from the centre. Individual shoots typically grow by a few centimetres each year, and each winter is marked by branches or slight 'elbows' in the stem and, in more recent growth, by the remains of rows of tiny leaves pressed against the main stem. With a little practice heather plants, and hence burnt patches in managed moorland, can be roughly 'aged' in this way.

The extent of heather cover seems to have increased across most of the Highlands over the last 6,000 years, in parallel with the decline in woodland, apparently because of a combination of natural processes and, more recently, human activity.

Cross-leaved heath (fraoch Frangach) *Erica tetralix*; bell heather (fraoch a' bhadain) *Erica cinerea*

These dwarf shrubs are almost constant features of heather moorland below about 500m, particularly in the west. They are, however, easy to overlook when not in flower, helping to perpetuate the common misapprehension that the ubiquitous ling heather is the only dwarf shrub.

Cross-leaved heath tends to grow as small, scattered plants amid the heather and *Molinia* on damp, peaty ground, and derives its name from the symmet-

Cross-leaved heath   *Bell heather*

rical whorls of four narrow leaves spaced regularly along the shoots, which have a characteristic turquoise-grey colour. In July and August, cross-leaved heath carries tight clusters of plump, pale pink bell-shaped flowers. Bell heather has finer, greener leaves with a slight gloss, which are arranged in groups of three. This plant is more common and vigorous on better-drained ground, often jostling for space with thick ling heather on steeper slopes. Bell heather flowers at around the same time as cross-leaved heath, forming slightly looser clusters of intense purple bells whose colour alone is immediately diagnostic.

Both plants keep their foothold in heathland vegetation by maintaining a high level of metabolic activity during the mild western winters, thus outflanking potential competition from more arctic-alpine dwarf shrubs.

Blaeberry (lus nan dearc) *Vaccinium myrtillus*; Bog blaeberry *Vaccinium uliginosum*

Blaeberry in flower and fruit

The well-known blaeberry is readily identified by the bright apple-green colour of its foliage, and by its photosynthetic stems, which are of similar colour and persist, leafless, through the winter. Blaeberry has broadly alpine tendencies and is very common in heather moorland, particularly towards the south and east, but becomes increasingly confined to cooler north-facing slopes towards the north west. Blaeberry is more snow-tolerant than heather and frequently extends to higher altitudes in various types of alpine heath.

The arctic-alpine bog blaeberry, or bog whortleberry, is also scattered on some higher slopes. The rounded, untoothed leaves of this plant have networks of very prominent veins and stand out from surrounding vegetation because of their turquoise tint. In common with many other alpine species, this plant largely maintains itself without sexual reproduction, and although individual shoots live for up to 60 years, the overall age of a given plant is almost indeterminable. A number of other adaptations may confer competitive advantage in these habitats, and the upper leaves are noticeably longer (up to 20–25mm) and strongly tilted, allowing more efficient capture of low-angled solar radiation. Both blaeberry species produce edible blue-black berries, offering a pleasant treat to passing hillgoers.

Crowberry (lus nam braoileag) *Empetrum nigrum*

Deep green, glossy mats of crowberry are very common in heather-dominated moorland and blanket bog, particularly to the east and at higher altitudes, and in other suitable habitats above the heather limit. Individual leaves are 4–6mm long and 1–2mm wide, and both look and feel 'fat', as their margins are rolled under, more than doubling their effective thickness. The margins meet below the leaf, giving the appearance of a white central stripe along the underside, which confirms the plant's identity. The black berry is edible, although slightly bitter.

In common with many alpine plants, the reproductive strategy of crowberry is adapted to the constraints of altitude. Above about 650–800m, this plant is largely represented by the distinct subspecies *E. nigrum hermaphroditum*. As the name implies, this variant has bisexual flowers, greatly increasing the efficiency of fertilisation in a hostile climate. This form of crowberry can often be distinguished, when in fruit, by the presence of residual stamens at the base of some berries. Subspecies *hermaphroditum* also has more rounded, stubby leaves than the low altitude form, whose leaves are parallel-sided, but this distinction is far from reliable. Within the UK, the hermaphrodite form is almost entirely confined to Scotland.

Cowberry (lus-nam-braoileag)
Vaccinium vitis-idaea;
Bearberry (grainnseag)
Arctostaphylos uva-ursi

Cowberry   *Bearberry*

Tom Prentice; Keith Miller

Cowberry and bearberry are distinguished from other dwarf shrubs by the dark and glossy appearance of their evergreen leaves, which are 1–2.5cm long, broad and untoothed. The leaves of both species are otherwise, however, quite distinct. The leaves of cowberry have blunter tips, often with a slight inward notch, and those of bearberry are broadest nearer the tip. The lower surfaces are respectively marked by visible dot-like stomata and a conspicuous network of veins. Both plants produce red berries.

Cowberry and bearberry are common in dry heath and blanket bog, particularly towards the eastern Highlands. Bearberry, however, favours marginally enriched soils and is poorly tolerant of shade, often growing as a creeping mat in bare rock debris where competition is reduced. The related alpine bearberry (*A. alpinus*) is scattered on gravelly, exposed ridges in the north-west, and has pointed, toothed and very crinkly leaves whose texture slightly recalls a tiny Savoy cabbage. This plant is deciduous and waits until the autumn to reveal its most startling characteristic. As the days shorten and its black berries ripen, the foliage of alpine bearberry turns to a rich blood-red.

Cloudberry (oighreag)
Rubus chamaemorus

The distinctive broad, crinkled, blunt-lobed leaves of cloudberry resemble those of bramble, and are up to 6cm across. They are commonly seen in blanket bogs and damp, peaty hollows at higher altitude, although the plant is rather more sparse in the west and north-west. Cloudberry flowers infrequently in Scotland, producing a characteristic fruit on a short stalk which resembles a solitary orange-pink blackberry, although with fewer segments.

Keith Miller

Cloudberry has a distinctly Arctic distribution, and is locally abundant in Scandinavia and mountain ranges elsewhere in northern Europe. This plant is commemorated by Beinn nan Oighreag, above Glen Lyon, and this name may well allude to the neighbouring Lairig Breisleach, memorably described in an old guidebook as a 'villainous bog'.

The fruit is edible, with a sweet taste that recalls cooked apples, and can be used to make sauces, preserves and a very passable gin. These culinary traditions are particularly well developed in Scandinavia. The gathering of berries is generally included in the Norwegian system of public access rights, known as *allemensretten*, but the right to gather cloudberries is reserved to the landowner in northern areas, where the plant is most abundant.

Creeping azalea
Loiseleuria procumbens

This diminutive dwarf shrub forms low, compact, creeping mats on high, windswept slopes and summits, often clinging to areas of bare, shifting gravel. Creeping azalea produces tiny pink flowers during May–July, but its identity is confirmed at other times of year by the small oval leaves, only a few millimetres long, which are dark above and pale below, and which are arranged in pairs on opposite sides of the shoots.

Mark Wrightham

This is one of our more extreme upland plants, with a wider distribution that is strongly centred on high mountain ridges and tundra to the north of the arctic circle. Wind-exposed ground does not accumulate an insulating snow blanket and the plant seems to have a number of physiological adaptations which are tailored to this extremely uncompromising habitat, allowing it to withstand temperatures as low as -40° C. Soil temperatures can oscillate dramatically in such situations during the spring, and the plant maintains exceptionally deep winter dormancy in order to avoid premature reactivation on warm spring days, followed by the sucker punch of a late freeze. Growth is extremely slow, with annual rings measuring no more than 0.1mm, but individual plants can survive for at least 60 years.

Least willow *Salix herbacea*

This tiny creeping plant bears no resemblance to the more typical shrub or tree form commonly associated with willows. Its leaves are typically 1–2cm long and almost circular, with a tendency to fold along their midribs. They are also quite shiny and can be seen, on closer inspection, to be edged with rounded teeth. The growth form of the plant is so low that the leaves almost seem to sprout directly from the ground.

Mark Wrightham

Least willow is a true arctic-alpine plant of higher altitudes and extends onto the highest Scottish summits. In common with many other such species, its lower altitudinal limit decreases towards the north-west, reaching down to 90m above sea level in Sutherland. This diminutive plant can only thrive where competition is relatively limited, and consequently tends to occupy two quite contrasting types of habitat. The plant can often be found on exposed stony surfaces which are scoured by wind and churned by frost, sometimes in relatively open *Racomitrium* heath, but also rubs shoulders with sedges and mosses in later snow-beds. The plant can sometimes also maintain a toe-hold on cracks and ledges in rock, and is quite common in the shattered gabbro of the Cuillin summits.

PLANTS

Bog myrtle (roid) *Myrica gale*

Bog myrtle is a small aromatic shrub which forms scattered clumps or thickets on low level blanket bog, wet heath and peaty seepage areas, especially in the west. The plant can reach over 2m but typically achieves less than half this height. In common with willows, individual *Myrica* plants carry flowers of only a single sex. Catkins appear in April and May, before the leaves, and it is at this time that the plant is perhaps most conspicuous. Both male and female catkins are of hard, scaly texture by comparison with willow catkins, and are respectively yellow-orange and of

Tom Prentice

stronger reddish colour. They are also of differing size, with male catkins reaching over 1cm in length while female catkins are rather smaller. The elegantly shaped leaves reach up to 6cm long and 2cm wide, and usually have a few vague teeth towards the tip.

The leaves and twigs of bog myrtle are dotted with very small yellow secretory glands which release a pleasantly fragrant resin when rubbed. The resin is an effective natural midge repellant, but the rather patchy distribution of the plant means that it is not always to hand in times of need.

Bog asphodel (bliochan) *Narthecium ossifragum*

The rich golden-yellow spikes of bog asphodel are a delightful and common feature of seepage areas and blanket bogs in the Scottish uplands, although the plant is less widespread and flowers less often at the highest levels. The flowering heads are carried on individual upright shoots, typically 10–20cm tall, which appear in July–August and persist, pale and bleached, well into the winter. Bog asphodel can

Mark Wrightham

be rather invisible amongst taller vegetation at other seasons, as the leaves are small and close to ground level, but the plant tends to be more obvious in open flushes dominated by mosses and liverworts. The curving blue-green leaves form small, stiff tufts, in which 3–4 blades lie together in the same plane like a partially unfolded Swiss Army knife. These die back in autumn, assuming a delicate salmon-pink hue.

Bog asphodel is more or less confined to oceanic north-west Europe. The botanical name refers to an alleged connection with rickets in grazing animals, although this might have been a case of guilt by association, as the vegetation of acid peatland habitats is generally low in calcium. Bog asphodel has traditionally been used as a source of yellow dye, providing an alternative to saffron.

PLANTS

Heath spotted orchid (mogairlean mointich) *Dactylorhiza maculata*

Tom Prentice

The attractive heath spotted orchid is scattered through the wet heaths of lower hill slopes in the Western Highlands, raising its distinctive solitary flowering spikes, which are around 15–25cm high, in June–August. The spikes are densely packed with complex flowers which are normally a delicate pinkish-white, finely patterned with deeper pinkish-purple lines or dots. The leaves are long and narrow, tapering to a point and typically carry large, conspicuous and roughly circular brown spots. This plant is rather variable and quite often occurs with white flowers, or without markings on the flowers or leaves, but these forms are still reasonably distinctive and unlikely to be confused with anything else that grows in these habitats.

Orchids, along with most other terrestrial plants, form an association with a fungus (known as a mycorrhiza) to increase the efficiency with which they can capture certain soil nutrients. Orchid seeds contain virtually no nutrient reserves and must establish this association at a very early stage if the seedling is to survive. In most mycorrhizae, the fungal partner obtains carbon from the plant, but this does not seem to occur in orchids – and it is unclear what benefit, if any, the fungus derives from this arrangement.

Lousewort (bainne na cuthaig) *Pedicularis sylvatica*

Tom Prentice

The complex flowers and intricate fern-like foliage of lousewort are common in western blanket bogs and wet heaths and will often be spotted when flowering between April and July – as small splashes of pinkish-purple amid the taller deer grass and *Molinia*. Each shoot typically stands around 10cm tall and is capped by a loose cluster of pink flowers, each with a distinctive upright 'hood'. This plant is only likely to be confused with its relative marsh lousewort (*P. palustris*), which is taller, more stiffly upright and rather less common, tending to occur in flushes where there is some nutrient enrichment.

This attractive plant has a mildly sordid semi-parasitic lifestyle, supplementing its nutrient intake by tapping into the roots of neighbouring plants. It acquired its charmless name because it was once believed to encourage disease and parasite infestations in grazing animals. In *The Herbal or General Historie of Plants* of 1633, John Gerard suggested that "*the herbe is not onely unprofitable, but also hurtfull, and an infirmitie of the medowes*" and that "*it filleth sheep and cattel full of lice*". Some may prefer to refer to the plant by its alternative name of dwarf red rattle.

PLANTS

Tormentil (cairt-lair) *Potentilla erecta*

Tormentil is one of the most ubiquitous Scottish hill plants and is dotted through grassland, dwarf shrub heath and blanket bog with a consistency that only flags at the very highest altitudes and in the more persistent snowbeds. The flowers of the plant appear between May and September and are easily recognised by their four neatly symmetrical, golden-yellow and more or less heart-shaped petals. Each flower is about 10mm across. Calcareous grassland and rock outcrops, particularly in

Tom Prentice

Breadalbane, can also harbour the somewhat rarer alpine cinquefoil (*P. crantzii*), which looks like a five-petalled tormentil. The leaves of tormentil are narrow and deeply-toothed, appearing as radiating whorls of five which faintly resemble the foliage of a cannabis plant.

In the Highlands and Islands, preparations of the root of tormentil were traditionally used for tanning leather and fishing nets. The modest size of the plant suggests that this would have been extremely laborious, and a 19th century commentator reported that one person would be occupied for most of a day in gathering enough material for a single infusion. The plant is also alleged to cure nervous diarrhoea and is sometimes conveniently available on belay ledges.

Heath bedstraw (màdar fraoich) *Galium saxatile*

This tiny, unassuming and very common plant occurs in a wide variety of upland habitats but can be found most consistently in grasslands, particularly of the relatively rich bent-fescue type. Its straggling shoots are very inconspicuous when the plant is not in flower, but can be identified (once spotted) by their whorls of 5–8 narrow leaves, 7–10mm long, which radiate from the stem at intervals like the spokes of a wheel. The leaves are broadest above their middle then taper fairly abruptly before culminating in a small, but distinct, point. The thin stems are square in cross-section and it is fairly easy to feel this by rolling them between a finger and thumb. As with most plants, however, identi-

Tom Prentice

fication is much easier when in flower, which occurs between June and August. Its minute cross-shaped white flowers, no more than 3–4mm across, can then be found sprinkled among the upland grasses and sedges with a simple and understated beauty.

This plant is a close relative of the similar but much larger common cleavers, or 'sticky willy' (*G. aparine*), a widespread plant of lowland scrub and waste ground which is familiar from its habit of sticking to clothing.

Heath milkwort (siabann nam ban-sith) *Polygala serpyllifolia*

Heath milkwort is often dotted through heather moorland and grassland at lower altitudes, and is perhaps most frequent in the extensive wet heaths of the west. This small plant is, however, likely to pass unnoticed unless it is in flower, which occurs between May and September.

Each shoot carries a loose cluster of small flowers, around 4.5–6mm across, which are usually a more or less deep blue. This colour is quite striking and differentiates this plant from almost everything else that grows in these habitats, but confusing variants with pink or white flowers are not uncommon. A closer look reveals that each flower consists of two petal-like structures and a central tube, slightly like a mini-daffodil, which is formed from three petals fused together. The delicate, quite narrow leaves occur in opposite pairs, at least on the lower part of each stem.

The name *Polygala* is derived from the Greek for 'much milk' and, along with the English and Gaelic names, reflects a historic belief that cattle grazing on pastures containing this plant would have higher milk yields. Milkworts were also thought to relieve enchantments which prevented milk from being converted into butter or cheese.

Tom Prentice

Devil's bit scabious (greim an diabhail) *Succisa pratensis*

Devil's bit scabious flowers between August and October, heralding the approach of autumn, and is unlikely to be confused with anything else that is common in the Scottish hills. The flower heads are 15–30mm in diameter and purple-blue in colour, while the leaves are untoothed and of classical pointed oval 'leaf' shape.

This widespread plant is dotted through a range of upland grasslands and dwarf shrub heaths, but is most abundant where seepage brings a little nutrient enrichment. Conversely, the plant is sparse or absent in blanket bogs, which overlie deep, acidic and impoverished peat soils. An apparently unique variety (*S. pratensis* var. *scotiaca*) has been described in Arran, The Trossachs and the Ben Nevis area, and is distinguished by several subtle characteristics including slightly smaller flowering heads (10–20mm in diameter).

The name of the plant is derived from its root, which ends abruptly as if chopped off. Tradition has it that the devil bit the tip away in an act of vengeance for the benefits which the plant bestows on humanity, although these principally consist of pigments which are useful for dyeing. The Gaelic name translates as devil's bite.

Tom Prentice

Wild thyme (luibh na macraidh)
Thymus polytrichus

'Wild mountain thyme' is widespread in the Scottish uplands, forming low, creeping mats which are fairly inconspicuous for much of the year. Each stem carries paired, oval evergreen leaves no more than 8mm in length, but definitive identification is achieved by rubbing, which releases the characteristic scent of thyme. Between May and August, the plant carries clusters of small, complex pink flowers about 5mm wide, and is then considerably more visible.

Wild thyme is a good indicator of calcium enrichment in grassland and on rock ledges, but can also eke out an existence on fine rock debris. Such areas can sometimes provide adequate nutrient inputs from relatively acidic rocks, such as the Torridonian sandstone of Ben Mor Coigach.

The juxtaposition of wild thyme and heather, referred to in the familiar song, is rather infrequent as these plants have distinct soil preferences. The two species do intermingle, along with common dog violet, in an unusual type of dry heath which occurs on some well-drained sites over the Inner Hebridean basalts and gabbros. This quirk may reflect a stand-off between the leaching and acidifying effects of very high rainfall, which favour heather, and nutrient inputs from the underlying rocks.

Keith Miller

Ladies-mantles (fallaing moire)
Alchemilla species

Two ladies-mantles are common in the Scottish hills and are most easily recognised by their distinctive leaves, as their small, green flowers are rather inconspicuous. Alpine ladies-mantle (*A. alpina*) is the more abundant, occurring at higher altitudes in short alpine vegetation, and on rock ledges and debris, with a moderate preference for more calcareous rocks. This plant is particularly prominent on the schists of Breadalbane and the volcanic rocks of the Inner Hebrides, occurring in large areas of grassy vegetation on

Alpine ladies-mantle

Stuart Rae

higher slopes, which at least partially reflect long-term grazing. The leaves have 5–7 narrow, deeply-cut lobes with a few teeth towards the tip, and have conspicuous pale margins.

The so-called 'common ladies-mantle' (*A. vulgaris*) has much less deeply-divided leaves, each of which is roughly circular, with a toothed margin divided into 7–9 shallow, rounded lobes. This plant is actually a complex array of very similar 'microspecies' and is strictly confined to calcareous grassland and ungrazed ledges.

The name derives from the former use of broader-leaved species as sanitary protection and as a poultice for wounds, although these plants are invariably dwarfed by grazing in open grassland, where the leaves only reach a fraction of their potential size.

Moss campion
(pocan ban/coirean-coinnich)
Silene acaulis

Mark Wrightham

Moss campion forms dense cushions in various types of alpine vegetation and on bare rock debris, and is most noticeable in July and August, when the cushions are dotted with 6–10mm wide pink flowers. These are carried on very short stalks and appear to sit on the cushion itself. At other times, these cushions are easily distinguished from those of thrift (below) by their leaves, which are less than 10mm long and taper gradually to a point.

This plant shows a distinct preference for soils with a relatively high calcium content, and is particularly abundant on the Dalradian mica-schists of Breadalbane. This requirement seems to relax with increasing altitude, and the plant occurs on the higher slopes and summits of many hills which are composed of acid rocks such as granite, quartzite and Torridonian sandstone. The deeply penetrating tap root and compact cushion form confer a high degree of wind resistance, often allowing the plant to exploit extremely exposed habitats on wind-scoured upper slopes.

Moss campion has an arctic-alpine global distribution and reaches 83° 9′ north in Peary Land, the northern extremity of Greenland. It is also among the highest occurring plants in the Alps, reaching 3700m in the Valais.

Thrift (tonn a' chladaich)
Armeria maritima

Mark Wrightham

This attractive plant forms small, dense cushions on exposed summits, most frequently in the west and north-west Highlands. Although most common in *Racomitrium* heath, thrift can also be found in other types of alpine vegetation, its abundance varying from hill to hill for reasons that are not always clear. Non-flowering thrift is distinguished from similar cushion plants, such as moss campion, by its very elongated leaves, which are generally at least 2cm long and about 2mm wide. The cushions assume a deep orange-brown colour in the winter months. Identification is easier in July–August, when the plant raises small pink flowers in stalked, globular clusters about 1.5–2cm across.

Along with some other Scottish alpine plants, thrift also occurs in coastal habitats. Thrift appears to have been more widespread during the early colonisation stages after the last glaciation, retreating in the face of growing competition from other species as the climate improved, and may now be concentrated on core habitats in which it enjoys a competitive advantage. The plant is well adapted to extreme wind exposure, which is characteristic of many alpine and coastal habitats, by virtue of its compact form and enormous anchoring tap root, which may reach 1.5m in length.

Roseroot (lus-nan-laoch)
Rhodiola rosea

Roseroot is very distinctive and is not difficult to identify. The upright, unbranched stems carry pale blue-green, fleshy, upward-curving leaves, which are occasionally tinged with pink. Between May and August, each shoot is capped by a dense, flat-topped cluster of tiny yellow flower heads. The waxy foliage assumes a gentle beauty on dreich days, when water pools as sparkling globules at the base of the leaves.

Gill Nisbet

   Roseroot is one of the many Scottish mountain plants that are strongly associated with calcium-rich soils, and is most often encountered on the Tertiary volcanic rocks of the Inner Hebrides and calcareous schists in the southern Highlands. The plant is very sensitive to grazing and is more or less confined to steep, rocky ground beyond the reach of sheep or deer. This requirement is satisfied by entire upper slopes and summits in the Skye Cuillin, where the plant can be found on open areas of rock debris.

   Extracts of *Rhodiola rosea* have been associated with a wide range of claimed or proven medicinal properties. These include a stimulant effect comparable to that of Korean ginseng and a capacity to promote endorphin release, counteracting some of the symptoms of stress.

Yellow saxifrage (clach-bhriseach-buidhe)
Saxifraga aizoides

Yellow saxifrage is easily recognised during June – August, when this plant produces flowers with five narrow, rather spaced petals which are carried on more or less upright stems. The petals are sometimes flecked with red specks, which form a more visible pattern under ultraviolet light and may serve to attract insects. The plant is equally distinctive, though less conspicuous, at other times of year, as its erect, unbranched shoots carry fleshy, pale blue-green leaves which are typically about 1cm long and 2–3mm wide.

Stuart Rae

   This attractive plant is a reliable indicator of calcareous soil conditions, and is particularly characteristic of the Dalradian schists of Breadalbane, and richer pockets amid the extensive Moine rocks of the Central Highlands. Within such favourable areas, yellow saxifrage is associated with areas of particularly marked calcium enrichment, including gravelly seepage lines and dripping vegetated crags. It can also be found in grasslands which experience some water movement, and where soils are enriched by the churning action of frost heave or, in some cases, human disturbance. Yellow saxifrage is patchily distributed across the mountain and arctic regions of Europe and North America, reaching 80° 49' North on Ellesmere Island in Canada.

Purple saxifrage
Saxifraga oppositifolia

The beautiful purple saxifrage is cited by many as their favourite mountain plant and its richly coloured flowers, which appear in April–May, signal the onset of spring. The flowers are roughly 10–20mm across with five petals and little or no stalk, appearing to sit directly on the underlying tangle of shoots. These are densely lined with opposite pairs of tiny leaves, 2–5mm long, which give the plant its Latin name, but it is easy to overlook when there are no flowers to catch the eye.

Tom Prentice

Purple saxifrage is a reliable indicator of calcium enrichment, occurring in springs, flushes, burnsides or sodden banks that are irrigated by calcareous water. It is most likely to be found over the Dalradian schists of the Southern Highlands, the Palaeogene volcanic rocks of the Inner Hebrides and isolated slivers of upland limestone, but the plant also marks out enriched pockets among acid rocks elsewhere. Even in favourable situations it is rarely abundant, spicing its appeal with a dash of mystique.

Purple saxifrage is particularly hardy, flowering under snow in the Alps, and this is among the most northerly flowering plants, reaching 83⁰ 39' N at Cape Morris Jessup in Peary Land, on the north coast of Greenland.

Starry saxifrage
Saxifraga stellaris

The delicate starry saxifrage is quite common at higher altitudes, most often in springs and seepage areas, sometimes fed by frigid meltwater from late-lying snowbeds. These habitats may be quite bare and stony or be carpeted by lush cushions of alpine mosses and liverworts. The leaves of this plant have very short stalks, a few marginal teeth and a sparse covering of hairs, and

Tom Prentice

form a flat 'rosette' close to the ground. The small white five-petalled flowers are 1–1.5cm across, with conspicuous red anthers, and are raised on thin, red, leafless stalks between June and August. A closer look reveals two yellow spots on each petal.

After the Ice Age starry saxifrage, in common with most Scottish alpine plants, would have spread from a limited number of 'refuge' areas to colonise the mountains in which it now occurs – which form a broad arc from the Alps to Scandinavia, Greenland and the eastern USA. DNA analysis suggests that most Scottish populations of starry saxifrage are closely related to those in Greenland, Iceland and Norway, but at least one Scottish population, in Glen Coe, is genetically distinct and probably results from a different phase of colonisation.

Sundews (lus-na-fearnaich)
Drosera species

These small but unmistakeable insectivorous plants are a frequent feature of wetter low-level blanket bog, particularly in the west. The most common species is the tiny round-leaved sundew (*D. rotundifolia*), followed by the larger great sundew (*D. anglica*), which has 7 elongated leaves up to 4cm in length and is confined to parts of the bog where the water table is highest. Both are instantly identified by the conspicuous sticky red tentacles around the rim of each leaf, tipped with the sticky secretion which gives the plant its name. Sundews produce simple but attractive flowers with five white petals,

Round-leaved sundew

Tom Prentice

which are carried on long, thin stalks and appear during June–August.

Insects trapped by the 'dew' provide a touch stimulus causing the nearest tentacles to bend inwards, often beginning within as little as 10 seconds. The leaf blade and remaining tentacles then curl inwards over the course of a day or more, to completely envelop the insect. The leaves remain shut for one to two weeks, eventually reopening to release residual indigestible fragments. Small insects less than 1mm in length form the bulk of prey, but surprisingly large invertebrates such as damselflies can also fall victim if trapped by several leaves simultaneously.

Common butterwort (mothan)
Pinguicula vulgaris

This insectivorous plant is so striking as to require little description, and resembles a small starfish roughly 5–15cm across. The pale green, fleshy, pointed leaves have upturned margins and are coated with a sticky mucilage, resulting in a characteristic greasy sheen. This secretion captures small insects, triggering the release of a cocktail of digestive enzymes. Common butterwort hoists solitary violet-like purple flowers in May and June.

Tom Prentice

This plant occurs sporadically in blanket bog and wet heath, but is most characteristic of peaty seepage lines with calcium enrichment. The plant is therefore most common over the volcanic rocks of the Inner Hebrides, Durness limestone and the schists of Breadalbane, extending up to the lower reaches of the alpine zone.

This curious plant has developed an extensive folklore. In some parts of the Highlands and Islands, butterwort was thought to grow wherever the wandering St. Maolrubha had touched the ground with his staff. The plant was also believed to confer protection against witchcraft and other misfortune, and it was said that travellers who carried nine roots of 'bog violet' were guaranteed to reach their destination in safety.

PLANTS

Purple moor grass (fianach-gorm)
Molinia caerulea

Tom Prentice; Mark Wrightham

This coarse grass is very prominent in low altitude blanket bog, wet heath and peaty flushes throughout the Scottish uplands, and particularly towards the west. The leaf blades are broad, flat and tapering, and of fairly soft texture, in marked contrast to the bristle-like leaves of mat grass. In areas of particularly rampant growth, *Molinia* sometimes forms large, lax tussocks over 30cm tall. In common with some other upland grasses, *Molinia* dies back in autumn, but the dead, straw-coloured leaf material persists for many months, forming long and distinctive ribbons which wind through the surrounding vegetation. These streamers are occasionally torn up by winter gales, giving rise to the old common name of this grass – flying bent.

Purple moor grass is commonly mixed with heather but can become overwhelmingly abundant, sometimes in conjunction with deer grass, where its competitive edge has been sharpened by grazing and burning. Although *Molinia* frequently occurs alongside mat grass, the two species become predominant in distinct situations. *Molinia* can often form homogeneous blankets on sodden valley bottoms and lower slopes, while mat grass tends to do this on slightly better-drained ground with a thinner peat cover, and extends to much higher levels.

Tufted hair grass (cuiseag-airgid)
Deschampsia cespitosa

Mark Wrightham

Tufted hair grass is quite common in the Scottish hills, occurring in alpine springs and on steeper slopes irrigated by snow-melt. The leaves are broad, flat and tapering, and of similar shape to those of purple moor grass, but this plant extends to much higher altitudes and, in these situations, forms smaller tussocks. These have a somewhat spiky appearance and stiff texture, and identification can be confirmed by pulling the base of a leaf away from the shoot, which reveals a membranous spike, or ligule, up to 1cm long. The leaves of tufted hair grass share the crystalline edging of mat grass, but are even rougher.

The tussock growth form may provide significant ecological benefits in the alpine zone. Dead leaves persist as bleached white tufts which provide a windbreak, raising the temperature around the growing tissues during the short summer season. This mode of growth also encourages the dead leaves to break down in situ rather than being blown away, thus concentrating recycled nutrients around the roots. This grass also occurs in a viviparous form (sub-species *alpina*), in which the flowering spikes carry complete miniature plantlets which drop off and take root.

Mat grass (carran) *Nardus stricta*

The sheer abundance of mat grass in certain situations can make recognition straightforward. The plant forms small and neat tussocks, typically around 15–20cm across, which are composed of fine, bristle-like leaves of quite stiff, wiry texture. These persist through the winter and spring, turning to the very pale straw colour which characterises many summit landscapes at these times. The flowering spikes are dark purple, very slender and curiously asymmetric, consisting of a row of spikelets which project in roughly the same direction. This is usually more obvious on the dead, pale

Stuart Rae

vestiges of the flowering head which can be seen later in the season. At higher altitudes, the next most common fine-leaved grass is sheep's fescue (*Festuca ovina*), which has softer leaves and frequently produces viviparous spikes covered with miniature plantlets.

Mat grass is naturally dominant over many upper slopes and summit plateaux and, where grazing has been persistent, can also carpet damp ground with a thin peat cover on lower slopes. This grass is encouraged by grazing because its foliage is edged with hard silicate crystals and is unpalatable to herbivores. This crystalline armour can be felt by sliding a leaf between pinched fingers.

Deer grass (lus-feidh) *Trichophorum cespitosum*

Deer grass is very widespread and common in blanket bog, wet heath and rough *Nardus* grassland, particularly in the west. This plant forms patches or tussocks composed of unbranched, apparently leafless shoots up to 30cm tall, each of which is capped by a simple flowering spike. This is of quite characteristic appearance and is seem-

Tom Prentice; Nick Kempe

ingly variegated with chestnut brown and yellow, due to the contrasting colours of outer and inner floral parts. The dying shoots can be strikingly patterned with fawn and orange, eventuallypassing to a mottled brown in winter. This plant is not particularly favoured by grazing deer and the name is instead derived from these autumnal colours.

Deer grass is usually less prominent than other plants such as heather, and the rank dominance of this species provides good circumstantial evidence of grazing and burning. In common with mat grass and purple moor grass, this increased cover can persist, once entrenched, long after these influences decline or cease. Deer grass is also very resistant to trampling, often surviving amid heavily used paths as bald tussocks, in which living shoots encircle the bare crown like a monk's tonsure.

Cotton grasses (canach)
Eriophorum species

The unmistakeable white heads of cotton grasses are a common sight throughout the Scottish hills. Common cotton grass (*E. angustifolium*) typically carries 3–5 heads on each stalk, although this is not always obvious unless the diffuse cottony tuft is rolled between finger and thumb. This widespread plant is perhaps most common in peaty seepage areas, blanket bogs and wet heaths.

Tom Prentice; Nick Kempe

Common

Hare's tail

The leaves are quite distinctive, tapering to a long, hard, triangular tip which turns to a vivid scarlet in autumn, the colour gradually seeping downwards to encompass the entire leaf.

The single-headed hare's tail cotton grass (*E. vaginatum*) is restricted to blanket bog, generally indicating peat at least 0.6m deep. Its fine, glossy leaves are of roughly triangular section for their entire length and can form vigorous tussocks up to 0.3m high.

Common cotton grass is widely distributed across northern Europe, Asia and North America, but hare's tail cotton grass is more skewed towards high altitudes and latitudes. This pattern is broadly reflected within Scotland and although both can occur from sea to summit, hare's tail cotton grass becomes more abundant on blanket bogs at higher levels and in the colder Eastern Highlands.

Stiff sedge (dur-sheisg)
Carex bigelowii

Sedges (*Carex* species) resemble grasses, but are more generally confined to infertile or waterlogged soils, occupying a fairly distinct ecological niche. *Carex bigelowii* is one of several sedges which are confined to higher altitudes, and seldom occurs below 600m. In summer, the plant produces a flowering spike with 3–4 small, dark heads, 5–15mm long, clustered at the top of a quite thick, stiff stem, which springs back when bent to

Stuart Rae

one side. In common with other sedges, the stem is triangular in cross-section, which is easier to feel than to see. The leaves have a central groove and are 2–7mm wide at the base, gradually tapering to a point. This leaf form is common to numerous *Carex* species, but this matters little on the high tops, where this plant is by far the most common sedge.

Carex bigelowii is frequent in a wide range of alpine habitats. It is commonly intermingled with mat grass on higher slopes and plateaux, and is strongly dominant in some 'snowbeds' on low-angled ground in the Central Highlands. The plant is also a more or less constant companion to woolly fringe moss in the *Racomitrium* heath of exposed slopes and summits.

Heath rush (bruth-chorcach)
Juncus squarrosus

The humble heath rush is very common on the Scottish hills, occurring in a range of situations and at various altitudes, typically on more or less poorly-drained ground. This is a rather tough and dourly functional sort of plant which somehow encapsulates bleak hill days when drizzle hangs in the wind and peaty soil slips and squelches underfoot. It often

Mark Wrightham; Tom Prentice;

grows alongside mat grass and is likewise encouraged by grazing.

   This plant is easily recognised by its straight, narrow, channelled and very glossy leaves, which are 1–2mm wide and radiate outwards to form symmetrical tufts that bend back strongly towards the ground. These are very stiff and sometimes push down surrounding plants to form sunken pock-marks in the vegetation, as the rush voraciously hogs the sunlight. Rigid stems, typically around 20cm high, rise from the centres of these rosettes and end in lightly branched heads with a few dense clusters of unassuming flowers or, later in the season, grain-like fruits (which are both largely chestnut-brown and are superficially similar at a glance). As winter begins to bite, the persistent dead heads stick up defiantly through shallow snow, sometimes edged with rime, keeping the promise of life until spring returns.

Three-leaved rush (luachair thri-bhileach)
Juncus trifidus

Juncus trifidus is one of relatively few plants which can thrive on the most exposed summits in the Scottish mountains, and is by far the most abundant species on the unstable rock debris of the Cairngorm plateaux. The plant is much less common elsewhere in the Highlands, reflecting the limited extent of comparable terrain, and is scattered on small areas of rocky detritus on wind-blasted ridges in the west and north-west.

   The stiff, unbranched shoots of the rush are up to 30cm tall, ending in a very compact, dark flowering head. This sits in the junction of 2–3 fine leaf-like structures which are several centimetres long (and strictly part of the flower spike, rather than true leaves). Clumps of shoots often twitch in unison in the gusting wind, as if joined like the springs of a mattress. In autumn, the foliage assumes a rich orange-brown hue.

Stuart Rae

   In the Cairngorms, tussocks grow laterally by 2–3mm per year, creeping downwind on the most windswept ground. The granite gravel fields drift like snow, with material blowing off exposed, actively eroding areas to accumulate in even the slightest of hollows, and the tussocks grow upwards or downwards at their margins as the ground level changes.

Soft rush *Juncus effusus*;
Sharp-flowered rush *Juncus acutiflorus*
(both species: luachair bhog fhlurach)

Soft rush is common at lower levels throughout the Scottish hills, often forming large, dense patches in wet pastures or seepage areas, frequently accompanied by *Sphagnum* or *Polytrichum* mosses. The clumped stems can reach 1.5m in height and carry small clusters of unassuming brown flowers which appear to project sideways from a point some way below the shoot tip. Around Loch Lomond, and elsewhere in the South-west Highlands, this rush is often replaced by the equally tall sharp-flowered rush, which has shoots tipped by branched clusters of brown flowers whose pointed extremities are spiky to the touch.

Soft rush

Soft rush is unpalatable to sheep and cattle, and its abundance on rough hill pasture generally reflects various combinations of grazing and ground disturbance. It is uncertain whether the plant is ever abundant as a result of more natural processes. Soft rush was widely used during the 18th and early 19th centuries to make so-called 'rushlights', to circumvent a tax which had been levied on candles. These lights were prepared by drying and peeling the shoots, then soaking the absorbent inner pith in animal fat, creating a kind of slow-burning taper. This lost skill could perhaps be revived for use in bothies.

Bracken (raineach) *Pteridium aquilinum*

Bracken is by far the most abundant fern in the Scottish uplands, where it has been estimated to cover over 1000km^2. Bracken can usually be recognised by its extent alone, and is typically vigorous, with large pale green fronds borne on tall stems which can exceed 2m in height. Unlike many other upland ferns, bracken never forms clumps of 'shuttlecock' appearance. Identification can be confirmed by the shape of the smallest lobes into which each frond is divided, which are elongated, up to 1cm long and completely untoothed. Several other large ferns form less frequent tufts or small patches in the uplands, and the only other species with untoothed 'pinnae' is lemon-scented fern, which releases its tell-tale aroma when rubbed.

Bracken commonly spreads by the outward growth of its bulky root system, forming genetically uniform patches which can be of enormous size. These roots comprise most of the biomass of this fern, and the rhizomes underlying a 0.25km^2 patch of bracken typically weigh between 250 and 500 tonnes. Bracken contains a formidable cocktail of toxins which are poisonous to grazing sheep or cattle. These include numerous carcinogens and hydrogen cyanide, which is released when the plant's tissues are crushed.

Sphagnum mosses (coinneach dhearg)

Sphagnum mosses often form large patches or hummocks, and are easily recognised by their symmetrically radiating branches and the small cap of densely clustered shoots which crowns each stem. Different species are variously bulky and swollen or fine and delicate, and vary in colour from lush greens and lurid yellows to deep crimson. The 30 or so Scottish species can be found in blanket bogs, acid flushes and other damp or humid habitats,

Mark Wrightham

occupying overlapping but distinct niches defined by nutrient status and the height of the water table. A gradation can often be seen around bog pools, with free floating aquatic *Sphagna* giving way to layered tiers of other species up the sloping pool margins.

The hollow cell structure of *Sphagnum* plays host to a remarkable diversity of animal life, including at least 145 species of Protozoa, which occupy different vertical zones within each plant according to their resistance to periodic dehydration. Tiny parasitic roundworms and other multicellular aquatic animals can also occur in considerable numbers, with up to four or five thousand per gram of moss. Many of these species occur in no other habitat, hinting at a complex and highly specialised microscopic ecosystem.

Polytrichum commune

The distinctive moss *Polytrichum commune* is abundant in the Scottish mountains. Its upright stems often exceed 15–20cm in height and carry dark, tapering leaves which radiate stiffly in all directions, so that large patches resemble miniature conifer plantations. This vigorous upright growth is made possible by a relatively well-developed system of water conducting tissues, which is unusual amongst mosses. In dry conditions, however, the leaves collapse against the stem to reduce water loss.

Nick Kempe

P. commune is most characteristic of seepage lines and, when present, is a reliable indicator of acidic water, often intermingling with vigorous soft rush and *Sphagnum* mosses. The plant nonetheless occurs in a wide range of upland habitats on acid soils, ranging from woodland to 'early' grassy snowbeds, often where there is a suspicion of burning or other disturbance due to land management. Its robust stems have been used for basket weaving, and examples have been found in Scotland which date from around 100 AD.

Several related species have the same general appearance, but are considerably smaller. *P. alpinum* is roughly half this size and is widespread at higher altitudes. *P. piliferum* forms tiny, dense tufts and is instantly recognised by the white hairs which tip its leaves.

PLANTS

Woolly fringe moss
Racomitrium lanuginosum

Racomitrium lanuginosum is quite easy to recognise with a little practice, and consists of soft, finely branched tufts which appear pale turquoise when dry and yellow-green when wet. The leaves are topped by fine white hair points, which give the whole plant a distinctive 'frosted' appearance. The purpose of these features is unclear, but the hairs may have a capillary function, drawing water over the outside of the plant towards the growing stem tips.

Tom Prentice

Woolly fringe moss is common in dwarf shrub heath and blanket bog at all altitudes, particularly in the west. On exposed upper slopes and summits, however, this plant can be identified by its sheer abundance, often forming very extensive carpets which are combed to the north-east by the prevailing wind to create a natural compass. *R. lanuginosum* is replaced by the smaller *R. ericoides* on some areas of loose soil high on the hills above Glen Coe and Glen Nevis.

The abundance of this alpine 'moss heath' on Scottish summits might be reflected by mountain names which include choinnich, such as Sgurr Choinnich Mor. *R. lanuginosum* is common in the more oceanic parts of North America, but is otherwise of restricted global distribution.

Hylocomium splendens

The elegant moss *Hylocomium splendens* is easily recognised by the combination of its red stems and golden-yellow fronds, in which each branch bears further side shoots to create an intricate tracery. The stem colour is less apparent when dry, but can be highlighted by moistening a shoot.

Mark Wrightham

This moss is very abundant in Scottish pinewoods, dry heaths and certain types of snowbed, and is a widespread feature of the boreal forest that encircles the arctic. Soil water can be limited in these habitats, and although many mosses draw water upwards over their exterior by capillarity, *H. splendens* is not well adapted to this mode of uptake. The loose feathery mats can, however, trap and retain rainfall, and the plant obtains all of its water requirements and certain key nutrients in this way. Phosphorus is not naturally abundant in rainwater, but is leached from the tree or dwarf shrub canopy as rainfall drains through, and is captured by the moss mat. The abundance of the moss in some western snowbeds is also likely to reflect these ecological characteristics, as these habitats have a relatively cool and humid microclimate and derive significant water and nutrient inputs from snow melt.

Pleurozia purpurea

Pleurozia purpurea is among the more frankly weird Scottish upland plants and is sometimes known by the ugly but apposite common name of purple worm liverwort, well capturing its appearance. The plant forms tufts or mats of smooth, upright shoots, each perhaps 3-4mm wide, which are typically deep purple but sometimes tinged red or yellow. Once spotted, it is impossible to mistake.

Mark Wrightham

Pleurozia is most conspicuous in western wet heath and blanket bog, where it is patchily distributed but locally abundant. It also occurs in dry heaths on cool, sheltered northerly slopes in the north-west, where rich mixtures of mosses and liverworts thrive in the humid underworld below rank heather and coarse boulders. This plant ranges well beyond Scotland, occurring for example in Norway, Alaska and the Himalaya.

There is more to any plant than meets the eye and this is particularly true of *Pleurozia*. Each leaf has two lobes, the lower of which forms a tiny closed sac sealed by a non-return valve. These sacs trap water, which could provide an obvious physiological benefit, but relatively recent evidence suggests that they can also attract and trap microscopic protozoa and that the plant may be carnivorous.

Fir clubmoss (garbhag an t-sleibhe) *Huperzia selago*; Alpine clubmoss (garbhag ailpeach) *Diphasiastrum alpinum*

The clubmosses are a curious group of plants whose great antiquity is matched by their primeval appearance. Two species are common in the Scottish uplands and are easy to distinguish on account of their quite distinct forms. The more widespread is fir clubmoss, which forms stiffly erect, spiky tufts of shoots up to 10cm tall, in dwarf shrub, grass- and moss-heaths towards higher levels. Alpine clubmoss has smaller, branching, slightly flattened shoots roughly 2mm across. These rather resemble miniature ropes, as the leaves are closely pressed against the stem. This species tends to be rather prostrate, forming small inconspicuous patches amid low, open vegetation in the alpine zone.

Tom Prentice

Fir clubmoss

Clubmosses are among the oldest known plants, appearing in the fossil record around 400 million years ago. In contrast to mosses, their well-developed water transport system allowed them to reach considerable sizes, with some species growing up to 40m tall during the Carboniferous. Although present day clubmosses are much smaller, their basic structure has altered little over time. An 18th century Highland folk tradition suggested that extracts of fir clubmoss have an extreme purgative effect which can induce labour.

Keith Miller

Alpine clubmoss

Cladonia lichens (crotal)

The diverse genus *Cladonia* contains all of the most common soil-dwelling lichens of the Scottish uplands. The most conspicuous species form dense clumps of fine branches a few centimetres across. At lower altitudes, perhaps the most widespread is *C. portentosa*, whose tiny branch tips curl in various directions. *C. arbuscula*, by contrast, is more common in the alpine zone

Cladonia arbuscula

and towards the east, and has branch tips which are all turned the same way. The much less branched *C. uncialis* is also frequent, and is of very distinctive appearance, resembling miniature discarded deer antlers only a few centimetres in length. A wide range of *Cladonia* species of completely different form are also common, often consisting of stalked cups like miniature golf tees, whose rims are sometimes adorned by bright scarlet fruiting bodies. All are more or less pale blue-green in colour.

Cladonia species are of great ecological importance in the arctic tundra, forming a critical part of the diet of reindeer and caribou at those times of year when higher plants are not available. However, they are extremely low in protein, and these herbivores have to metabolise muscle to make good this deficit until more nutritious grazing becomes available.

Map lichen
Rhizocarpon geographicum

A variety of lichens, mosses and liverworts can be found on rock surfaces in Scotland's mountains, playing out similar ecological battles to those which shape plant communities on the ground. These species are not always easy to identify precisely on the hill, but one of the more widespread and prominent is the so-called map lichen, which occurs on a variety of relatively acid rocks at all altitudes from glens to summits.

The 'body' or thallus of this lichen is smooth to the touch, forming a hard crust on the rock, and is a distinctive pale greenish-yellow, dotted with very small, subtle and embedded black fruiting structures. An underlying black layer highlights both cracks in the surface and the edge of the thallus where it abuts against its neighbours, creating a fancied resemblance to areas marked on a map.

Common and yet otherworldly, rock-dwelling lichens may be the only visible life in some areas of summit blockfield and in the high alpine zone of bigger mountains beyond the UK. *R. geographicum* is abundant, for example, above 1500m in parts of Norway, imparting its eerie yellow tinge to stark landscapes high in the Rondane and Jotunheimen areas.

137

Invertebrate Life

Keith Miller

Mating northern eggar moths (female on left; male on right)

Introduction

Invertebrates, or animals without a backbone, comprise about 95% of animal species worldwide. This is also true of our mountains and during the summer, the observant hillwalker may well find 20 species of invertebrate for every sighting of a vertebrate. Invertebrates play a variety of important roles in upland ecosystems, which include pollinating flowers, consuming plants and dead plant or animal material, and providing food for other animals, including other invertebrates. Thus they play a vital part in various food chains.

Although the invertebrates of Britain are probably the best known in the world, as a result of more or less continuous study since the 19th century, the depth of this knowledge is not spread evenly either geographically or across habitats. In Scotland, and especially the Highlands and Islands, there have been, and still are, relatively few local people studying invertebrates and much recording has been undertaken by visiting naturalists. These limitations have been compounded by factors such as the small size of many invertebrates, identification difficulties, nocturnal habits and the relatively remote nature of many Scottish mountain areas. There have consequently been few systematic studies or surveys and most attention has inevitably focussed on more easily accessible areas and habitats, and sometimes on specific sites where rare species are known to occur, such as Ben Lawers, Rannoch and Strathspey.

Our knowledge of the distribution, life cycles and other ecological aspects of many Scottish mountain invertebrates is far from complete, and considerably less than that of lowland species. This provides great potential for enthusiastic amateurs to generate new information through fairly simple observation and recording.

A tremendously wide variety of familiar animal groups are invertebrates, including spiders, butterflies and moths, midges, bluebottles, bumblebees, centipedes, snails, slugs, ticks, earthworms and woodlice. These clearly have a considerable range of body structures and apart from the absence of a vertebral column, different groups of invertebrates often have little in common. Some knowledge of the main differences between the groups of invertebrates and their life cycles considerably facilitates identification and understanding of how different species survive in their habitats.

Body structure and sensory organs

Most invertebrates, around 85% in Scotland and 93% globally, are arthropods. Arthropods found in the uplands include millipedes, centipedes, woodlice, spiders, ticks and mites, and a wide variety of insects such as dragonflies, beetles, butterflies, grasshoppers and flies. The most obvious characteristics of arthropods are a segmented body, pairs of jointed limbs and a thickened cuticle forming an 'exoskeleton' which covers the surface of the body. The exoskeleton is a complex multilayered structure containing the chemical chitin combined with protein, producing a very strong and lightweight material. Movements of the body or body parts are dependent on muscles which are attached to the exoskeleton.

Of the terrestrial and freshwater invertebrate species known from Scotland, about three quarters are insects. Besides the usual arthropod characteristics, most adult insects have a number of other more or less obvious external features. Their bodies are divided into three regions, the head, thorax (the middle section) and abdomen. The head has one pair of antennae and a pair of compound eyes, which are composed of a number of separate visual units or 'ommatidia', each with its own lens on the eye surface. Three pairs of legs and two pairs of wings are usually attached to the thorax, though there is considerable variety in their appearance. In some groups, the hindwings are considerably smaller than the forewings and in the true flies, the hind pair of wings are reduced to small club-shaped structures which act as balancers in flight, enabling the fly to sense changes in movement and direction. Beetles, by contrast, have hardened forewings, or 'elytra', which protect the flimsy hindwings when not in use.

Adult insects are well served by sense organs: antennae act as feelers and pick up the presence of airborne chemicals (akin to smell), while compound eyes pick up visual stimuli. The number of ommatidia determines visual acuity and tends to relate to the requirements of the insects' life styles. Those with mainly subterranean lives, such as worker ants, have relatively few (in this case around 600 per eye) and rely more on their antennae. At the other extreme, the compound eyes of dragonflies cover most of the head and are composed of up to 30,000 ommatidia, enabling them to catch prey in flight. The mouth parts of insects often have sensory projections known as 'palps', and the body may be clothed with sensory hairs.

An important feature of insects which differs from other animal groups, though it is not visible to the naked eye, is the respiratory system. Vertebrates and most other invertebrates have special breathing organs (lungs or gills), along with a blood system which transports oxygen from these organs around the body. However, insects have a system of fine air tubes or 'tracheae' that spread throughout their bodies. Air enters through pores, or 'spiracles', along the surface of the thorax and abdomen, and passes into the tracheae, from where oxygen diffuses into the tissues of the body.

The great diversity of insects, and the success of some species, results from several factors. These include their exoskeletons, which provide effective protection and reduce water loss. Their relatively small size enables them to occupy an extremely wide variety of niches, and their ability to fly, which is unique among invertebrates, can clearly facilitate their dispersal to new areas of suitable habitat.

By contrast to insects, another familiar group of Arthropods, the spiders, harvestmen, ticks and mites, have bodies which are generally divided into a combined head and middle section (cephalothorax), which carries four pairs of legs, and an abdomen. Furthermore, they have simple, rather than compound, eyes and their sensory faculties are largely provided by bristles and hairs, known as 'setae', rather than by eyes or antennae. These hairs cover much of the body and each is supplied with a nerve.

Non-arthropods are also very diverse and include flatworms, roundworms, slugs, snails, mussels, leeches and earthworms, some of which are common in the hills, though often unseen. At least 44 species of flatworm and roundworm, for example, have been recorded as parasites of red deer.

Life cycles

Most invertebrates lay many small eggs from which immature young, usually called 'larvae', emerge. This immature stage generally needs to feed for further growth and development. Life cycles vary considerably between invertebrate species, with development to maturity taking anything from several days to a few years. Slower developing species spend most of their lives as larvae.

Insect life cycles are fascinatingly varied, but there are two main types, which are known as 'complete' and 'incomplete' metamorphosis (or change of form). Butterflies, moths and two-winged flies, for example, undergo complete metamorphosis which has four stages: egg, larva (a caterpillar or maggot), pupa (or 'chrysalis') and adult. Dragonflies and damselflies, on the other hand, undergo incomplete metamorphosis which has three stages: egg, larva (or 'nymph') and adult. With a few exceptions, such as the larger caterpillars, larvae are generally harder to see on the hill than adults. While the adult stage tends to be relatively short, it is primarily devoted to finding a partner, mating and egg laying, a period of intense activity which helps to make the insect conspicuous.

Larvae are basically 'feeding machines' and may be very specialised in their food requirements; the larvae of some species of butterfly or moth, for example, are associated with just one plant species. The presence of an exoskeleton means

Almost fully grown (c6cm long) emperor moth caterpillar

Larval case (exuvia) of hawker (Aeshna sp.) dragonfly (c4cm long)

that, in order to grow, a larva must shed its old one, known as an 'exuvia', and expand its body into a fresh stretchable one which hardens on contact with air. This generally happens between four and ten times, and each time the larvae are especially vulnerable to predation. Once shed, exuviae are very light, fragile and rarely seen except for those from which adult dragonflies emerge.

Most Scottish insects overwinter as larvae, though some do so as eggs, pupae or adults. Insect breeding cycles also vary so that some species have one brood per year and others two, but very few moths can complete two generations in the year where lower temperatures prevail. It is not infrequent for species that manage two broods in southern Britain, such as the common carpet moth of grasslands and moorlands, to have only one brood in Scotland. For most invertebrates, suitable conditions for breeding must occur each and every year and as a result they are generally relatively sensitive to changes in environmental conditions.

One significant ecological and conservation implication of these complex life cycles is that the different stages may have quite different niche requirements. For some invertebrates, one of these requirements may be a mammal or bird host. A familiar example in the uplands is the sheep tick, which also uses red and roe deer and other mammals as hosts.

Survival in the mountain climate

Unlike mammals and birds, invertebrates are 'cold-blooded' and the temperature of their bodies varies with that of their surroundings. They are therefore dependent on external heat sources for their physiological requirements. In the Scottish mountains the prevailing climatic conditions make warmth unpredictable, and although strong winds can facilitate their dispersal, such conditions also create many constraints for these small creatures. Despite these unfavourable circumstances, numerous species of invertebrate are resident in, and some are restricted to, the Scottish mountains.

The reason for this is that for most invertebrates, it is the micro-climate of the habitat that is crucial for their survival. Even in the mountains, the fine details of topography, ground surface and vegetation can provide the necessary conditions of warmth and shelter. However, there is also plenty of evidence of physiological or behavioural adaptations to the prevailing weather. Some invertebrates of the upper slopes and summits, such as the black mountain moth, have adapted to windy conditions by spending more time crawling as opposed to flying. Northern or mountain populations may also have life cycle adaptations to help them cope with climatic constraints. In some species of insect, such as the northern eggar moth, development takes two or more years rather than a single year further south. It is thought that for full larval development each species requires a certain time above a specific temperature threshold and for these insects, one short cool summer is insufficient for complete development.

Another phenomenon associated with some northern and upland species is 'melanism'. Darker surfaces absorb more of the sun's radiation than paler ones. This enables adult moths with dark wings to warm up and so become active faster. Several day-flying moths from the Scottish mountains illustrate this feature, including the black mountain moth and the netted mountain moth.

Historical background

There is evidence from beetle research that even Arctic tundra species did not survive the last Ice Age. As the ice retreated from Britain and the climate ameliorated, invertebrates would probably have recolonised from the then land-linked European mainland. The ice re-advance about 13,000 years ago affected much of Scotland and some species ill-adapted to colder conditions may not have survived, even in areas which remained ice-free. As the temperature subsequently rose again, colonisation recommenced to an increasingly wooded country, and it was during this period that the majority of our invertebrate fauna would have arrived. While some cold-adapted species became extinct, others, such as the northern dart moth, survived on Scotland's mountains.

Once sea-level rise separated Britain from continental Europe, non-flying invertebrates could only arrive with assistance, either from their hosts (for species such as bird fleas), from humans (accidentally or deliberately), or through transport by wind or water. Stronger flying insects could still reach Britain unassisted. Previously unrecorded species are still arriving by these routes, especially in southern England.

Most of the invertebrates on Scotland's mountains are comparatively widely distributed 'generalists' which, while not having specialist adaptations, survive by finding sufficient places places within the uplands that meet their less specific requirements. Those that are largely restricted to hill country can be loosely divided into two categories; those limited to higher altitudes, above the limit of potential tree growth, and those that occur in lower altitude habitats, such as heather moorland and upland woodlands. Two similar and closely related butterflies that broadly illustrate these distributions are the mountain ringlet and the Scotch argus, which are both dark brown with orange bands and black spots towards the outer margins of each wing. The mountain ringlet has a more restricted distribution, occurring on open mountain grassland between around 350m and 900m, whereas the Scotch argus occurs in damp grassland up to 500m, but also in woodland clearings.

The diversity of invertebrates generally decreases with altitude due to the more severe climate, lower diversity in the structure of the vegetation and other factors, some of which are not fully understood.

Glens and lower slopes

Lochs, rivers, pools and flushes

Many invertebrates are associated with water, either specifically or within a wider habitat, such as pools in moorland, blanket bog and wet heath. Particular species tend to be adapted to either flowing or still waters, though for some species larvae and adults have different requirements. Other important factors include the acidity, temperature and depth of the water, the type of substrate (stony or peaty), the amount of pollution and the concentration of dissolved oxygen, which is

Small bog pools such as these beside Loch Maree, provide habitats for various invertebrates including dragonflies

greatest in fast flowing water. Some of these properties can change on a seasonal basis and this variation can also be important. Due to the acidic nature of most of Scotland's rocks and soils, calcareous water, where it occurs, tends to support rare species. These specific requirements mean that some groups or species can be used as indicators of particular environmental conditions.

The insect species of stoneflies, mayflies and caddisflies (p158) are all intolerant of pollution. Stonefly nymphs show a strong preference for flowing water, particularly with stony substrates, and are primarily found in upland areas. Mayflies and caddis flies occur in both flowing and standing water across Britain, but are more common in the lowlands. Nymphs of all three insect groups form an important component of the diet of freshwater fish and so are familiar to fly fishermen.

Blackflies (family Simuliidae) are also important food for fish (p219) both as larvae and adults. Females of these small two-winged flies require blood meals to produce eggs, which are laid in running water. On hatching the larvae attach themselves to a rock with tiny hooks at the end of their abdomens and passively filter-feed on suspended organic matter in the flowing water. The larvae pupate inside a brown cocoon then as adults, float to the water's surface in an air bubble in late spring to begin their short flying stage.

Dragonflies and damselflies are among the most conspicuous and beautiful upland invertebrates and of similar general appearance. Most prefer water with a soft sediment substrate, and are more associated with slow-flowing or standing waters. Bog pools are often particularly important for this group of insects, as they are relatively shallow and thus heat up quickly, and are distinctly acidic, reducing the range of larger animals present. Under these circumstances, the carnivorous larvae are often the top predators, feeding on almost any creature that comes their way, even smaller larvae of the same species. Adult dragonflies are also superbly adapted predators, with highly developed eyes and wings that beat independently of each other, giving them the amazing ability to fly back as well as forwards.

Male large red damselfly (total length c.36mm), showing wings held along abdomen as is normal for most damselflies.

Keith Miller

The conditions in their favoured habitats are generally comparatively stable, and the soft sediments and associated vegetation provide the larvae with both invertebrate food and shelter. The larvae of large dragonflies may live for two to four years in the sediment of the water bodies in which the eggs are laid, where they can both overwinter and survive periods of summer drought. The final exuviae left by emerging adult dragonflies may be seen attached to plants such as rushes and cotton-grasses growing from bog pools, lochans and other water bodies. Adults live for only a few weeks, which provides enough time to reproduce.

Different dragonfly species in the uplands can occupy distinct habitats. Some species, such as the azure hawker, use bog pools as small as two metres across and 20cm in depth, but with a significant layer of detritus at the bottom. By contrast, the four-spotted chaser is a widespread and much less discerning dragonfly, which is found around a wide range of pools on moorlands and bogs. The large and prominently coloured golden-ringed dragonfly is unusual in that it uses flowing waters, normally less than two metres wide.

The abundance of standing water in the Scottish hills also provides habitats for a variety of other freshwater invertebrates. These include familiar species from lowland ponds, such as pond skaters, water boatmen and whirligig beetles, although these are generally confined to modest altitudes in the Scottish mountains.

Heather moorland and grassland

A considerable number and variety of invertebrates live in moorland habitats, and some are particularly attractive. These include a diversity of moths whose larval foodplants include common 'ling' heather, bell heather, cross-leaved heath, blaeberry, crowberry, bog myrtle and a variety of grasses. Even the smaller, more indistinct moths fulfil important roles in the ecosystem, for example providing food for breeding birds such as meadow pipits, wheatears and skylarks.

The adults of several species, such as the emperor, northern eggar, magpie and fox moths, are large, distinctively marked and day-flying, and are therefore easy to identify on the hills. The bright green emperor and hairy dark brown fox moth caterpillars are equally conspicuous. Both of these are around 6cm long when fully grown and may be seen on moorlands during the late summer and autumn. A butterfly found on wet moorland and bogs up to 750m is the large heath, whose caterpillars mainly feed on hare's tail cotton grass. In Britain this is predominantly a Scottish species, though it does occur in Wales and northern England. A distinctive bright green butterfly, the green hairstreak, also occurs on some moors, its caterpillars feeding on blaeberry.

Numerous moorland and grassland plants rely on insect pollination, particularly towards lower altitudes. Species which play key roles in this process include some two-winged flies, such as craneflies and hoverflies, along with butterflies, moths, bees and wasps. A distinctive, but apparently declining, species pollinating some moorland plants is the bilberry bumblebee, which may be seen on blaeberry during early summer and thereafter on other plants especially bird's-foot trefoil, bell heather and ling.

A variety of both carnivorous and herbivorous beetles may be seen on moorland and grassland. 'Ground beetles', including the large black flightless species *Carabus glabratus* and *C. problematicus*, may be seen hunting amongst vegetation on the ground. The distinctive green tiger beetle may also be seen on bare ground or sparse vegetation, or in a short flight. 'Click beetles' are often conspicuous and may be readily identified by their ability to "jack-knife" their body, an adaptation enabling them to right themselves when lying on their backs. This action, which is accompanied by an audible click, is enabled by an unusually mobile joint between the first and second segments of the thorax.

As its name suggests, the heather beetle feeds principally on ling, both as adult and larva. The adult beetle is brown and about 6mm in length, and can be abundant in some years – a population peak occurred, for example, in Strathspey and parts of south-east Inverness-shire in 2004. In such years extensive areas of heather moorlands may be affected, resulting in large swathes of dead heather. Heather beetle outbreaks, however, are of relatively modest impact by comparison with those of some other upland invertebrates. The larvae of the pine beauty moth feed on the needles of Scots and lodgepole pines, and major outbreaks of this moth started in Sutherland and Caithness lodgepole pine plantations in 1976. These outbreaks have sometimes more or less destroyed entire tree crops over areas of several square kilometres. Interestingly, major infestations of pines by this moth had not been recorded in Scotland prior to the large-scale planting of lodgepole pine and other conifers, though it was a well known pest of Scots pine in central Europe.

Various other invertebrates can be conspicuous on the lower hill slopes. Slugs and snails are common and the large black slug, *Arion ater*, is very noticeable, as it can be 10–15cm in length when fully extended. Spiders' webs and their waiting occupants are a common sight, though there are also a number of non web-making species present. Spiders generally protect their eggs within egg sacs, which are varied structures and may, depending on the species, be attached to leaves or vegetation, stuck under stones or carried around by the female. Most species guard

Well grown (c6cm long) northern eggar caterpillar on ling, one of its main foodplants

Female Araneus quadratus web-making spider (abdomen c1cm across)

Keith Miller

the egg sacs, and some wolf spiders are particularly attentive parents, periodically re-opening their sacs, providing extra fluid and re-sealing them. Eventually the nymphs, or 'spiderlings', emerge from the egg sac. The females of some species feed their spiderlings with regurgitated food, while others leave large prey for them to feed on, and in species where the female has abandoned the egg sac, or has died, the spiderlings fend for themselves. Wolf spider nymphs cannot escape from the egg sac, which must be opened by the female, and the mother then carries the spiderlings around on her back for a week or so before they disperse.

The Highland midge is much harder to see unless close up, when it is all too familiar to hillwalkers. This tiny fly undergoes complete metamorphosis, and its life-cycle is particularly well adapted to the environment found over much of the Scottish uplands. Eggs are laid on the moist soils of the blanket bogs, wet heaths and acidic grasslands that are common in the Western and Central Highlands, and damp conditions are crucial for their survival. The eggs hatch after only a few days, and the tiny aquatic larvae burrow into the soil and slowly mature during the autumn and winter, sometimes at extremely high densities. It has been estimated that up to 2,400 midge larvae may occur in a square metre of suitable ground. The larval stage lasts for up to 10 months and after a short pupal stage, the midges emerge as flying adults and mate. Although the first batch of eggs is laid without a blood meal, females must feed on a suitable host animal to ensure the development of subsequent batches of eggs.

Ticks are another group of invertebrates of moorlands, grasslands and woodlands that are familiar because of their bites. Like midges they have four stages of development. Eggs are laid on the ground in mid- to late summer and hatch into small, colourless six-legged larvae less than 1mm long, either after a few weeks or in the following spring. Before further development can take place, the larvae need a blood meal and crawl into vegetation to await a warm-blooded host, such as a small mammal or bird. Ticks do not possess eyes, but have finely tuned sensors located on their front pair of legs, which can locate passing animals and birds by vibration, heat and the CO_2 from their breath. Once on a host, a tick larva moves to a suitable feeding site, embeds its barbed mouthparts into the skin, injects an anticoagulant and feeds on blood. After a couple of days, when gorged, it drops off, moults and emerges as an 8-legged nymph.

The cycle is then repeated as the nymph seeks out a host, and this is the stage of tick development at which humans are most frequently bitten. The nymph feeds, drops off, moults and emerges as an adult male or female, which is 2–4mm in diameter before feeding. As adults, it is principally the females which feed, while males search for females with which to mate. After feeding and being fertilised, females lay up to 2,000 eggs and the whole life cycle starts again. Sheep ticks have a total life span of up to four years in colder northern climates and two to three years in warmer areas. They may be abundant in suitable habitat and in an Austrian forest the number of sheep ticks has been estimated as around 20 larvae, nine nymphs and one adult per square metre. As drought is the major factor limiting tick numbers, equally large populations may well occur in optimal habitats in the Highlands.

Upper slopes and summits

The diversity of invertebrates is much reduced on the higher slopes and summits. Most species are relatively small and inconspicuous, spending much of their time on the ground amongst the rocks and the short and often sparse vegetation. As at lower levels, however, they play important roles in the ecosystem, and resident, dispersing or migrating invertebrates provide a significant high altitude nutrient resource for birds such as snow buntings, and for carnivorous invertebrates.

Some invertebrates are well suited to these windswept habitats, in part because their exoskeletons help to prevent water loss and reduce the likelihood of desiccation. Their life cycles can be short with, in some species, development from egg to adult taking only a few weeks. In the mountains, this attribute allows growth and reproduction to take place during the relatively short periods with suitable conditions, and these rapid cycles may also, in the longer term, give rise to rapid evolution. Their relatively small size enables them to occupy an extremely wide variety of niches, and their varied characteristics have enabled them to colonise and survive in almost all mountain habitats; even the barren Cairngorm plateaux.

Smallish, rather nondescript day-flying moths, such as the northern grass-veneer and alpine grey, are known to occur at high elevations, though little is known about the larvae of either species. However, there are some more conspicuous, identifiable and interesting species that live at altitudes above 600m, such as the northern dart, black mountain moth and mountain (or Scotch) burnet. The known larval foodplant of each of these species is crowberry, which is widely distributed across British upland areas. However, the distribution of each moth is much more restricted and the reasons for this are not entirely clear. The northern dart has been recorded from scattered upland sites in northern England and Scotland, including the Outer Hebrides, Orkney and Shetland. The black mountain moth, by contrast, occurs mainly on the Cairngorms and Monadh Liath above 600m, and the mountain burnet is only known from between 700m and 850m on a small number of mountains in the eastern Cairngorms.

Many beetles found on the upper slopes are non-flying. Ground beetles are found in almost all habitats from the seashore to the highest mountain summits and, as their name suggests, spend much of the time on or under the ground. Although they are all good runners, some species are completely wingless or their elytra are fused together. One such species is *Nebria gyllenhali*, which is widespread and found in a variety of habitats and altitudes right up to the summits. The very similar but much rarer *Nebria nivalis* is an arctic species known only from a number of mountain summits across the Highlands and Inner Hebrides and is sometimes associated with areas of late lying snow. It is only possible to guess at the number of equally specialised invertebrates that remain to be discovered.

'Rove beetles' are predators or scavengers, and generally have an elongated

Keith Miller

Red admiral butterfly, a visitor to the summits, basking on rock

body with distinctively short elytra which leaves much of the abdomen exposed. One such species found on some of the highest tops is the endangered *Eudectus whitei*. This beetle appears to prefer exposed summit areas, where it lives amongst the sparse short vegetation, mosses, stones and rocks, and it has been found in particularly barren parts of the Cairngorm plateau.

Various flies also occur on the high tops, and upland craneflies, such as *Tipula montana*, are of particular ecological importance. These frequently have a synchronised emergence during the early summer, which results in large numbers of adults appearing over short periods, and several upland birds, notably dotterel and golden plover, take advantage of this abundance to feed their young. In some species, a second mass emergence may also occur in the autumn. The co-ordinated timing of this metamorphosis is believed to be a survival adaptation, as predator populations are not able to multiply sufficiently rapidly to consume a high proportion of individuals (see p183).

Most spider species inhabiting the windswept upper mountain slopes are non web-making, to avoid problems associated with wind damage, and live under stones. Many of these are 'wolf spiders', which can be seen running on the ground and actively hunting, though some live in silk-lined burrows or silk tubes from where they ambush their prey. The hairs or setae that cover their bodies are very fine and extremely sensitive to air movement and vibration, enabling spiders to sense both potential prey and predators, and this adaptation greatly assists species which hunt by these methods.

A variety of invertebrates, both dead and alive, may frequently be seen on the surface of high level snow patches which remain through spring and into the summer. These include some 'lowland' species of spider which use air currents as a means of dispersal. This is sometimes called 'ballooning', and involves the spiderling (or adult spider) climbing to a high point and releasing strands of silk from its spinners. These are caught by air currents and carry the spider away, in some cases for considerable distances. Some of these airborne spiders will be eaten by birds, land on unsuitable terrain or water, be caught in spiders' webs or be carried off to high altitudes, but enough reach appropriate habitats for this to be an effective dispersal mechanism.

Many other types of invertebrate have been recorded flying, or drifting on air currents, from lower to higher elevations. The species recorded from snow patches are a clear indication of the variety reaching the summits and plateaux. For instance, a study in June 1979 recorded at least 130 insect and spider species from snowfields above 1100m on Ben Macdui and Braeriach. Only 10 of these were species which normally breed on the upper slopes, typically above about 600m.

Of the others, 50 were believed to be altitudinally widespread species breeding both below and above 600m, although probably nowhere near the altitude of the snowfields, and 28 were 'lowland' species. The remaining 42 species were insufficiently well known to categorise.

These visitors from lower levels help to enliven the hill scene. During bright, warm, sunny weather, flashes of colour from adult small tortoiseshell and red admiral butterflies may be seen up to the summits. The small tortoiseshell is a very common and widely distributed species often associated with human activities, and its larval food plants are nettles. On the other hand, the red admiral, though often an abundant and widespread butterfly, is a migrant with influxes from southern Europe and North Africa. It does not normally overwinter in Britain, but has been observed to do so in the south of England. Both species are strong fliers and can easily reach the high tops.

In recent centuries the main influence on invertebrates in Scotland, as elsewhere in Britain, has been human activity. High grazing levels have reduced the extent of some habitats that are potentially important for invertebrates, including tall-herb vegetation and alpine willow scrub, which are now largely confined to isolated steep rocky slopes and ledges. Knowledge of invertebrates associated with alpine willows is far from complete, though at least six species of the sawfly genus *Pontania* are associated with these plants. These insects are not easy to see, but they stimulate the formation of abnormal growths, or 'galls' on leaves, in which the larvae feed, and which may be very obvious. Grazing has also significantly reduced the range and abundance of many plants that are important food and nectar sources for invertebrates. At some sites, such as Meall nan Tarmachan, Ben Lawers, Creag Meagaidh and Coire Sharroch in Glen Doll, conservation efforts are underway to redress this situation and the invertebrates that are associated with, or confined to, these scarcer habitats may have a better long-term chance to survive and prosper.

Red gall, containing larvae of Pontania herbaceae, on least willow

Mountain invertebrates also appear to be entering a period of considerable uncertainty due to the effects of climate change. The generally predicted increase in temperature is likely to facilitate a northwards range expansion of some species, and this has already been recorded in England and southern Scotland for a few species of butterfly, moth and dragonfly. Those invertebrates that are restricted to Scotland's mountains due to their requirements for cooler temperatures may have limited scope to adapt, as they will have to move upwards and may have nowhere higher to go. Time will tell.

Mountain (or Scotch) Burnet
Zygaena exulans

Burnets are an unmistakeable colonial group of day-flying moths with green- or blue-black forewings, with red spots or patches, and predominantly crimson-red hindwings. In the mountain burnet, each forewing has five red spots (wingspan 2.5–3.5cm) and the colouration is subdued but identical in adult males and females.

Unlike the widespread, though in Scotland mainly coastal, six-spot burnet (*Z. filipendulae*), the mountain burnet is restricted to a few hills in the eastern Cairngorms near Braemar, occurring between 700–850m. It is believed, however, that the populations are stable and not threatened.

Adults fly strongly in sunshine between mid-June and the end of July. Caterpillars hatch during July and August, and feed principally on terminal shoots and unripe berries of crowberry, though cowberry and blaeberry may also be used. Overwintering takes place as caterpillars and development continues in the spring. Caterpillars are stout, grow up to 2cm, and are dark greenish-black in colour, with a prominent line of yellow spots along each upper flank. Due to the environmental conditions found at this altitude it may take several years for caterpillars to achieve full growth; when they do, pupation takes place in June.

Roy Leverton

Northern Dart (gainne thuathach)
Xestia alpicola

This medium-sized moth of northern latitudes and the alpine zone occurs above 450m on the upper slopes of some mountains in Scotland and northern England, extending to lower altitudes in north-west Scotland and Shetland.

The northern dart's upper forewing (wingspan 3.5–4cm) generally has a variegated brown, reddish or greyish background with prominent brown or black markings, of which one is kidney- and a second oval-shaped. Its hindwings are pale brown. If seen clearly, these markings readily identify this species.

Roy Leverton

Adults mainly fly at night during late June to August, but also in hot sunshine. Hatching from eggs laid in July or August, caterpillars feed primarily on crowberry and develop slowly, spending two winters as larvae. After the second winter caterpillars are almost fully grown (3–3.5cm long) with dull purplish-brown or reddish-brown wrinkled skin and a pale line along the back. Pupation occurs amongst moss in late-May or June. Observations indicate that this life-cycle is locally synchronous, with adults in Scotland emerging in even-numbered years, though in odd-numbered years in the northern Pennines. The reason for this periodicity is not fully understood, though interaction with a species of parasitic wasp appears likely.

Emperor moth (an iompaire chorcaraich) *Saturnia pavonia*

A common, unmistakeable species of moorland, bog, heath and open woodland, the adult emperor is a large moth with a wingspan of 5.5–8.5cm and prominent eye-spots in the middle of each upperwing. It flies in April and May and males can be seen flying rapidly in sunshine; females fly at night, and are less often seen. Adults do not feed, their time being spent locating partners, mating and egg-laying. Males have large and prominent feathery antennae with which they pick up chemicals called pheromones released by females.

Keith Miller

Female (slender antennae)

The caterpillar is equally unmistakeable, having a bright green body with generally broken black bands on each segment, each with pink or yellow warts and short black bristles. During late May to August the caterpillar feeds on a variety of mainly woody plants, including common 'ling' heather, before spinning a brownish pear-shaped cocoon amongst the vegetation, in which the pupa overwinters. The entrance to the cocoon is defended by a circle of spines.

This species occurs in suitable habitats throughout much of mainland Britain, the Hebrides and Orkney. Worldwide, the family (Saturniidae) to which the emperor belongs contains around 1,300 species, though only the emperor is resident in Britain.

Northern Eggar (ughach tuathach) *Lasiocampa quercus callunae*

The northern eggar is a common, very large and distinctive moth (wingspan 7–9.5cm). The uppersides of its wings are a rich dark brown in the male and buff in the female; both sexes have pale bands across each wing and a white central spot on each forewing. Females are distinctly larger than the males. Adults fly from late May to July, males during daylight, especially afternoon sunshine, and females

Roy Leverton

Male, with feathery antennae, in front; female behind

from early dusk. Males have an obvious rapid, zigzagging and apparently erratic flight.

This species is widespread across Britain but occurs in different forms. In southern England, where it is called the oak eggar, it has a one-year life cycle and larval foodplants include a variety of trees and shrubs. Northern populations have a two-year life cycle, with the principal larval foodplants being ling, bell heather and blaeberry, and are found predominantly on heather moorland. There appears to be a transitional zone in central England where sometimes one-year and sometimes two-year cycles occur. Eggs hatch after 2–3 weeks. In northern areas, the first winter is spent as a small larva whereas the second winter is spent as a pupa inside a tough brown cocoon amongst leaf litter.

INVERTEBRATES

Magpie moth (leomann phioghaideach) *Abraxas grossulariata*

Keith Miller

This widespread and locally common moth is found in a variety of habitats, especially heather moorland in Scotland, and is most common in the West and North-west Highlands, and the Hebrides. The adult flies in late June–August and is medium-sized (wingspan 4–5cm) with a yellow body and distinctively black and white wings, with a narrow yellow band across each forewing. The proportion of black and yellow markings on white can vary, though extremes are rare. The only similar moth is the clouded magpie (*A. sylvata*) which is rarely found north of the Southern Uplands and lacks the black spots on the edges of its wings.

With one generation each year, the magpie overwinters as a small larva then actively feeds in the spring, frequently on ling in Scotland, before pupating in late May to mid-June. The pupa is yellow and black, and is clearly visible through its open-weave cocoon attached to the ling. Local populations appear to fluctuate greatly, with periods of abundance and scarcity, though the reasons for this are not clear. The coloration of the magpie in all its stages is an excellent example of markings which act as a warning to potential predators.

Black Mountain moth (leomann dubh na beinne) *Glacies coracina*

Roy Leverton

The black mountain moth is fairly well distributed across the Cairngorms, Monadh Liath and some other Highland areas and is largely confined to the summits, upper slopes and plateaux above 600m. This small moth (wingspan 2–3cm) is unusual in that both fore- and hindwings are of a similar size. Their uppersides are dark brownish-black, with a darker central band and a small black spot centrally positioned on each forewing. Both sexes appear the same size. No similar species occur in its habitat; alpine heaths with crowberry.

Adult males fly in sunshine during June and July, while females crawl around on the ground and vegetation, but when conditions are too cool or windy, both sexes crawl readily. Both this and the dark wings, which absorb heat more readily than paler moths, appear to be adaptations to the harsh mountain environment.

The caterpillar is grey with black chevrons along the middle of the back, and its foodplant is crowberry. The moth spends its first, and probably its second, winter as a caterpillar. This two-year life cycle is a feature of many alpine species, and adults are generally more abundant in odd-numbered years. However, full details of its life cycle are not known.

Mountain Ringlet (amlag na beinne) *Erebia epiphron*

The relatively rare mountain ringlet is the only true alpine butterfly in the British Isles. The uppersides of its wings (wingspan 3.5–4cm) are dark brown with red-orange blotches near the outer margins, each containing a black spot; the undersides are similar but paler and less distinctly marked.

Keith Miller

Its principal known larval food plant is mat grass, and the mountain ringlet is generally found on mountain grassland dominated by this species between 450m and 750m (its overall altitude range is c350–900m). It has also been recorded from species-rich grassland and sedge flushes where mat grass is present in the area. Although mat grass is extremely common across much of the British uplands, the mountain ringlet is restricted to the Central and Southern Highlands, from Ben Nevis in the west across to Creag Meagaidh and south to Ben Lomond, with an outlying population in Glen Clova; plus the English Lake District.

There is one short adult flying period from mid-late June to early August, but activity is strongly dependent on air temperature (>13–14° C) and sunshine. Because of the weather that is frequently experienced in Scotland's mountains, it is more often seen on being disturbed than in active flight.

Scotch Argus (argus albannach) *Erebia aethiops*

The upperwings of the scotch argus (wingspan 4–5cm) are very dark brown to black, with an orange-red band near each outer margin which contains black spots with white centres. The undersides of the hind wings have alternating bands of light and dark, which are more prominent on females. Similar in appearance to the mountain ringlet, this species can generally be distinguished by altitude, habitat and flight period.

Paul Kirkland

Occurring across much of the Scottish uplands, its habitats are damp grassland and open woodland up to 500m. The main larval foodplant in Scotland is purple moor grass, and caterpillars feed on the leaf tips after dusk. Overwintering takes place as small caterpillars, which resume feeding in the spring and from mid-May are large enough to be found. They are up to c2.6cm in length and pale ochre in colour, with a dark brown line along the back and paler lines along the sides, and sparsely covered in short bristles. They pupate during late June.

The adult flight period is from the end of July to early September, and sunshine encourages males to fly almost continuously and females to bask. During poorer weather, both sexes are more likely to be disturbed than seen flying.

Large Heath (dealbhan mor an fhraoich) *Coenonympha tullia*

This butterfly of bogs and wet moorland occurs from sea-level to c750m. At one time it was thought to be three distinct species, so variable are its markings, and today three forms are recognised in Britain. It is medium-sized (wingspan 3.5–4cm) with, in the northern form, pale yellow-brown upperwings and, perhaps, a few indistinct pale spots (often dark-centred). The hindwings, and outer parts of the forewings, are pale greyish beneath. There may be a dark spot

Keith Miller

with a white centre towards the apex of the forewing underside and this can often be seen, since the large heath rests with its wings closed. Females are paler than males.

Adults fly between mid-June and August, but this varies considerably with altitude. Provided the air temperature exceeds around 14° C, it will fly during dull weather conditions. Eggs are laid at the base of hare's tail cotton grass shoots, with caterpillars soon hatching, feeding and then hibernating low down on the same species. The large heath lives in colonies, some very large with up to 15,000 adults reported, though defining a distinct colony can be difficult. Adults are sedentary, with most moving less than 100m and a maximum recorded movement of 450m.

Common hawker (Aeshna juncea) Azure hawker (A. caerulea)

The large common hawker dragonfly is widely distributed throughout upland Britain and is 7.5cm long, with a wingspan of 9.5cm. The azure hawker is mainly found in the Western and Northern Highlands and is slightly smaller at 6cm long, with a wingspan of 8cm.

Both favour blanket bog, breeding in pools up to around 600m, but the common also breeds in other acid pools and lakes, and in slow-moving water runnels. The azure prefers shal-

Male azure hawker basking on sunlit rock

Keith Miller

low, often small, bog pools with abundant Sphagnum moss. The larvae of both species live for 3–4 years in water before emerging and becoming strongly-flying adults. The azure is on the wing from late May to late August, while the common flies from mid-June to October.

Common hawker males have dark brown abdomens with blue and yellow spots, and yellow thoracic stripes, while the azure male looks distinctly blue (paler in cold weather), with blue and dark-brown abdomen (no yellow spots), blue stripes on a dark brown thorax and bright blue eyes. The female of both species is generally brown with variably coloured markings on the abdomen, and may be easier to distinguish by the markings on the brown thorax; the common has narrow yellow stripes, the azure doesn't.

Four-spotted Chaser (tarbh-nathrach na ceithir spotan) *Libellula quadrimaculata*

Found around still water habitats, such as bog pools, this dragonfly has a brown thorax and a brown tapered abdomen, with yellow spots along the sides. Each wing has a dark brown base and two dark spots along the leading edge. It has an overall length of around 4.5cm and wingspan of about 7.5cm.

Keith Miller

During the flight period (May to August) males aggressively defend an area of pool or bog against other males. They perch on tall vegetation from which they fly swiftly to attack other males, or attempt copulation with females, often returning to the same perch. Females spend much of the time away from water and may be seen perched on branches. Aerial mating takes place very quickly (5–20 seconds) and then females lay eggs in shallow water, either by flicking them or by dipping the tip of the abdomen. The eggs are encased in jelly which enables them to stick to submerged vegetation, where they hatch after a few weeks. Larvae take to to four years to develop before emerging from the mud or bottom debris and becoming adults. Like other dragonflies, the adults feed on insects which they catch in flight.

Golden-ringed dragonfly (tarbh-nathrach cearcaill-oir) *Cordulegaster boltonii*

Associated with upland burns that have slow to moderate flow, the adult golden-ringed dragonfly is the largest Scottish species of dragonfly, with a wingspan of around 10cm and an overall body length of around 7.5cm (males) and 8.5cm (females). It is very distinctive, with both sexes having bright green eyes and a black body with bright yellow bands.

Keith Miller

Flying between June and September, males patrol low along several hundred metres of water-

Female, with ovipositor visible at tip of abdomen

course, to which females pay visits. When a female is encountered the male grasps the back of her head with anal appendages located at the end of his abdomen. They then fly off in 'tandem' and mate perched on vegetation. After copulation, females use their long, specialised egg-laying organ (ovipositor) at the tip of the abdomen to lay eggs in gravel, silt or mud at the shallow edge of the watercourse. Larvae spend 2–4 years, and sometimes longer, growing in this sediment before crawling up vegetation at night and transforming into flying adults. Adults feed on other insects, including bumblebees, damselflies and other dragonflies, and it is believed that they only live for a few weeks.

Heath bumblebee (seillean-mor an fhraoich) *Bombus jonellus*

The queens, workers and males of this small species of bumblebee have two yellow bands on the thorax and one at the front of the abdomen, with the end of the abdomen being white (though this is orange in Shetland and the Western Isles). Males have distinctive yellow hairs on the face.

Murdo Macdonald

Its face is blunt, being as wide as it is long (in contrast to the similarly coloured garden bumblebee (*B. hortorum*) whose face is much longer than wide) and its tongue is short. These features strongly influence the food sources of the heath bumblebee, which can only reach nectar in small and short-tubed flowers. Various plants are utilised, but bell heather, cross-leaved heath and ling are favoured when flowering. Later in the season, devil's bit scabious is often important.

The heath bumblebee is widespread, though it is believed to be declining and becoming more localised. It may be found in a variety of habitats, but is particularly associated with heaths and moorlands, and is fairly frequently seen at high altitudes. In coastal areas it also favours machair grassland. In Scotland, the flight period of queens mainly begins in May, but they are not common until mid-June.

Bilberry bumblebee (seillean-mor nan cnaimhseag) *Bombus monticola*

A small bumblebee, the queens, workers and males all have two bright lemon yellow bands on the thorax, though the rear one is frequently narrow and less obvious, and over half of the abdomen is a distinctive reddish-orange.

Helen Boulden

This is principally an upland species of heather moorlands, and the Grampians are currently considered its main stronghold. It is strongly associated with blaeberry, and queens emerge after hibernation to coincide with its flowering in late April–May. Until late June, blaeberry is used almost exclusively for both nectar and pollen by queens and workers, but other plants are used thereafter, including cross-leaved heath, bell heather and ling. Males appear during the late summer and feed on nectar from later flowering plants.

Once widespread, it has undergone a significant decline in range and numbers across Britain, and is still believed to be decreasing. The reasons for this are not fully understood, though overgrazing of upland habitats, which can reduce the quality and quantity of blaeberry, is one possibility.

23 species of bumblebee occur in Britain, of which 18 are found in Scotland, but only the bilberry and heath bumblebees are frequently seen on the hills.

INVERTEBRATES

Green Tiger Beetle
Cicindela campestris

The adult of this medium to large-sized beetle (c1.5cm long) is readily identified from its distinctive bright green colour, with a few small pale (yellowish) markings on the hardened forewings or 'elytra'.

David Whitaker

It is a widely distributed, warmth-loving beetle that is most readily seen in sunshine. The adults are active during spring and summer, when they may be found on open bare ground such as paths, tracks and estate roads, or in sparse vegetation on moorland and grassland. Its long legs enable it to be an active and fast runner, but when disturbed it often takes flight in a flash of bright green, though it rarely flies any great distance. A fiercely carnivorous species preying on other invertebrates, it hunts using its sharp eyesight, provided by large compound eyes, to locate and capture prey.

Breeding takes place during the spring and the carnivorous larvae dig a small vertical burrow in suitable ground, in which they wait for prey to come near enough to catch without releasing their grip. Larvae remain in the burrow until fully grown, when they pupate in an excavated chamber. Adults remain in the chamber until the following spring.

Ground beetles (daolagan na talmhainn) Carabus glabratus, Carabus problematicus

Ground beetles are so named because they spend much of their time on the ground, neither of these species being able to fly.

Carabus glabratus is an alpine species in Britain, primarily occurring on peatland and damp moorland, and favouring dwarf shrub heath with ling and *Sphagnum* mosses. *C. problematicus* is more common and is probably the most likely ground beetle to be seen in the uplands. It is found in a wider variety of habitats, but especially upland woodland and moorland.

Roy Anderson / www.habitas.org.uk

Carabus problematicus

They are both large black beetles (2–3cm long) that may show metallic blue margins to the elytra. There are longitudinal ribbed lines along the elytra of *C. problematicus*, whereas the fused elytra of *C. glabratus* are smooth, without any lines or rows of depressions.

Adults of both species are carnivorous, hunting invertebrate prey on the ground and amongst vegetation. From June to September, adults are active during the day, with *C. glabratus* even being active during rain. *C. glabratus* has a biennial life cycle, spending the first winter as larvae and the second as adults before breeding. In the uplands *C. problematicus* also tends to have a biennial life cycle.

Craneflies (Corra-bhainne) *Tipulidae*

Craneflies, or daddy-long-legs, are a familiar group of two-winged flies occurring in most habitats. The greatest variety of species is associated with damp or wet habitats. Adults have one pair of narrow membranous wings attached to the thorax, with club-shaped balancers behind (see p138), prominent long dangling legs which break off easily if handled and, in most species, a slender body.

Tipula montana, a northern and alpine species, occurs in the Highlands, especially across the Cairngorms above around 600m, but is believed to be under-recorded. It is particularly associated with *Racomitrium* heaths and generally has a two year life cycle, overwintering twice as larvae. Adults emerge synchronously and fly during June and July, generally close to the ground. Larvae and adults provide a food supply for dotterel, snow buntings and other birds.

Adult cranefly, with forewings and rear balancers visible

Laurie Campbell

Adult *Tipula montana* are c1.5cm long, have mottled wings (wingspan around 3.5cm) and long palps (part of the mouthparts) which are visible from close up. In Britain three other similar species of *Tipula* fly above about 300–400m, but only *Tipula alpium*, which flies in May–June, has an overlapping flight period. These two species can only otherwise be readily separated through more detailed anatomical study with the help of a hand lens.

Horseflies (creithleag-nan-each) Tabanidae

Horseflies are two-winged flies and a familiar sight in the Scottish hills. They are stout-bodied fast-flying insects with large, often iridescent, compound eyes. Clegs, the frequent and widespread horseflies, *Haematopota pluvialis* (literally 'blood drinker of the rains') and *H. crassicornis,* are active from May to early September. They grow to around 12mm long and have dull, predominantly grey bodies. At rest or when feeding their mottled brownish wings are held roof-like over their bodies, not in a flat 'V' as in most other horseflies. The dark giant horsefly (*Tabanus sudeticus*) is

The Notch-horned cleg (common horsefly), Haematopota pluvialis; about 11mm long and clearly showing a large iridescent compound eye.

Keith Miller

also seen in our uplands and is the heaviest fly in Europe, with a body length of 25mm.

Males feed on nectar but females are voracious bloodsuckers, requiring a blood meal before they can reproduce, and feeding on a range of large mammals including humans. Bites are painful and caused by very sharp mandibles; anti-coagulating fluids are injected into victims enabling females to lap up blood with their labellae, spongy lobes extending from their mouthparts. Females lay eggs on vegetation or rocks near water; on hatching, the carnivorous larvae live in moist soil and develop for 1–2 years. Adults only live for a few days, enough time to mate and reproduce.

Mayflies (Ephemeroptera), stoneflies (Plecoptera) and caddisflies (Trichoptera)

These groups (orders) of insects are generally dull and often brown in colour, and are associated with unpolluted fresh water, providing important food for trout, salmon and birds like the dipper. Being generally intolerant of water pollution, these insects are often used as water quality indicators by ecologists. They are generally weak fliers and are rarely seen far from water.

Stuart Crofts / Buglife

Mayfly (Ameletus inopinatus), with characteristic resting posture of wings held vertically over the body

Mayflies have very slender bodies with short antennae and transparent wings, the hind pair being much smaller than the fore. At rest these wings are held vertically over the body. Most mayflies have three long

David Pryce / Buglife

Stonefly (Brachyptera putata), showing resting posture with wings folded flat over the body

'tails' known as cerci. Uniquely for insects, they have two flying stages: nymphs metamorphose in or on water into weakly flying sub-adults (known as the 'fisherman's dun') which then, within a few hours, moult into adults. These live for a few days at most and often only a few hours. Their scientific name is from the Greek *ephemeros*, meaning short-lived, literally "lasting a day".

By contrast the membranous hind wings of stoneflies are larger than the fore, and at rest are folded flat over the body. Males of some stoneflies are almost wingless, especially among high altitude species. They often have two long cerci and long slender antennae. Stoneflies favour streams with stony or gravely bottoms, and are particularly intolerant of water pollution.

Caddisflies are moth-like but have hairy, not scaled, wings which are folded roof-like over the body at rest. Their antennae are slender and generally long, but they do not possess long 'tails'. Larvae of many caddis species make cases from suitable material such as sand grains and plant fragments to protect their soft abdomens. These cases are open at both ends and body movements ensure throughflow of water, providing the larvae with a supply of oxygen.

Stuart Crofts / Buglife

Caddis-fly (Philopotamus montana), with wings folded roof-like over the body.

'Highland' midge (meanbh-chuileag *Culicoides impunctatus*

34 species of biting midge (*Culicoides*) have been recorded in Scotland, though only four or five attack humans. Most of these species are rare or uncommon, and the most widespread and familiar species of Scottish upland areas is *Culicoides impunctatus*. This fly is tiny, with a wingspan of about 1.4mm, a feature highlighted in its Gaelic name, which means tiny fly. There are six or seven dark blotches on the wings, and their pattern differentiates this species from others. This is not visible with the naked eye, so the species cannot be distinguished by sight alone.

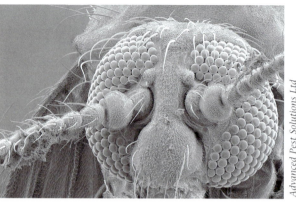

Advanced Pest Solutions Ltd

Head of a midge showing the ommatidia (see p139) of its compound eyes and the bases of the antennae

Adults of the Highland midge first emerge during May, with most of the early hatching being males, which do not bite and therefore often go unnoticed. Subsequently the biting females start flying and persist throughout the summer and into September.

Although midges are generally associated with warm humid weather, cloud cover is the principal factor which determines their activity levels. They are sensitive to light and are prevalent in cloudy conditions, when sunlight is obscured, and during evenings when the sun is starting to set. The other environmental factor that restricts their activity is wind; when this exceeds about 5mph, they find shelter amongst vegetation.

Sheep tick (mial-chaorach) *Ixodes ricinus*

Some 18 species of 'hard tick', which have a rigid chitin dorsal shield (see p139), have been recorded in Britain. The sheep tick is widespread and abundant particularly in upland areas, occurring in woodland, moorland, rough grassland and areas dominated by bracken. An adult sheep tick, with its mouth parts embedded in the skin and its abdomen sticking up in the air, is all too easy to recognise, especially if engorged with blood, when it can reach the size of a small pea. In order

David Whitaker

to develop, larvae and nymphs also require hosts on which to feed on blood, though they are much smaller and less obvious. Ticks can be found on or near the top of plants such as grasses, bracken and small shrubs, where they wait in ambush for a passing mammal or bird, to which they transfer once contact is made.

Ticks are inactive in cold temperatures and are vulnerable to drying out, but thrive in warm moist conditions. They are particularly abundant where coarse vegetation with associated leaf litter, ground flora and humus provide a humid micro-climate for most of the year, and good populations of mammals and birds on which to feed.

Large black slug (seilcheag mhor dhubh) *Arion ater*

This widespread and generally common slug is the largest British species, and occurs in a wide variety of habitats including woodland, grassland and moorland. Slugs need to avoid desiccation, are mostly nocturnal and during dry periods remain amongst vegetation or even burrow deep into soil. It is not unusual to see this slug in the Scottish hills, especially during damp periods or after rain.

Tom Prentice

When mature its extended length is 10–15cm, though when disturbed it characteristically contracts into a hemispherical shape and may sway from side to side if touched. It is very variable in colour with black, brown, grey, red and orange individuals being recorded. Typically in Scotland adults are entirely black, though the foot fringe and sole may be lighter. Juveniles are smaller and paler. Behind the head lies a distinct area known as the mantle, which is roughened, and the respiratory opening lies on its right hand side; the rest of the dorsal surface is covered with raised elongated tubercles.

Although predominantly herbivorous, *Arion ater* will feed on decaying animal matter and may frequently be seen feeding on red deer and sheep droppings.

Deer Ked *Lipoptena cervi*

An adult deer ked is 3.5–5.0mm long and has a tough flattened body which is mainly brown in colour, though part of the abdomen is greenish. The legs are stout with large claws and are adapted to crawling through hair and fur. Deer keds have a wingspan of some 12–14mm.

Adults fly from September through the autumn looking for their deer host, principally red and roe. After finding a host the adult crawls through its fur and sheds its wings which break off near their bases. The deer ked feeds on its host's blood and then mates. The female produces a single larva which is retained in her body to develop until it is ready to pupate.

The fully developed larva falls from the host and pupates in the soil. A winged adult emerges and the cycle is repeated.

Malcolm Storey / www.bioimages.org.uk

In the early autumn adults may occur in large numbers and often land on walkers, when they are readily noticed due to their crawling movements being rather 'itchy'. Adults can bite humans and bites are reportedly very irritating and painful. They are not known to reproduce on hosts other than deer nor to transmit any disease to humans.

Mountain Birds

Stuart Benn

Introduction

Birds add so much to our hill days. They give us vitality. The first wheatear of spring, the skylark's exuberance and the boundless *joie de vivre* of a raven all lift the spirits, like the clouds tearing apart to reveal a view on a day of mist and rain. They enrich our lives. Although first encounters are often the most memorable, there is something new to see every time we go to the hills. But above all, birds fire the imagination. Their capacity to survive in a harsh environment inspires us. Their migrations make us wonder. And their flight makes us dream, as it did the poet Robert Warren:

> "They fly
> In air that glitters like fluent crystal
> And is hard as perfectly transparent iron, they cleave it
> With no effort."

Although the lack of cover makes it easier to see birds on the open hill than in woodland, even an eagle is dwarfed by the scale of the Scottish landscape. But there are ways to shorten the odds, and the best of these is to listen out, as hill birds often have far-carrying calls and songs. Even on a good track, it is difficult to walk and look up at the same time, so it is always worth stopping, letting your breathing still and having a good look around. Birds use the hills in predictable ways, so try to think as they do. How will the wind be hitting the ridge to make it easiest for a raven or eagle to fly? Where are the patches of sun-warmed vegetation that a ptarmigan might feed on when all else is iced up? Finally, most hillwalkers follow the same routes at the same time of day, and while some birds tolerate regular disturbance, others schedule their activities to avoid people, or are just less active in the middle of the day. There is much to be said for getting out early or late, choosing a less popular route or visiting quieter hills.

To understand Scotland's mountain birds, it is important to appreciate what makes them tick. All birds have common basic needs, which could be loosely summarised as survival, feeding and breeding, and these present various challenges in a mountain environment.

Survival

Cold, wet, wind and mist are the norm in the hills and upland birds are well adapted to these conditions. Birds are relatively resistant to windchill because of the insulating properties of feathers, and spend much time close to the ground, where wind speeds are lower than those experienced by hillwalkers a few feet higher up. They also tend to avoid particularly severe weather by taking shelter and riding out the storm, and rarely die as a direct result of such conditions.

The embryos of some northern species are also remarkably resistant to prolonged chilling, and eggs have been known to hatch even after burial in snow or immersion in water. Young chicks, however, cannot regulate their own temperature and can suffer heavy losses if left unattended in bad weather. Harsh conditions generally have a much greater indirect effect on birds by influencing food availability. If severe weather is particularly prolonged then only carrion feeders benefit, and other birds must either move or die.

Birds must also reduce the risk of predation and have evolved a range of adaptations which even out the contest between hunter and hunted. Most hill birds are dull in colour and avoid detection by blending with their surroundings, and by only moving when they have to. Those that must travel any distance often do so in flocks and use the topography for cover, and pigeons, for instance, will fly along the sides of glens rather than right down the middle if they are in peregrine country. Nevertheless, predation is inevitable and prey species tend to make good any losses through high breeding rates. In general, predators and prey therefore tend to stay roughly in equilibrium.

Significant numbers of birds are also killed as a result of human activities. Some of this is accidental, as when black grouse and capercaillie fly into deer fences, or ptarmigan collide with wires at ski areas. Red grouse and ptarmigan are shot during legally defined open seasons, while crows are trapped in the course of legal predator control. Birds of prey are also killed, but illegally, and there is a very strong correlation between recorded cases of poisoning and managed grouse moors. If this persecution were to stop, golden eagles would live twice as long on average and, with other birds of prey, would become much more common.

Feeding

The abundance and availability of food are among the chief factors determining bird numbers and distribution. Herbivorous birds can eat various parts of plants, but are surprisingly rare given the amount of material that seems to be available. This is because special adaptations are required to handle a very high cellulose diet. Grouse are one of only a few birds to have these refinements, including a well-developed large intestine for microbial digestion of fibre and a muscular gizzard for grinding up plant material. They also eat small quantities of grit to aid this process. Red grouse and ptarmigan are generally restricted to where there is good growth of dwarf shrubs. The nutrient content of these plants is strongly influenced by the underlying geology, and these birds tend to be more abundant, and breed more successfully, over more calcareous rocks in the Southern and Eastern Highlands. Fruits and seeds are more nutritious, but only occur at certain times of the year and in unpredictable amounts and places. The older growth of many common hill grasses is generally of very low feeding value and no bird can survive on them alone.

In contrast, invertebrates are highly nutritious and easily digestible, and occur in extraordinary numbers. There have been estimated to be up to one billion flying insects above every square mile of Scotland, although anyone who has camped in Glen Brittle in July may consider this to be an underestimate. Such plenty is replicated on vegetation, in the soil and underwater, and consequently, in summer most of the common hill birds are insectivores. As in the case of herbivores, the abundance of these birds is influenced by the local geology, and they tend to be more numerous where richer rocks, and hence richer vegetation, result in a greater abundance of prey.

Nevertheless, being an insect eater has its drawbacks. Huge numbers are needed to keep the bird alive, so high feeding rates must be maintained and any break in supply can have fatal results. This is particularly so in winter when most insects are absent, locked in the frozen earth, or appear at unpredictable times. Before winter starts, most insectivorous birds therefore head for the lowlands or migrate south. Only dippers, wrens and stonechats remain. Dippers can find aquatic invertebrates in rivers even in mid-winter, feeding briefly under a surface covering of ice where necessary. Wrens are so small that they can seek out invertebrates in the dwarf shrub layer beneath a covering of snow. Stonechats, however, have no special adaptations, and perish in large numbers during hard winters. But, just as vultures have learned to perch next to minefields in Africa, some upland birds are beginning to adapt to changing circumstances. Milder winters are gradually making the appearance of insects more reliable, and meadow pipits and golden plovers are seen on the winter hills with increasing frequency.

The fortunes of carnivorous birds generally mirror those of their prey. The larger predators, such as eagles and buzzards, can find sufficient grouse or carrion in winter to remain on the hills, but merlins, which chiefly feed on small insectivorous birds, must follow their prey to the lowlands. Fish also tend to be unavailable in winter as they move deeper and out of reach, or because lochs freeze over, so fish-eating birds, such as divers, leave for the coast too.

Breeding

The annual reproductive cycle can begin early in the year and although it doesn't always feel like it, the sight of an eagle or raven displaying in midwinter is a sure sign that spring is near. Other birds follow suit as the season progresses, and they become very conspicuous at this time. Displays are aimed at keeping a partner and discouraging rivals, so they are always most vigorous when other birds are close by. This is taken to extremes by black grouse and capercaillie, where males compete against each other at communal display grounds, known as leks, in the presence of several females. The male that successfully occupies the centre of the arena tends to mate with all the females, so the benefit of being 'top dog' is clear.

Birds must also be able to find a nest site. Although meadow pipits need little more than a hollow under a tussock and can nest virtually anywhere, most species

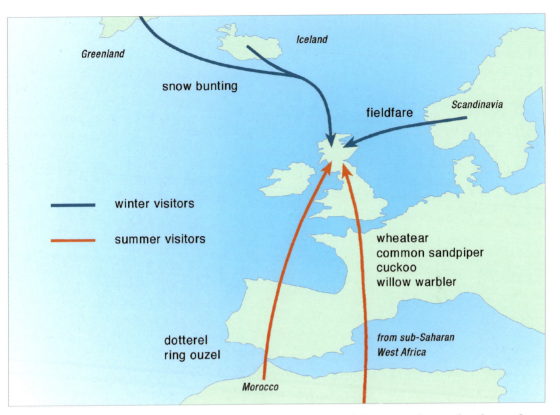

Summer visitors come to Scotland's hills to take advantage of the seasonal superabundance of invertebrates. Those in winter do so to escape harsher conditions further north

have more exacting requirements. For example, eagles and ravens seek shelter from sun, wind and rain and do not nest at high altitude, as is often supposed, but seek out north- or east-facing crags well down the hill. The distance between adjacent pairs depends largely on nest site availability and food supply. Herbivores and insectivores can occur at comparatively high densities, with up to 50 pairs of meadow pipits per square kilometre, but the prey of carnivores is relatively scarce and each pair defends a larger area to provide for all their needs. For eagles, this territory can be well in excess of $100km^2$.

The date of egg-laying varies between species and is timed to ensure maximum food availability when the young are being reared. Many ravens are on eggs by February, so that hatching coincides with the late winter and early spring mortality of sheep and deer. Snow bunting and dotterel, by contrast, do not have clutches until late May or June, in order to benefit from the summer flush of insects. Not surprisingly, there is some variation according to regional climate, and birds which nest in the alpine zone tend to do so later than their compatriots at lower levels. In the case of meadow pipits, this delay amounts to about one day for every 40m of height gained. Unusually benign conditions in any given year shift the season forward, and our steadily warming climate means that most species now nest several days earlier than they did 50 years ago.

Birds tend to become unobtrusive when they have eggs, relying on their camouflage to protect the nest. If discovered at this time, they are liable to desert, but when the eggs hatch, the adults once again draw attention to themselves if

Eagle usually only rear two young where there is plenty of live prey and this tends to be in the east

they feel that the young are threatened, sometimes undertaking elaborate distraction displays. Biologically, this makes sense, as the adults have invested relatively little effort in reproduction early in the season and their own survival is more important. Later on, it is worth taking some risks to ensure the survival of their young.

Birds use two main strategies to maximise their lifetime reproductive output. One is to be long-lived, rearing few, if any, young each year, but attempting to do so over a very long period. The alternative is to 'live fast, die young' and lay many eggs or several times in the one season, and most small birds do this. Either way, over the course of their reproductive lifetimes, any pair of birds only needs to rear two young to adulthood to replace themselves.

Historical background

Although the fossil, archaeological and, until recent times, written record is scant there have clearly been major changes in the diversity and distribution of Scotland's upland birds during the Holocene. During the more extensive Ice Age glaciations, only the hardiest birds, such as ptarmigan and snow bunting, would have been able to survive. However, as the temperature rose and the ice retreated, birds of the tundra and, in time, native woodlands, colonised Scotland. At the height of forest development around 7,000–8,000 years ago, it is reasonable to assume that Scotland's birds would have been similar to those currently found in Scandinavia. Further climatic change and increasing human influence led to the expansion of blanket bog, heath and grassland at the expense of woodland, and by around 2,500 years ago, with few exceptions, all our familiar hill birds would have been present. These comprise a unique mix of far northern species such as ptarmigan, dotterel, snow bunting and divers, which have been 'left behind' in areas of suitable habitat, and birds of wider global distribution like crows, golden eagle, raven and black grouse.

Since that time, human activity has become the key influence on birds and although the species have remained much the same, their numbers and distribution have changed considerably. Birds were rarely written about prior to the Middle Ages unless they could be hunted or eaten, but the clearance of forests and drainage of bogs must have benefited open country species at the expense of those of wetlands and woodlands. More recently, agriculture, sport shooting and forestry took on increasing importance, each ebbing and flowing depending upon the inclinations and finances of private owners and the state.

Mixed agriculture, largely based on crops and cattle, was once commonplace in the uplands, but was virtually abandoned following the Clearances and largely superceded by sheep. Varied patchworks of habitats were therefore replaced by poor quality grassland, leading to the decline or disappearance of many small birds and waders that would have been familiar to Victorian mountaineers.

Birds have been hunted for sport in Scotland since the introduction of falconry in 980 AD, and game species have been specifically protected since the 1400s. Driven grouse shooting became popular in the Highlands during the mid-19th century, due to a number of developments. These included the building of rail links in the 1840s, the invention of the breech-loading shotgun in 1847 and Queen Victoria's purchase of Balmoral in 1852. The consequent preservation of heather prevented much of the Scottish uplands from being turned into poorer habitats like sheep walks or conifer plantations, and undoubtedly benefited many birds. However, birds of prey were seen as a threat, and the level of killing was so great that several species, including red kite and goshawk, became extinct by the early 20th century. Unfortunately, this legacy lives on and illegal persecution continues in many areas to the present day.

The Clearances also paved the way for the growth of the Victorian deer forests, and the associated pattern of management resulted in large increases in the overall red deer population. With the added influence of sheep in many areas, this level of grazing has often affected the extent or condition of upland habitats. Although carrion feeders benefit to a point, many hill birds would be more common if these herbivores were more in balance with their habitats.

The planting of non-native conifers began in the 18th century,

Mark Wrightham

What Scotland could look like with less grazing? Willow and dwarf birch growing profusely at 1200m in Norway.

Oystercatchers are amongst the noisiest and showiest of birds where farmland meets the hill

but increased greatly after the timber shortages of the First World War, which brought about changes in government policy. Huge areas were planted with dense, uniform blocks of trees, putting pressure on birds of open hill country. However, relatively recent changes to the grant system now encourage the restructuring of these plantations and the planting of native woodland. This is beginning to reverse some of these adverse effects and will, in time, benefit many upland species.

These positive changes have to be viewed within the wider context. Even by the end of the 19th century, naturalists were beginning to note the greatly reduced bird numbers that had occurred within their lifetimes and, unfortunately, this trend has continued. The east has been less affected and the semi-natural habitats there generally remain in reasonably good condition, supporting relatively healthy bird populations. In contrast, and while there is much variation, lower slopes across much of the Southern Uplands and Southern Highlands, and parts of the Western Highlands, have been turned into large expanses of poor grasses or plantation. Although still of some conservation value, these areas support far fewer birds than they would under more sympathetic management.

Glens and lower slopes

Although Scotland's hill birds often range widely across the mountain landscape, most are broadly associated with particular types of habitat.

Heather moorland and grassland

The lower slopes of hills are covered by patchworks of heather moorland and rough grassland (see p94) and are sometimes flanked by low-intensity farmland in the floors of glens and straths. These habitats are well used by upland birds, and while most are found on the lowest slopes, often using adjacent farmland for feeding, other species push into more rugged hill country.

Many of Scotland's best known upland birds are waders, and the moorland fringes, especially in the east, come alive in spring with their vivid calls and energetic displays. Lapwings and oystercatchers are particularly attractive, flashing black and white, and although curlews don't quite have the same visual impact, their appeal is just as great. It has been said that "a moor without a curlew is like a night without a moon", and Burns also captured the depth of emotion: "I never heard the loud solitary whistle of the curlew on a summer noon…without feeling an elevation of the soul". These waders rarely reach far up the hill and are soon left behind on the climb, but on ranges like the Cromdales which rise steeply from fertile ground, their cries can drift right up to the tops on the warm breeze.

Snipe can frequent wetter fields, but they are equally at home in boggy glens, so push deeper into the uplands and much further west. Unobtrusive at most times of year, they are also best seen in spring, when they sit on fence posts or perform their diving displays over bogs and marshy pastures. Then, their calls and 'drumming' are amongst the most distinctive sounds early and late in the day, often continuing well into the night and keeping campers awake. The 'drumming' is produced by the passage of air over their stiffened outer tail feathers as they plunge earthwards, and defies phonetic description. But one of their Gaelic names is *gobhar-athair*, or 'father of the goat', and the sound perhaps bears some resemblance to a distant bleating.

Although they need unfrozen ground to feed, small numbers of snipe sometimes remain on the hill in the winter, as they can tough out a few days of hard weather by drawing on their reserves of fat. However, if the cold continues and the damp flushes freeze hard, they are forced down to the coasts and lowlands. In autumn, migrant woodcock from Scandinavia also turn up on the hills, particularly after November's full moon, which is known as the 'woodcock moon'. Woodcock look superficially like snipe, and flush up from underfoot in the same way, but are bigger, darker and silent. These birds will pitch down and feed awhile on the hills before descending to winter in damp woodlands.

The next major group of upland birds are the 'passerines', or perching birds. Meadow pipits are the commonest, and probably outnumber all the other hill birds put together. Only the rankest of vegetation is avoided, and they are otherwise found almost everywhere from the lowest slopes to the highest summits. The pipits arrive in March and breed, then little flocks begin to gather from June onwards, and only the odd straggler is left after September. Even their most ardent supporter would have to admit that they are not much to look at, or even to listen to, but without them the hills would be much quieter. Surprisingly for something so familiar here, they have a very restricted world distribution, and are

David Whitaker / www.highlandwildlifephotography.com

Lapwings have a wide variety of country names, including green plover

Skylark – unassuming plumage, wonderful song

David Whitaker / www.highlandwildlifephotography.com

virtually confined to northern Europe.

Meadow pipits can breed at such high densities that most walkers will eventually stumble upon a nest. Mark where the bird has come out from underfoot, gently part the grass, and there will be a beautifully constructed little cup with four or five dark eggs or cheeping young-sters. If you look at enough nests perhaps, once in a lifetime, you will find a cuckoo's egg or chick instead.

The cuckoo's habit of laying in other bird's nests is well known and in the uplands, meadow pipits are the main victims. Each female cuckoo lays up to 25 eggs, one per nest, similar in colour to those of the host. Shortly after hatching, the young cuckoo evicts the eggs or chicks of the host and receives all the food brought in by the parents. Once it fledges, the young cuckoo is on its own and must make its way to Africa without any assistance; in fact, it never knowingly sees its real parents.

Cuckoos use bushes, trees or telegraph wires as song perches or look-out posts from which to spy out pipit nests, or their favoured food, hairy caterpillars. They are able to deal with the irritant hairs by coughing them up in pellets, and have specialised gizzards whose lining is periodically sloughed off and regurgitated. This combination of food and habitat requirements restricts cuckoos to the lower hill, but here they are common and familiar.

Besides the pipits, several other small passerines are common in these habitats. Wrens and stonechats may be seen where there are bushes or long heather, while skylarks and wheatears prefer areas of insect-rich bent-fescue grassland, kept short by sheep. In some areas, rabbits also help maintain these swards, and wheatears can derive an added benefit by nesting in abandoned burrows. These birds are real characters, flicking their wings and tails or sweeping up to boulders, white rumps flashing.

On particularly favoured hills, skylarks can be abundant and the spring air is filled with their song. The length of time the male stays aloft and sings is an indi-cation to his mate of how good a father he will be. Other females eavesdrop as well, and like many species, both sexes are not averse to sneaking an extra mating if they feel it is with a better quality partner. Although a lark has been heard singing continuously for over an hour, most flights last just a couple of minutes. The torrent of notes, though, is overwhelming and the collective term for larks, an 'exaltation', is very appropriate. Formerly, both skylarks and wheatears were caught and eaten in vast numbers. 300 larks were made into a pie to celebrate the opening of the Forth Rail Bridge in 1890, and Mrs Beeton gives a recipe for wheatear, helpfully noting that 'they are seasonable from July to October.'

Ring ouzels are birds of rougher, craggier country and they too have a wonderful song, ringing out across cliff and glen, as bright and clear as a cumulus. The ouzels stay all summer, but two other members of the thrush family are shorter-term visitors, passing through in the autumn on migration from Scandinavia to their wintering grounds in lowland Britain. Fieldfares are commonly seen ranging over the hill in rather ragged flocks, grey and long tailed, 'chakking' away. Redwings, in contrast, are rarely seen, but fly over in huge numbers in clear weather at night. Anyone camping in October may hear their thin, high 'seeps' punctuating the long dark hours.

Although waders and passerines enrich the upland scene, it is red grouse that most define Scotland's heather moorland. Red grouse are virtually dependant upon ling heather and the fortunes of these species closely mirror each other. Heather tends to be less extensive and in poorer condition in the west, so grouse are less common here, but over the drier eastern hills, heather grows well and the grouse respond. These rolling hills are also more suitable for driving birds over guns, and have been managed to provide even more favourable conditions. Red grouse need long heather to nest in and young shoots to feed on, and Burns, as ever, was a keen observer when he referred to "ye grouse that crap the heather bud". Rotational burning of the oldest heather ensures a steady supply of fresh growth, and the resulting patchwork of old and new is a familiar sight on many hills. Wetter areas are also maintained and encouraged, the female grouse feasting on the protein-rich seed heads of cotton grasses in the spring, in preparation for egg-laying. In June, these flushes provide important food for grouse chicks, which are insectivorous in their first few days of life.

On managed moors, red grouse can increase to densities of hundreds per square kilometre, well in excess of any other hill bird. Such unnaturally high densities cause some problems, and the birds are particularly prone to infestation

Muirburn on Dun Mor above the Sma' Glen

Larsen trap – a decoy crow is used to attract other crows inside, where they become trapped

by a parasitic intestinal worm. Keepers seek to counter this by providing small piles of grey medicated grit, which the birds eat to aid their digestion. In the past, the numbers of red grouse shot have sometimes verged on the incredible, the record Scottish bag being 2,523 on Roan Fell in the Southern Uplands, on 30th August 1911, with another 1,266 shot eight days later. Grouse numbers had steadily decreased through much of the last century as heather was lost to forestry or grassland and as gamekeeper effort declined. However, recent intensification of management on many moors has led to an upsurge in numbers and a return to large bags.

Predatory birds form the top tier of the upland ecosystem. Crows can stay in the uplands all winter, living on carrion or raiding feed troughs, but they welcome the spring arrivals and flap slowly across the hill looking for nests to plunder. Snipe are beautifully patterned and usually escape detection, but waders which lack such camouflage rely on vigorous defence of their territories, getting up *en masse* to drive crows away. These persistent predators nonetheless take many eggs and young. They also have a reputation as killers of lambs, but this has little basis and almost all lambs eaten by crows are already dead or moribund.

Crows are routinely killed throughout their range and can be legally shot or caught in certain kinds of trap. These can be found on the hill in tucked-away corners and either look like giant wire cages with a one-way 'lobster pot' entrance, or boxes consisting of several compartments, one of which contains a captive bird as a lure; the so-called Larsen trap. Where control is very intensive, particularly on heavily-keepered grouse moors, holes can appear in the distribution of crows, but they are still among the most successful, common and obvious of birds.

Buzzards can also be seen over much of the uplands, though, like crows, they rarely penetrate far into the hills, tending to be a bird of mixed habitats on the lower slopes. In favoured areas, and particularly early in the season, up to a dozen may be seen circling in the air at once, their mewing calls clearly audible. The fledged young are especially noisy in the height of summer, and their skirling calls ring out from crags and woodland. Once largely confined to the north and west, buzzards have greatly increased since the early 1990s and have expanded across most of the British Isles. Much of this has been due to high rabbit numbers and an assumed reduction in persecution in the lowlands. Mammals, birds or carrion are located from a prominent perch or whilst soaring, but earthworms can also form a significant part of their diet, and any buzzard standing in a field is likely to be on the lookout for them.

This catholic diet means that buzzards can find enough food to survive in many areas, whereas peregrines need a steady supply of live birds and consequently struggle in the north and west. A peregrine in full flow is an impressive sight, said to be the fastest living thing that flies as it stoops onto its prey. They are perhaps the ultimate aerial predators and are superbly adapted, with acute eyesight, strong legs and sharp talons to grip their prey, and a notched beak to deliver the final *coup de grace* with a quick bite to the neck. Their bones comprise just 5% of their entire body weight, and their nostrils contain cones that allow them to keep breathing at extreme speeds. All these tools mean nothing without their amazing flying ability, and that has to be learned. The price of failure is high, and two thirds of all young peregrines die within their first year.

Peregrines nest on cliffs and readily betray their presence with harsh screeching

Female peregrine falcon. Like many birds of prey, female peregrines are bigger and more bulky than males and can feed on larger prey

Short-eared owls can often be seen in bright sunshine

if they feel that a walker is coming too close. Favoured sites can have long histories, with many crags which provided birds for medieval falconry still being used today.

The two smaller falcons, kestrels and merlins, are more widespread. Both keep largely to the lower slopes of the heathery hills, though merlins can also be found in some very rough country in the north and west, as long as there is a ready supply of small birds. Meadow pipits can comprise up to 90% of their diet and jinking chases can sometimes be seen, though nine times out of ten the pipit is likely to escape.

Hen harriers and short-eared owls were once restricted to heather moors, but they are now less common in these areas, at least partly because of persecution. Young forestry plantations and rough grassland provide both cover and food, and a trip to Orkney, the Uists, the Inner Hebrides, Argyll or Arran is most likely to produce a sighting. Despite suitable habitat, both are absent from Shetland, Lewis and Harris, probably due to a lack of voles, which never colonised these islands. These birds hunt by keeping low, using the terrain or vegetation to hide their approach, ready to pounce upon an unsuspecting vole or pipit. In the popular imagination, owls are birds of the night, the familiars of witches, heard but rarely seen. Not so the short-ear, which hunts during the day, flapping slowly over heather or rough areas. They perch readily on posts or the ground, their big yellow eyes staring unblinkingly, right at you.

Woodland

The native pine and birchwoods of the lower slopes (see p99) provide important habitats for a number of birds, and little flocks will be encountered, particularly in winter, searching the trunks and branches for insects. These are mostly familiar species of our parks and gardens, but keep an eye out for bullfinches; handsome, plump birds with red fronts, black caps, white rumps and a call as soft as falling snow. Willow warblers can be frequently heard in the summer, their rather sad, falling songs coming from all but the densest plantations, while stonechats, whinchats and tree pipits frequent areas of scrub and small trees. The eastern pinewoods are home to some rare specialities, such as capercaillie, crested tits and crossbills.

Exotic conifer plantations are now much more extensive than native woodland, and are initially of some benefit to birds. The fencing of hillsides and removal of grazing lead to an early surge of vegetation growth, including heather previously suppressed by browsing, and result in a great abundance of voles. These conditions provide excellent habitats for some birds, including hen harriers and short-eared owls. Once mature, the main species to benefit are crossbills, goldcrest, coal tit, siskin and goshawk all of which, with the exception of crossbill, usually remain well hidden and are often identifiable only by call or song.

Black grouse are found in transitional habitats where areas of scattered trees are mixed in with heather moorland and farmland. Usually offering just a brief view when flushed, they are best seen on early spring mornings when they gather at their leks, but this is only for early risers, as the activity starts before dawn and is over by seven or eight am. The males face up to each other, posturing, flapping and indulging in mock battles, their breath condensing in the chill air. All the while they make an odd, continuous, low cooing that can carry for up to a mile on still mornings, and following this sound is the best way of locating a lek. Anyone lucky enough to chance upon one should not to disturb the birds, as this forms a vital part of their breeding cycle. While Boswell talked of black grouse being extraordinarily abundant on Raasay in 1773, their numbers and range then greatly declined. They can colonise new areas very quickly if conditions change and have benefitted from new native woodland plantings to expand out from their previous core areas of Perthshire, Deeside, Strathspey and Inverness-shire.

Rivers and lochs

Upland rivers and lochs provide comparatively rich bird habitats and are always worth a look, even when the hills are quiet. The dipper is the most likely bird to be seen, either flying away along the stream or standing on a rock in the middle of the burn. Scotland generally provides excellent dipper habitat, but the more acidic waters are less rich in invertebrates, so they tend to be most common on eastern streams over richer rocks. Only the most prolonged freezes drive them off their territory and they brighten up many a midwinter day, when the river and the dipper's back may be the only dark colours in a white world.

The other two distinctive river birds, grey wagtails and common sandpipers, are both summer visitors to the hills. Long-tailed and elegant, grey wagtails are rather inappropriately named, for while they are grey on the back, their undersides are a lovely lemon yellow. These colours are well seen as they run around the water's edge, pumping their tails or sallying up to snap insects from the air. Common sandpipers also enliven loch shores and the shingly lower reaches of rivers, as they flick away on stiff wings, calling loudly. Dippers, wagtails and sandpipers all bob up and down habitually and this is believed to be a means of communication, visual cues being more reliable than sound carrying above a noisy river.

Many Highland lochs harbour a few ducks like mallard, teal or red breasted

Black-throated divers are so sleek and streamlined that it can be hard to believe that they are covered in feathers

merganser, along with common gulls. Black-headed gulls were once widespread on small wetland areas, but have declined in the uplands. This is perhaps linked to the reduction in mixed agriculture, as they obtained vital supplementary food by following the plough.

Greenshanks also occur alongside lochs or the wider, shallower rivers of the glens and straths, but have a much more restricted distribution within the Highlands. Found right across Eurasia to Kamchatka, they nest in huge numbers on the great forest bogs of the taiga but in Scotland, uniquely, greenshanks favour open areas with high rainfall and poor drainage, leading to an abundance of standing or running water. Although this sounds like a fair description of much of our uplands, the most suitable conditions are provided by the flows of Caithness, Sutherland and Lewis, and other rough, low ground in the north and west. Greenshanks are rather scarce in the generally drier east, but their presence brings a touch of the exotic to the wild headwaters of some of our greatest rivers, including the Spey, Geldie and Tarf.

A few lochs hold black- or red-throated divers. Despite their Latin name of *Gavia arctica*, black-throated divers breed further south than any other diver species. Even so, Scotland is about as far south as they get, and their haunting wailing cries, cutting across the still of a Highland loch early or late in the day, are a wonderfully evocative addition to the hill scene. In contrast, red-throated divers are amongst the most northerly of aquatic birds, occurring right to the northern tip of Greenland. Much commoner than black-throats, the bulk of the population is found on the low lochan-studded moors of the Northern and Western Isles, and the Flow Country, but they are also fairly common on small lochs and tiny dubh lochans from Kintyre to Cape Wrath. These rarely provide sufficient food, so the divers must fly to larger lochs or the sea to fish. Their flight call is a sure sign of one passing overhead or preparing to splash down in a cloud of silver spray.

All divers are supremely adapted for life in the water and are expert swimmers, remaining submerged for up to two minutes as they pursue fish. However, their legs are set so far back on their bodies that they are incapable of walking, and must shuffle about on their bellies when on land. Their nests therefore have to be close to the water's edge and, if loch levels change, can either get flooded or marooned out of reach. Red-throats tend to be less affected, as their dubh lochans have small catchments, but the water levels of the large lochs favoured by black-throats are not so consistent, particularly if used for hydro production. In recent years, artificial floating islands have been provided and these rise and fall with the water level, providing secure nesting places.

Autumn also sees geese and whooper swans arriving in Scotland from their breeding grounds further north, to winter in lowland and coastal wetlands. They are frequently seen on the return journey in April and May, and many of these flights go through the hills. On fine mornings with light southerly winds, listen out for the honk of greylag geese, or the higher pitched yap of pink footed geese. A glance upwards will reveal a straggling skein overhead, sometimes involving hundreds of birds beating steadily north-west straight for Iceland, their departure having been timed to reach landfall in one non-stop flight.

The alpine zone

Many of the birds of the lower slopes are also found on the high tops, albeit in smaller numbers. Skylarks like the short, wind-scoured vegetation and their songs are a frequent accompaniment in spring and summer, while meadow pipits also push uphill to nest at 1000m and beyond. Wheatears 'chack' from stones and build their nests, lined with ptarmigan feathers, in the shade and shelter of summit boulderfields. The headwalls of many corries have an attendant pair of ring ouzels, dodging over the cliff edge or singing far below. And common gulls can nest on water bodies which are surprisingly high in the hills, particularly in the Cairngorms. Loch nan Stuirteag, between Cairn Toul and Monadh Mor, is perhaps the best known example, though Loch Etchachan is higher still at an altitude of 930m. The gulls take to the tops to feed during hatches of the large, nutritious alpine cranefly *Tipula montana* (see p158).

Upland birds are not confined to the more fashionable summits, and many species frequent the vast high-level blanket bogs of, for example, the Monadh Liath, Gaick and Atholl. Many walkers are content to go into these areas once, bag such high hills as there are, and head out again, glad that they need never return. But such fleeting visits do not do justice to their special qualities of time, space, and those rarest of modern commodities, peace and quiet. The solitude is most keenly felt in midwinter as the wind comes scything across the tops and at this time red grouse are usually the most obvious birds, often banding together in impressive packs. Otherwise, only the odd eagle, raven or snow bunting marks the passing miles. In summer these areas are much busier. This is golden plover country par excellence, the tussocks and mounds providing perfect lookout posts, while dunlin trill from beside peaty pools.

Golden plover reach high densities on mid-level moors and hills, but walkers most often meet them on the higher tops. One of the first birds to return in spring, they are often back on territory by March, though late snows put a brake on their activities and send them back down to the farms and crofts to await the thaw. Repeated periods of snowfall and melt can lead to much to-ing and fro-ing before courtship begins in earnest. They also leave the territory during

Golden plover nest with chicks. In common with many other upland birds, golden plover nest at greater densities on richer eastern tops

incubation, when the males often travel up to 10km at night to feed on surrounding farmland.

When they have young, the plovers are amongst the most obvious of birds. As Charles St. John put it in *Wild Sports*, in 1846: "the golden plover has a plaintive and rather sweet note as he flits rapidly around the traveller who intrudes on his domain". This call is a signal to the chicks to freeze, keep their heads down and rely upon their camouflage to avoid detection, whilst the adult tries to gently lead the danger away. In autumn, on some of the high-level grasslands, look out for migrant golden plovers en route from Iceland. These birds behave very differently from the breeders. Rarely allowing a close approach, they rise up and swing away with the wind, calling softly as they go.

To many, the golden eagle is the bird that most epitomises the Highlands, and is often imbued with power, strength, aloofness, nobility and wildness. Eagles are undoubtedly magnificent and inspiring, but they are also widespread, and sightings need not be the 'once in a lifetime' experience that many people believe. With a bit of effort, eagles can be seen on many hill days.

The swirling mist in a high corrie shows how complex air movements can be in the varied terrain of the Scottish hills. Eagles are superbly adapted to harness the lift from updraughts and thermals, and despite being as heavy as a well-stuffed day sack, they can remain airborne for long periods with minimal effort, relying solely on subtle movements of feathers or wings. They also spend plenty of time in the glens, but few people have sharp enough eyes to spot them against dark hillsides, so the classic view, for most, is of an eagle hanging on the wind over a corrie edge or spiralling high above the hill.

Scotland has about 450 pairs of eagles, perhaps 1000 birds if young are also taken into account, but they are not evenly distributed. A few pairs cling on in the Galloway hills and the lower hills south of the Central Belt, but man's intolerance prevents them from fully occupying these areas. The core of their range is therefore within the Highlands. Eagles are much more common in the west but, outside grouse moors, breed most successfully in the east. The reasons for this difference are complex, and are likely to include the abundance of prey in summer and winter, the availability of nest sites, and persecution.

Eagles are particularly active from autumn to February or March, when the pairs often soar close together, or indulge in spectacular rollercoaster displays, to strengthen their bond. This is the best time to look for them. Pick a breezy day, particularly when it is brightening after heavy rain, as eagles tend to sit out wet periods and become more active when they have passed. Choose just about any Highland glen, find a sheltered spot with a good view of plenty of sky, make yourself comfortable and scan along the tops of the ridges. Be prepared to give it some time and an eagle will almost certainly appear.

Another useful way to locate eagles is to follow the flight of ravens, which have much better eyesight than humans and will frequently rise to mob intruding birds of prey. The raven has a much more positive public image than the other all-black bird of the hills, the crow, and this is surely down to the appealing character of these gregarious, inquisitive, playful and noisy birds. To stand in one of the great corries with ravens rolling and tumbling above, their resonant 'pruuks' reverberating between the walls, is a wonderful experience.

One of the most widespread species in the northern hemisphere, ravens can thrive in a Death Valley summer, the depths of an arctic winter and most wild places in between. However, they haven't always been pushed to such extremes

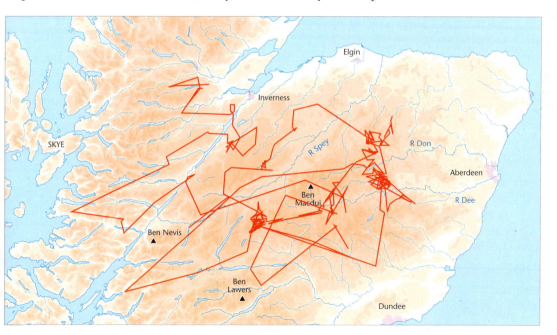

Golden eagles mature and set up territory when they are four or five years old and spend the time before then learning the lie of the land. Recent advances in satellite tracking have allowed us to find out more about these wanderings, which can be substantial. For example, this bird was fitted with a satellite tag in the Cairngorms and covered much of the Highlands within the first seven months of learning to fly (data RSPB)

The Cairngorm landscape offers a mix of three-leaved rush heath, mat grass and boulder fields, favoured by dotterel, ptarmigan and snow bunting

and used to be familiar associates of man, protected because of their useful function in scavenging refuse. Although still common in Edinburgh in 1600, they went into decline as the streets became cleaner, and the last pair nested on Arthur's Seat in 1837. Once equally widespread in the countryside, ravens were ruthlessly persecuted by sheep-rearing interests from the mid-1600s and then, a century later, by gamekeepers. By the beginning of the 20th century, they only survived in the most remote areas, the long rough miles being the best defence against gun, trap and poison.

Although it still goes on, the intensity of persecution has certainly declined in recent years and ravens have reclaimed much of their former range, although they are still most common in the north and west. The birds in the eastern hills tend to be non-breeders, but they can occur in sizable flocks. Such gatherings have a number of functions, including as an information exchange on the location of food. Ravens feed largely on carrion and anything freshly dead will soon be found. Carrion or sick and injured animals may be detected by smell or by watching the movements of other scavengers and predators. In Scotland, ravens would once have followed wolf packs for the pickings from any kills, but it may be a long time before they can do so again. In the meantime, they have learned to use man as a surrogate wolf. Ravens follow stalkers and know that the sound of a shot means a meal, the bird often getting in at the grallochs whilst they are still warm.

Although skylarks, plovers, eagles and ravens are all birds of the tops, for many people the term is best reserved for the three alpine specialists – snow bunting, dotterel and ptarmigan. In winter, there are few small birds around, and although a wren may 'churr' from deep cover or a stonechat flick from a heather stem on lower slopes, the upper hill is left to snow buntings. A truly arctic species with a wide circumpolar distribution, the buntings reach further north than any other bird and even frequent nunataks amidst the Greenland ice sheet. However, even these hardy little birds cannot survive the winters at such latitudes, and thousands stream south from Iceland, Greenland and arctic Canada, to reach the relatively benign conditions of the Scottish hills and coasts. These flocks can be encountered just about anywhere, scouring the hills for seeds where the sedges and grasses are not covered by snow. They have also learned to take advantage of human scraps and often feed around ski areas like sparrows.

By May, most will have returned north, but a few stay to breed on the very highest tops, our closest equivalent to the arctic. In summer, invertebrates form the greater part of their diet, and at these altitudes, there is very little competition from other birds. Their nests are tucked away in rock crevices, under boulders or in screes, and are often located near insect-rich habitats such as flushes or, more especially, long-lying snow patches. These provide easy feeding as they trap insects, which are carried up on air currents and immobilised by the cold. Over much of the arctic, the short summers mean that snow buntings only have time to rear one brood, but the longer season in Scotland gives them the opportunity to lay a second time. However, few young survive from this second round, as hatching occurs after the midsummer flush of insects has passed.

In May, just as the snow buntings are establishing their territories, dotterel are returning to the tops, having spent the winter on the arid plains of north Africa. But whilst the buntings favour the corries, cliff edges and boulder fields, dotterel seek out the moss and rush heaths which carpet the broad ridges and plateaux (see p104). This largely confines them to above about 800m but, like ptarmigan, they can be found at surprisingly low levels on the exposed tops of the north-west, where suitable habitats creep further down the hill. Numbers vary greatly from year to year, but they are always most common on the great sprawling hills of the Central and Eastern Highlands.

Attractive to look at, endearing in behaviour and living exclusively in places that are so special, it is no wonder that seeing a dotterel is one of *the* treats of the Scottish hills. But perhaps it is their elusiveness that really cements their appeal. Although dotterel live amongst vegetation that is only a couple of centimetres tall, it is easy to walk within a few yards of one and be quite unaware

Alan Ross

A common village bird in the Arctic, snow buntings are found only on our highest hills in summer

Dotterel nest showing the use of Cladonia lichens to insulate the incubating eggs while the nest is unoccupied

of its presence; even the most experienced fieldworkers, in perfect conditions, find less than half of the birds on the hill at any one time. Not for them the noisy peeping of the plover – instead, dotterel prefer to run off quietly or crouch down, relying upon their superb camouflage to melt into the background. They can take a bit of finding, but when located, they offer an experience unlikely ever to be forgotten. Often remarkably confiding, this characteristic is recognised by their Gaelic name of *amadan mointich* or 'moss fool'. Their common name is also descriptive, as it is derived from a Middle English word meaning 'easily caught', etymologically related to the Portuguese root that gave us 'dodo'.

Dotterel have a fascinating life history too. The newly arrived groups, or 'trips', are especially approachable, and a close look will show that some birds are brighter, others duller. Basic biology might suggest that the showy birds are males but this is not so, as dotterel are one of the very few bird species in which the sex roles are reversed. The more brightly coloured females take the lead in courtship and, once the eggs are laid, seek out another mate in Scotland or even Norway. Such repeated laying is possible because dotterel, unusually for waders, produce only three light eggs in each clutch. Females do not necessarily stop after two partners. One Scottish hen was reported to mate with five males in succession in one season, the last of which had only one foot.

After laying and the departure of the female, the male must do all the incubation himself. This means he has to leave the nest unattended in order to feed, which is potentially hazardous in such a cold and unpredictable environment. Cooling of the eggs is reduced by keeping the feeding trips reasonably short, and by lining the nest with the lichen *Cladonia uncialis*, whose hollow tubular structure offers some insulation from the ground. In very poor weather, when the risk of chilling is greatest, he tends to sit tight, and in severe summer storms, male dotterels have been observed with just their heads poking above the freshly fallen snow. If the conditions are persistently bad, the sitting male must eventually leave the eggs to keep himself alive and many of these nests undoubtedly fail. However, there are records of males returning after absences of up to 10 hours to eggs that had fallen in temperature to $0°$ C. Remarkably, these subsequently hatched, having apparently gone into a state of suspended animation, to become reactivated on rewarming.

On their feeding trips, dotterel prefer to work the short vegetation of the *Racomitrium* heaths, where their invertebrate prey cannot easily hide. A wide range of insects, spiders and beetles is taken, but on the Scottish hills, their diet is dominated by the cranefly *Tipula montana* (see p158). This insect hatches in large numbers within a short time window, and the timing and scale of these events varies greatly between years. Emergences are not completely synchronous between hills or even necessarily on different parts of the same mountain, so the north end of Beinn a' Bhuird may be covered in craneflies whilst the south hardly has any. *Tipula montana* has a two year life cycle, so this spatial variation is roughly reversed in alternate years. Dotterel breeding success is linked to cranefly abundance, so the males, which do not maintain exclusive feeding territories, will move some distance to feed where they are most numerous.

It is whilst off the nest that the males are most likely to be seen, busily searching for food with their stop-start little runs over the mosses. Females and, later in the season, males with chicks, tend to be somewhat more obvious, but

Ptarmigan, midway between winter and summer plumage. Even in this state the bird is remarkably well camouflaged among Schiehallion's boulders

Ptarmigan nesting near the summit ridge of The Cairnwell

even so, any hillwalker will certainly be seen by many more dotterel than the other way round. Most dotterel have left the tops by late August, although odd stragglers remain into September. Before long, they too have gone south, making a non-stop flight to Morocco and leaving our hills a slightly duller place until their return in the spring.

The summits would be quieter still but for the one bird that remains on the tops all year. Ptarmigan are far more common and widespread than either dotterel or snow bunting, and are found on most hills with any amount of alpine vegetation, though rarely straying far from the stony ground, boulders and block screes that afford them song posts and shelter. Generally more common in the east, largely because of the extent of suitable habitat, their numbers are also influenced by the underlying geology. The rather infertile granites of the Cairngorms hold relatively few, not usually exceeding 30 pairs per square kilometre, whilst the richer Dalradian schists towards Glen Shee and Glas Maol can support about twice this number. Their populations tend to fluctuate, though, on cycles of around 10 years, at least over poorer rocks. Some outlying ranges, for example on Skye, Mull and Arran, retain small populations, but these are always vulnerable to extinction if insufficient young are produced to maintain numbers. Ptarmigan rarely move any distance, and it is unlikely that these isolated refuges would be recolonised under present climatic conditions.

Although they can be obvious whilst displaying in the spring or flocking together in the autumn, ptarmigan are usually unobtrusive and would be easily missed but for their rattling calls, or when they take flight. In summer, they take on the greys, browns and whites of the rocks and gravels, but during the autumn, falling temperatures trigger a moult and they turn white. So effective is this camouflage that, early and late in the day, their shadows can be more obvious than the birds themselves. Ptarmigan, and indeed grouse, have feathered feet and toes and their Latin name, *Lagopus*, means 'hare foot'. In winter, these feathers become longer and more dense, and their claws, which are normally long to allow the birds to run up rocks, also increase in length. The overall effect is to increase the surface area of the feet fourfold and improve their grip, like a combination of snowshoes and crampons, allowing them to walk more easily on both soft snow and ice.

The female incubates and, like male dotterel, only leaves the eggs briefly in order to feed. The young leave the nest as soon as they have dried after hatching, and can fly after two weeks, or even earlier with the aid of a favourable wind. Care of the young is also largely carried out by the female, and family parties are often encountered in June and July, the hen performing a desperate distraction display. Sometimes several broods come together in creches, presumably as an anti-predator device. From August onwards, ptarmigan begin to form mixed-sex flocks, which persist throughout the winter in poor weather. The largest recorded flock in Scotland was of 470 birds, but this is exceptional and these groups typically comprise less than 30 individuals.

The survival ability of ptarmigan may seem remarkable, but this view may be coloured by the hillwalkers' experience of severe winter conditions. Like the Inuit, ptarmigan seek shelter behind boulders or in the lee of a hill, rather than fighting a blizzard. They will even take cover within snow drifts, landing directly on the surface and digging in to avoid leaving a scent trail that predators could follow. Here, like snow-holers, they remain insulated from the wild weather above. The prostrate alpine heaths favoured by ptarmigan occur in relatively exposed parts of the upper slopes and tend to be blown clear of snow, so unless conditions are exceptionally severe, the birds will usually be able to find sufficient food. In fact, ptarmigan can survive in areas with much worse weather than that of Scotland, and winter far into arctic Canada, where the mean January temperature can be as low as -40° C. Indeed, Adam Watson has suggested, with good reason, that Scotland is actually "an unusually mild outpost in the species' range".

While these are the birds that are most characteristic of Scotland's high summits, there are also some local specialities. Manx shearwaters nest on the high ridges of Rum, attracted by well-drained soils deep enough for burrowing, which overlie weathered bands of peridotite. A summer visit to these breeding colonies is an unforgettable experience, with the birds flapping past in the half-light, their demonic cries filling the night. Like many Hebridean hills, Trallval was named by the Vikings, and it has been suggested that they may have heard the shearwaters' cackles from their anchorages and fancied that the hill was the lair of trolls.

There is very little evidence that direct human pressure from recreation has had anything other than local effects on the numbers and distribution of the birds of the alpine zone. Ptarmigan are no longer found in the Western Isles and Southern Uplands, and in the latter area, dotterel have all but disappeared, but these losses are probably associated with long-term deterioration of their habitats. This trend is probably linked to grazing, burning and atmospheric nitrate deposition. Now, perhaps the greatest threat of all is climate change. Although this will have complex and unpredictable effects, these may include the loss of certain species, and of some of the richness of the Scottish hills. The implications of these changes are discussed in the final chapter.

Many of the environmental processes which shape the lives of upland birds also influence the numbers and distribution of mammals, reptiles, amphibians and fish, which are considered in the next chapter.

Ptarmigan (tarmachan)
Lagopus mutus

Ptarmigan are shaped like small, slender red grouse, but their plumage makes them unmistakable. In winter, the pure white is only relieved by the black outer tail and, in males, a thin black line from eye to bill. In summer, their wings and belly remain white, but they otherwise change to a mottled blend of subtle greys and browns, flecked like Cairn Gorm granite.

The birds are both beautifully camouflaged and unobtrusive and were it not for their calls or other signs it would be

Male in summer

Stuart Rae

easy to think that they were absent from the hill. Like other grouse species, ptarmigan have particularly resonant calls, in this instance a peculiar mechanical sounding rattle or croak, which is mainly given in flight. Apart from droppings, the most obvious traces left by the birds are their moulted white feathers, and it can be safely assumed that any found high on the hill originally belonged to a ptarmigan.

Along with capercaillie, ptarmigan are the only birds whose English names derive from the Gaelic, and there are several tarmachan hills, the most widely known being Meall nan Tarmachan above Loch Tay.

Mark Wrightham

Ptarmigan droppings; these appear identical to those of red grouse but may be distinguished according to habitat if, for example, they occur well above the heather limit

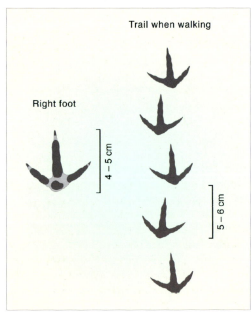

Ptarmigan tracks: these are very similar to those of red grouse, though as for droppings, habitat may provide a useful distinction

Red grouse (male: coileach-fraoich female: cearc-fhraoich)
Lagopus lagopus

Red grouse are medium-sized, stocky reddish-brown birds and look essentially the same throughout the year. The males are somewhat darker and have distinctive red combs above each eye, which are particularly obvious on displaying birds in a state of sexual arousal. Most vocal early in the morning and in late winter and spring, the

George Higginbotham; Tom Holden

Female

Male

crowing cocks are hard to miss as they boldly proclaim their territory. At other times, activity tends to die down and the birds are more likely to flush up from underfoot and skim away low over the heather on downcurved wings, giving their guttural alarm call, a rattling 'ak ar-ar-ar-ar ak ak ak ak'. The droppings of grouse are frequently found and tracks can also be seen under suitable snow conditions.

Natural fluctuations of grouse populations are sometimes accompanied by sudden crashes. Such was their economic impact that the issue was investigated by a Committee of Inquiry, set up in 1905. One of the members was Edward Wilson, an eminent scientist of the day, but now chiefly remembered as a member of Scott's ill-fated South Pole expedition.

Black grouse (male: coileach dubh/female: liathchearc)
Tetrao tetrix

Male and female black grouse are known as blackcock and greyhens, respectively, reflecting their markedly different appearances. Blackcock are unmistakable, and are glossy blue-black in colour with striking white patches on the wing and under the tail, which are best shown off during their displays. They are some 30% longer than greyhen, largely because of their bizarre lyre-shaped tails, which trail behind

David Whitaker

Male displaying

in flight to give a distinctive silhouette. Greyhen can be confused with red grouse but are slightly bulkier, distinctly greyer, and have a faint pale wing bar and notched tail. Red grouse, by contrast, have a rounded, darker tail. Although both species can occur together, habitat is usually a fairly reliable guide, with black grouse preferring the more wooded and farmed fringes, while red grouse favour pure heather moorland. Another useful distinguishing feature is their behaviour, as black grouse take off silently when flushed, tend to fly higher off the ground and readily alight in trees, with some preference for birch and larch.

The blackcock's distinctive tail feathers have been used for a variety of decorative purposes, and have adorned the glengarrys of the pipers of several Scottish regiments.

Meadow pipit (didig) *Anthus pratensis*; Skylark (topag) *Alauda arvensis*

Meadow pipits and skylarks are the definitive 'little brown birds' of the uplands. Abundant and widespread, one or the other will be present on practically any hill walk between March and September. Superficially similar when seen on the ground, they are essentially brown above, pale and speckled below, and have white outer tail feathers. Skylarks are bulkier, have a slight crest and, when flushed, show a white trailing edge to the wing.

The best way to tell them apart is by their displays and calls. Both perform their songs in flight, singing on the way up and down, but meadow pipits stay aloft for shorter periods and parachute to earth with a gentle spiral compared to the fast plummet of the skylark. A pipit's call is a rather thin and weedy seep and the song is little more than a repeated, slowly accelerating series of such notes. By contrast, skylarks have a full-bodied, fruity 'chirrup' and their song is a loud, sustained and complex outpouring. Many poets and writers have sought to describe the skylark's song and instil it with wider meaning to humanity, but none have so far been sufficiently moved to pen 'To a meadow pipit'.

Meadow pipit

Jill Pakenham

Snow bunting (eun an t-sneachda) *Plectrophenax nivalis*

In summer, male snow buntings are splendid little birds with a pure white head, body and inner wings, and jet-black back and outer wings. Females are dowdier and are mottled grey above and pale below. Both sexes are buff-coloured in winter, giving such excellent camouflage against the bleached grasses that they are likely to be overlooked until they take flight. Listen out for their tinkling calls or look for the big white flashes on their wings, tail and body, which give them their nickname of 'snowflakes', as they flicker past.

Male in winter

David Whitaker

These sparrow-sized birds are commonest in winter, when small, restless flocks are often encountered, even well down the hill. From April to July, however, just a few dozen males give their high, rapid, musical song from prominent perches on the highest tops. The rims of the great corries of the central Cairngorms, Ben Nevis and Lochnagar are good places to look and the birds go about their business quite unperturbed by passing walkers.

Snow buntings from different areas have distinctive dialects, and it is said that the Inuit could navigate at sea in thick fog by noting which variety of song drifted across from the hidden land.

Wheatear (brugheal)
Oenanthe oenanthe

A male wheatear is amongst the most handsome of birds, with his black 'robber's mask', grey head and back, dark wings and buff underparts. The female is similar but paler, and both sexes share the main distinguishing feature, the flashing white rump that gives the bird its English name, a bowdlerised version of 'white arse'.

Of the smaller hill birds, only meadow pipits and skylarks are more widespread, and where there is a mix of boulders and short turf, there will usually be a pair of wheatears. Noisy birds, they call repeatedly, with 'chacks' that sound like two pebbles being struck together, interspersed with sharp 'wheets' like unoiled machinery. The song consists of a short, vigorous warble with some harsher notes thrown in, and often includes accurate mimicry of other birds.

Jill Pakenham

Male

The earliest summer visitors to arrive, wheatears are often back on the hill by the end of March, and the first sighting is usually of *that* rump flitting away from the roadside. Despite this early start, each pair normally rears just one brood and their brown-winged young are very obvious in June and July. Only a few birds remain after August, when they leave to winter in Africa.

Stonechat (clacharan)
Saxicola torquata

Perched erect on a gorse bush 'like a guardsman on duty', and constantly flicking its wings and tail, a male stonechat is amongst the most conspicuous of birds. Its song and calls, which are readily given, are very similar to those of wheatear, and the two birds are best distinguished by their appearance and habits. Stonechats have dark, unpatterned heads, white half collars and reddish fronts,and are therefore quite distinct from wheatears. They usually perch on vegetation or fences, whilst wheatears prefer stones, boulders and walls.

Derek Belsey

Male

In summer, the stonechat might be confused with the much rarer whinchat, but the latter has a white eyestripe and 'moustache' and pale patches at the sides of the tail. Whinchats winter in Africa but stonechats stay in Scotland, albeit largely on the lower slopes and in the more temperate west. Harsh weather kills many birds, but stonechats counteract this by breeding several times in the one season, starting so early that the first chicks are on the wing by May. The female leaves the care of the preceding batch of young to the male whilst she lays and incubates the next clutch, and given a run of mild winters, the numbers soon bounce back to previous levels.

Golden plover (feadag) *Pluvialis apricaria*

Pigeon-sized waders, male golden plovers have black and gold-spangled backs, and a black face and front set off by a broad white border. The females share this pattern but are less well marked.

Golden plovers are noisy birds and are particularly noticeable during late March or April, when indulging in their fantastic territorial displays. The males circle with wingbeats as slow as an owl, excitedly 'coo-rooing' or giving their characteristic two note call. The first note is short and less clear from afar, but the second is stronger, more prolonged and falling. Later in the season, the birds

Male

David Whitaker

once again become conspicuous if their territory is crossed, and the 'too' of an alarmed bird as it keeps a wary eye out is one of the most distinctive, and to human ears, sad, sounds of the tops. The calling bird will often keep just over the skyline with only its head in view, gently leading the intruder away from its young.

Autumn birds are likely to be moving through from further north and will be in their less distinguished winter plumage, the overall impression being of a light golden-brown bird with a pale belly and white wing stripe.

Dunlin (gille-feadaig) *Calidris alpina*

Waders little bigger than a starling, dunlin are only on the hills from mid-April to early July. Easily overlooked, they are often first located by their soft purring little trill, which they readily give during their displays, or as they flush up from underfoot. Males and females are similar in appearance, with short, slightly downcurved bills, red-brown backs and white undersides, with a conspicuous black patch in the middle of the belly. On the tops, they often nest semi-colonially amongst bog pools, in groups consisting of a few pairs.

On their breeding grounds, dunlin often form an unusual association with golden plover, and to a much lesser

Stuart Rae

extent dotterel, which has led them to them being called 'the plover's page'. The dunlin will often stand beside a plover, call when it calls and follow closely behind when it flies. This can look somewhat comical, with the larger plover apparently being chased by the tiny dunlin. It is thought that the dunlin derives some protection from predators by using the taller plover as a lookout. What the plover gets out of the deal is less clear.

Dotterel
(amadan-mointich)
Charadrius morinellus

Slightly smaller and slimmer than golden plover, and much less obvious, dotterel are masters at blending with the summit mosses and grasses. By far the best way to locate them is to learn their call – a 'kwip' so soft that it makes the gentle piping of the golden plover sound positively harsh.

Dotterel reverse the usual sex roles in birds, and the females are more brightly coloured than the males. They have dark caps, broad white eye stripes (which meet in a 'V' on the nape of the neck), white faces and dove-grey chests and backs, with a white chest band. Their bellies are the orange-red of a rainbow towards the front, shading into black underneath. Males share this colour scheme and pattern, and though slightly more muted are still splendid.

Stuart Rae

Male

Little is ordinary in the life of the dotterel. These birds were thought to breed only in the arctic tundra or the alpine zones of northern Europe and Russia, so it came as something of a surprise when a small population was found nesting on agricultural land in the Dutch polders, four metres below sea level.

Snipe
(croman-loin/gobhar-athair)
Gallinago gallinago

Secretive and inconspicuous on the ground, snipe rely upon their cryptic plumage for camouflage amongst the grasses and rushes. Often waiting until the last moment before bursting from underfoot with a harsh 'scaap', the most frequent view is of a smallish bird, brown above and white below, zig-zagging off into the distance. The bill comprises a quarter of the length of the bird and is often carried in a characteristic 'head down' way.

Tom Holden

In spring and early summer, boggy glens and flats are filled with the sounds of snipe, which consist of a 'chicka chicka chicka' as the pair keep in contact, or the strange, atmospheric vibrato 'drumming' given during their display flights. These displays give a chance to get a more prolonged view, but this still tends to consist of a long-billed silhouette zipping about against the sky.

Snipe feed with their heads down, using the flexible and sensitive tips of their bills to locate prey underground. This makes them potentially vulnerable to predators, and to counter this, their eyes are set remarkably high and far back on the head, enabling them to see forwards and backwards at the same time.

BIRDS

Curlew (guilbneach)
Numenius arquata

One of the largest waders in the world, curlews are otherwise rather nondescript – a mottled grey-brown above and pale below, with a large white patch at the rump extending some way up the back. Their most useful distinguishing features are their long legs and their elegant downcurved bills, some 10-15cm long.

Tom Holden

In spring, curlews are noisy birds and their calls and display song are both easy to recognise. The call is a whistling 'coor-lee' which gives them their English name, while the song is a rapid, accelerating bubbling, and both can be heard from a considerable distance. The song is given in flight as the bird flutters steeply up, then slowly glides back down with wings, head and tail stiffly outstretched. In the 17th century, the alarm calls of curlew were said to have betrayed the presence of Covenanters to searching government troops.

Ben Gulabin, the attractive Corbett overlooking Glen Shee, carries the Gaelic name of this bird, and the lower ground adjacent to this hill well illustrates the mix of habitats in which they are most often encountered, with heather moorland and enclosed farmland in close proximity.

Greenshank (deoch-bhuidhe) *Tringa nebularia*

Perhaps our most elegant hill bird, greenshank are medium-sized, greyish waders with pale undersides, long greenish legs and long, slightly upturned bills. Apt to go unnoticed as they feed quietly along the edges of a loch or large river, they are much more obvious in flight, with dark wings and a flashing white wedge extending up their backs. The birds arrive back from their estuarine wintering grounds in April and can be noisy at that

Tom Holden

time, giving a shrill and far-carrying 'tew tew tew' if they are flushed. They are even more conspicuous when they have young later in the season, and any hillwalker going near a greenshank territory will soon have the adults yelping around their head.

Like all waders, greenshank chicks can leave the nest soon after hatching, and the parents often move them some distance to favoured feeding areas. This can necessitate some remarkable feats for tiny balls of fluff weighing less than an ounce. There are records of young swimming 70 yards across the River Garry and, perhaps even more amazingly, crossing 3.5kms of the roughest country in Sutherland within two days of leaving the egg.

Red-throated diver (learg-dhearg)
Gavia stellata

Duck-sized but slimmer and more streamlined, red-throated divers can be seen, or more frequently heard, in the north and west between April and August. Most often noted in flight as they give their rapid quacking call, a quick glance upwards will reveal the hunch-backed diver arrowing over-head on narrow, swiftly beating wings. These sightings are most common at lower altitudes, as the birds travel to and from their feeding areas.

Derek Belsey

On the water, their territorial calls give them away. These consist of repeated, rhythmical and rolling crow-ings, which are audible at some distance. When seen in these situations, they are often in silhouette, but their habit of holding the head and bill upwards at an angle is distinctive and quite unlike a duck or black-throated diver. In good light, the striped hindneck and plain back are good recognition features and it is only then that throat colour is a helpful clue; otherwise the deep wine-red just looks dark.

In Shetland, red-throats are known as rain geese and Martin Martin, in his 17th century account of his travels to St Kilda, states that they "make a doleful noise before a great rain".

Black-throated diver
(learga-dhubh) *Gavia arctica*

Although black-throated divers are only marginally longer than red-throats, they are much heftier birds, with a particularly thick head and neck. Most likely to be located by sound, their flight call is deeper and throatier than a red-throated diver's and slightly resembles a rapid succes-sion of raven's croaks. When on their territories, they give a series of shrill, rising wails that culminate in a whistling peak.

David Whittaker

Individuals' calls are indistinguishable to the human ear, but analysis of sonograms has shown that each bird has a unique vocal 'fingerprint'.

When seen well on the water, their plumage is bold and showy with chequer-board backs, dove-grey heads and hind necks, and dark, iridescent throats. Even so, they have an amazing ability to 'disappear' on open water, particularly if there is a surface shimmer.

Black-throated divers need plenty of room to take off, running along the surface like a swan to become airborne, and this generally confines them to larger lochs than red-throats. The odd pair hangs on in the south-west and Perthshire, but most of Britain's 200 or so pairs are found north and west of the Great Glen.

BIRDS

Buzzard (clamhan) *Buteo buteo*

Buzzards are compact, dark, medium-sized birds of prey. Nobody ever mistakes an eagle for a buzzard, though the inexperienced or hopeful frequently manage the converse, and confusion is most likely when the bird is in flight and can't be accurately sized. In these circumstances, the overall 'feel' of the bird is the best guide. In contrast to eagles, buzzards have short heads, thick necks and short rounded tails. The wings also look relatively short and rounded and their rear edge is convex in silhouette.

Tim Melling

If seen together, their respective dimensions become very apparent; buzzards are about two-thirds the size of an eagle, but only 20% of their weight. Plumage is not a particularly safe guide, as buzzards are notoriously variable and can range from dark chocolate brown to almost white underneath. However, one reliable feature is that a buzzard's underwing usually has dark areas along the trailing edge, and at the tip and 'elbow'.

Buzzards call frequently (a mewing 'pee-yah'), hover readily, often perch on telegraph poles or in fields, and regularly allow a close approach. If a bird does any of these then it isn't an eagle.

Golden eagle (iolair-bhuidhe) *Aquila chrysaetos*

Most often seen in flight, adult golden eagles generally appear uniformly dark below and have long, broad wings with an 'S'-shaped trailing edge and clearly splayed feathers at the tips. The upper wings often have pale 'shoulders', and the golden nape can be obvious. The young have large white patches on their wings and at the base of the tail, which gradually reduce in size until maturity at four or five years. Sea eagles may be seen in the west and have massive straight-edged wings. The adults have pale heads and gleaming white tails, whilst the young are dark all over.

Ronan Dugan

Golden eagles leave characteristic signs around regular perching places where prey is plucked or digested. These are generally small mounds with a commanding view, and the regular input of nutrients makes them much greener than the surrounding ground. The long streaks of 'whitewash' are obvious, but eagle feathers and regurgitated pellets, comprising fur and bones, can also be found. The pellets are precisely the size and shape of a vole, but without the characteristic twisted ends of mammal scats.

Peregrine (seabhag) *Falco peregrinus*

Peregrines are large, crow-sized falcons, dark blue-grey above, with an obvious 'moustache', and finely barred black and white below. However, plumage details are often hard to discern against the sky, and they are best identified by their swept-back wings, which impart a characteristic anchor shape when the bird is seen in silhouette. Exceedingly noisy at their nesting cliffs, their harsh screeching carries some distance.

Their hunting ability is legendary and they can kill just about any bird, up to the size of a raven, in flight. Folding their wings in and diving, or 'stooping', on their prey from great heights, speeds in excess of 200 mph have been reliably recorded. When pulling out of a dive, the birds experience a positive force of 25G; without special suits, humans lose consciousness if subjected to much above 9G. Grouse or racing pigeons are preferred prey. Their fondness for the former marks their card on many moors, and the distinct lack of either over much of the north and west explains the peregrine's rarity there. Sightings are most likely on the Southern Uplands and some unmanaged eastern moors, where birds can occasionally be flushed up from kills.

Tom Holden

Merlin (meirneal) *Falco columbarius*

Merlins are Britain's smallest falcon, little bigger than a blackbird. Males are light blue-grey above and pale below, whilst the females are more generally brown. Kestrels, the other commonly seen small falcon of the uplands, have reddish-brown backs and inner wings, and frequently hover.

Close or prolonged views of merlins are a rare event to the casual observer, and often the best that can be hoped for is a fleeting glimpse as the bird flashes past close to the ground. Merlins are noisy as they set up territories in April and early May, drawing attention to themselves with their 'tecking' and chittering calls. In the middle part of the season, they tend to be inconspicuous, but from late June they once more become demonstrative if the young are approached too closely.

Tom Holden

Female

Like eagles, they often betray their presence with signs. Having caught a small bird, the merlin takes it to a prominent spot to pluck, so in heathery country it is worth checking the tops of large boulders for little bundles of feathers; the remains of one of the 450 or so pipits, skylarks or wheatears that a pair with young need to sustain them through the breeding season.

Mammals, Reptiles, Amphibians and Fish

Rob Raynor and Roger Owen

The mountain hare is Scotland's only true arctic-alpine mammal

Introduction

To the casual observer, the only animals that appear to live in the uplands are the ubiquitous black-faced sheep, deer and the occasional frog or mountain hare. Most of the other species found in our mountains are either scarce, elusive or nocturnal, or a combination of these, and seeing them requires effort and a reasonable quotient of luck. However, these animals often leave signs of their presence, and the ability to recognise these adds a whole new dimension to hillwalking. Wild camping, with early morning and evening forays around the campsite, where time can be spent quietly observing and investigating, significantly increases the chance of both seeing and finding evidence of animals.

While large herds of deer roaming the hillsides are undoubtedly an impressive sight, the reality is that compared with the major continental mountain ranges, Scotland's upland fauna is relatively impoverished. The reasons for this include climate, geographic isolation, persecution and large-scale land management practices that favour particular species. Unlike the other major mountainous regions of Europe where several species of mountain specialist have evolved, Scotland has only one; the mountain hare. All our other mountain animals are not restricted to higher ground and have adapted their lifestyles to the uplands.

Many of the difficulties associated with this environment are similar to those experienced by birds (see p162-3). Mammals, like birds, are warm blooded, and this allows them to remain active over a much wider range of temperatures than cold-blooded species, provided there is adequate food. The disadvantage is that their energy requirements are much greater than for a similar-sized cold-blooded animal. Consequently, many upland mammals, notably red deer, are forced to retreat to lower ground during winter, when food is scarce, and to avoid excessive exposure at higher altitudes. Those mammals that remain include some small rodents such as voles, which can find shelter underground, and the mountain hare, which has a number of adaptations to cope with the extremes of this environment. These include a moult from its blue-grey summer coat to the thick white winter coat, and the fur on the undersides of its toes, which can be spread widely to create miniature 'snow shoes'.

Despite the apparently serious disadvantage of being cold-blooded, reptiles and amphibians can survive in the uplands, as elsewhere in cool temperate climates, by hibernating during the winter. The unpredictability of the Scottish climate, particularly during the spring when these animals start to become active again, can place particular physiological stresses on them. An early mild spell can bring them out in February, only to be followed by heavy snowfall a week or so later and the resumption of hibernation. Sudden changes in ambient temperature can be particularly serious for reptiles when their bodies are not sufficiently warmed up. Consequently, adders and viviparous lizards are sometimes 'caught out' in the open by a sudden wintry shower in the early spring, seemingly incapable of retreating to shelter, because their body temperature has fallen too low.

Scotland's native fish are also cold-blooded but are nonetheless well adapted to a cold climate. Salmon, trout and charr can easily survive in Scottish winter temperatures, even under a surface ice cover, so long as there is sufficient depth of oxygenated water. Because their metabolic rate is related to temperature, the rate of feeding and growth then slows drastically or ceases altogether. By contrast, various other species, including eels, burrow into deep sediments to survive winter temperatures. Non-native fish species, which have been introduced by man to Scottish upland waters, are less well adapted, although some can survive at moderate altitudes.

The nutritional requirements of upland mammals also create various opportunities and constraints. Larger herbivores tend to graze preferentially and seek out the most productive areas (see p91), while the populations of smaller, less mobile herbivores often vary according to the richness of the underlying rocks.

Those animals that feed primarily on invertebrates, such as shrews and bats, enjoy a relatively bountiful food supply in summer, but in winter, they are obliged either to switch to the few species that are still available, or find an alternative solution to dealing with this lean time of year. In the case of bats and hedgehogs, the solution is to hibernate, although they do not remain in this state continuously throughout the entire winter period.

Carnivores such as foxes rely to a large extent on scavenging, and spend some of their time in the winter foraging on the open hill for deer and sheep carcasses. This behaviour is not restricted to winter, but the scarcity of suitable live prey at this time, combined with the high energetic cost of finding and killing it, means that scavenging is usually a more cost-effective winter feeding strategy.

The relative lack of food and shelter in turn mean that for many animals, the population density and the number of offspring produced per female are significantly lower in the hills. Wood mice, for example, have only one or two litters per year in the uplands, compared to up to four in the lowlands. The clearance of native woodland has further restricted the availability of food and shelter in the hills, although the expansion of commercial forestry and recent moves towards native woodland restoration have benefited some species, such as the pine marten.

Historical background

Our range of mammals reflects the combined effects of natural colonisation, selective extinctions and introductions by man. The most important factors influencing their distribution and abundance have been, and continue to be, human activities.

Natural colonisation

During the Ice Age, Britain was linked to continental Europe by a land bridge and the more mobile species, including arctic and tundra specialists such as the arctic fox, Norway lemming, musk ox and reindeer, were able to colonise Scotland. As the ice retreated, so did the distribution of these animals. At the same time, temperate species, including many of those we have today, moved into the new post-glacial woodlands and marshes, gradually expanding their ranges northwards. Natural colonisation of Britain ceased when the land bridge was severed due to sea-level rise around 9,500 years ago, although colonisation within the British Isles continued for some time after this. Once separated from mainland Europe, any loss of animal species, whether from hunting or habitat change, could not be offset by further immigration from larger source populations elsewhere.

Large mammal extinctions

There is some uncertainty about when the major post-glacial British mammal extinctions occurred, due to the small number of sites where remains have been found. Much of our information comes from the famous bear caves in the glen of the Allt nan Uamh, west of the Corbett Breabag, near Inchnadamph.

The change from tundra to woodland did not favour reindeer and their extinction, around 8,300 years ago, was almost certainly due to this loss of habitat. By contrast, the aurochs, the wild ancestors of all domestic cattle, were hunted to extinction in the British Isles and subsequently became totally extinct, probably by Roman times. The elk succumbed to a similar fate in Britain, but its Gaelic names (lon or miol) accurately describe its appearance and gait, suggesting that it may have survived until around 1,000 years ago. The wild boar and beaver clung on for much longer, perhaps until the late 16th century. The beaver was hunted both for its pelt and for its castoreum, a valuable secretion from the scent glands that was used in perfumery and for medicinal purposes, as it contains salicylic acid, better known as aspirin.

Of the carnivores, the brown bear probably became extinct around 2,000 years ago, and although woodland clearance caused progressive fragmentation of the bear's habitat, hunting pressure ultimately led to its demise. The lynx suffered a similar fate, although this forest-dwelling cat may have survived until around 1,500 years ago. Of all the large native carnivores, the wolf survived the longest, and the last British one was supposedly killed by a Highlander, MacQueen, on the River Findhorn in 1743. Wolves are less restricted to forested areas than lynxes or bears, and this ability to adapt readily to other habitats may have enabled them to survive so long, despite relentless persecution.

Although extinct in Britain as a native wild species, free-ranging reindeer from a semi-domesticated herd in Glen More may be encountered in the Cairngorms

Introduced mammals

The other major factor that has shaped the mammal fauna of upland Scotland is the introduction of new species by humans. Some of these, such as the feral goat and rabbit, were introduced so long ago that they have been assimilated into our native fauna, and if they had an adverse effect at the time, we are no longer aware of this. More recently, the introduction and spread of feral American mink, sika deer and in some areas, the grey squirrel, has been more problematic.

Introduced species can interact with the native fauna in several ways. Predation can have catastrophic effects, particularly where the prey species is already under some other form of ecological pressure, such as habitat degradation. The introduction of mink has severely affected our native water voles in this way.

Closely-related species may hybridise with each other, and when an introduced species is involved, particular characteristics which are unique to the native species may be lost forever, with an overall loss of biological diversity. Sika deer were introduced to Britain from 1860 and have adapted well to upland forestry plantations, where they interbreed with red deer. The hybrids, like pure sika, are more likely to occupy dense thickets than are pure red deer, making them more difficult to cull, although they also occur on the open hill. A consequence is that the numbers of sika and hybrids are likely to increase in proportion to pure red deer and if this process is allowed to continue unchecked, the only 'pure' red deer left will be confined to islands. In parts of Scotland it is already impossible to distinguish sika-red hybrids from 'pure' red deer or 'pure' sika deer. Hybridisation also threatens the Scottish wildcat, in this case through interbreeding with domestic and feral cats.

An introduced species may also oust a native by some competitive advantage, as in the case of the American grey squirrel and the native red squirrel. Greys appear better adapted than reds to broadleaved woodlands, especially those comprising trees such as oak that produce large seeds. Grey squirrels also carry the squirrel pox virus, which does not appear to affect them, but is fatal to reds. Although there is still potential for further range expansion northwards by greys, the Highlands still remain uncolonised.

Influence of human activities

Besides extinctions and introductions, human land use has increasingly determined the abundance and distribution of many species, as in the case of red deer. After the extinction of our larger carnivores, hunting initially prevented deer numbers from increasing. Indeed, hunting pressure was such that a series of 16th century Acts of Parliament was passed to 'conserve' deer, primarily for the benefit of royalty. Their numbers probably reached a low point in the mid- to late 18th century, when large areas were stocked with sheep and deer were regarded as competitors. Then, during the 19th century, sheep were cleared from many areas and much hill land became 'deer forest', managed for the increasingly fashionable sport of deer stalking. Deer numbers were allowed to increase, with a brief dip during the Second World War due to increased shooting and poaching, before rising again to the current total of between 360,000 and 400,000. In many areas, elevated deer populations have now resulted in decades of overgrazing and suppression of native woodland, including natural treeline and alpine scrub.

Public policy is now to reduce deer numbers by voluntary means, though this has been difficult to implement in practice. A successful example can be seen at Creag Meagaidh National Nature Reserve, where Scottish Natural Heritage has achieved impressive natural regeneration on the lower slopes by a progressive reduction in deer numbers. Nevertheless, despite an annual cull of around 100,000 the overall deer population continues to increase.

Mammals

Grassland, heather moorland and the alpine zone

In the glens, there is generally a greater variety of habitats than at higher altitudes, combined with more shelter. Common lowland species such as rabbits are more likely to be encountered here, but also other less obvious species including shrews, hedgehogs, bats, mice and voles. Several of these small mammals are equally at home on the open hill, sometimes to summit level.

Buildings provide excellent shelter and food for an array of species including the brown rat and the house mouse, both of which can occupy bothies at a range of altitudes. Rats are unlikely to be confused with anything else in such places, but a mouse that is seen in or around buildings could either be a common house mouse or a wood mouse, if suitable habitat is present nearby.

Moving upwards, agriculturally improved grassland rapidly gives way to rough grassland and heather-dominated vegetation, both of which are ideal for field voles and shrews. Unlike voles, which are rodents and almost exclusively herbivorous, shrews are voracious predators of small invertebrates and belong to a different taxonomic group, the Insectivora. They have a very high metabolic rate, a physiological characteristic common to many small mammals, and are active throughout the year, both day and night. Both common and pygmy shrews occur on the Scottish hills, although the latter are generally scarcer.

Shrews are essentially solitary, territorial animals, and are frequently aggressive to one another. In order to fuel their very active lives, they need to eat 80-90% of

The weasel is our smallest carnivore and a specialist predator of small rodents

their body weight every day, and twice this when feeding young, dying if deprived of food for more than a few hours. Although rarely seen in the open, their high-pitched shrieks ('tzi-tzi') can often be heard, particularly in the summer as they scurry relentlessly about in the vegetation. Shrews have scent glands along their flanks, which produce a musky odour that is distasteful to many predators, but this 'defence' does not always prevent the shrew from being killed, and it is not uncommon to find dead shrews lying out in the open.

The field vole also occurs, sometimes at high population densities, in extensive areas of rough grassland at all altitudes, and feeds mainly on the leaves of grasses. This rodent is a key prey species for many predators, and like many other small rodents, its populations show substantial cyclic peaks and troughs over time, typically with a peak once every three to five years. These cycles are incompletely understood despite numerous scientific studies, but in turn affect the breeding success of their predators. In the uplands, rank and tussocky purple moor grass provides one of the best vole habitats. Here, their runs can often be seen as small tunnels disappearing into the morass of the previous summer's leaf litter to form complex labyrinths within the vegetation. Runs are also created under snow and these are very obvious just after the snow has melted. They are active both day and night and may occasionally be glimpsed as they dart across the more exposed sections of their runways. Runs have been reported from nearly 900m on Ben Hope.

The stoat is one of the more visible ground predators that can be encountered on the open hill, usually close to cover such as a collapsed drystane dyke or shieling. Both stoats and their smaller relatives, weasels, may be active by day or night, but tend to be more diurnal during the spring and summer. They are naturally inquisitive and if disturbed, will often reappear to watch you, provided you are quiet and remain still. They can sometimes even be enticed out from cover by making squeaking noises, and particularly by an imitation of a squealing rabbit, which is a staple prey species. Both the local distribution and population density of stoats are closely related to those of rabbits.

Both stoats and weasels are also attracted to young conifer plantations, which often support large numbers of small rodents, and both habitually enter the tunnels of their prey. Weasels are especially well suited to following field and bank voles along their runs and burrows, including tunnels formed beneath snow, while stoats are restricted to wider burrows, such as those of water voles, rats and rabbits. Both may be encountered at all altitudes, if suitable prey is available.

The diet of the upland fox includes field voles, rabbits and mountain hares, along with ground-nesting birds, invertebrates, berries and the carrion of sheep and deer

Stoats though tend to be more common than weasels in hill country possibly because there is less prey and the weasel's smaller size restricts its choice of victims. They have even been reported from the summit of Ben Nevis.

Of all our carnivores, the fox is arguably the most adaptable, being found in almost every habitat that exists in the British Isles. Not surprisingly for such an opportunistic animal, the upland fox's diet is varied and includes small mammals such as field voles, rabbits and mountain hares, along with ground-nesting birds, invertebrates and berries. Sheep and deer carrion is also important, especially in western ranges, where mountain hares and grouse are more scarce.

Foxes are mainly active at night, or at dawn and dusk, but also during daytime where they are not disturbed. The basic family unit is a pair, but an adult male and several vixens may share a territory, which may be as extensive as 40 km² in the uplands, roughly equating to the entire area of a small mountain group such as Ben Mor Coigach. As foxes are usually much more scarce in the hills than elsewhere, they are less likely to be seen there than in other habitats. However, fox scats are commonly found along hill paths and are amongst the more obvious mammal field signs that hillwalkers will encounter.

Fox dens or 'earths' are sometimes excavated where the soil type allows, but as in the case of badgers, upland dens are usually located in natural cavities such as rock fissures or boulder piles, several of which may be used within a territory. Dens may also be used by a badger or even an otter, so it can be hard to distinguish between these respective animals' shelters. Breeding begins in January and this is when foxes are most vocal. The average litter size is four to five, with the cubs born during March and April. As with many other species, the family may be moved to alternative dens if disturbed.

Foxes, stoats and weasels are controlled on many estates because of the damage they can cause to poultry and to sporting interests, although the fact that they are also important predators of rodents and rabbits often seems to be overlooked. However, despite a long history of intense persecution, their populations do not appear to have been adversely affected. This is in stark contrast to the polecat, which is believed to have been completely eradicated from Scotland by keepering pressure. Following deliberate releases there are now localised small populations in Perthshire, the Trossachs, east Sutherland, and possibly also Argyll. Similar looking polecat-ferrets also occur in some areas, including Strathspey and some of the islands.

The very rare and elusive wildcat is one of the most enigmatic of our carnivores and the least likely to be seen by the hillwalker. Any potential sighting is also complicated by the uncomfortable truth that it is difficult to distinguish wildcats from 'lookalike' hybrids. There is a longstanding and unresolved taxonomic debate over whether the wildcat exists as a separate species from the domestic tabbie, or whether 'wildcats' are simply a distinct group within the same species, but with certain characteristics that set them apart from other cats. This is not a purely academic debate, because it impacts on the legislation that aims to protect the Scottish wildcat from persecution, and there is a perception amongst some gamekeepers that they can get away with killing any cat on their patch that is not obviously a domestic 'moggy'. For all this, and despite the possibility of 2,000 years of interbreeding between wild and domestic cats, there are still a few cats out there that conform to our 'traditional' understanding of a wildcat, based on a combination of coat markings, body-form characteristics, such as skull size, and genetic markers. The best evidence for these surviving wildcats comes from the Cairngorms, parts of north east Scotland and the Morvern-Ardnamurchan area. These areas are now the focus of an ambitious conservation initiative designed to protect the remaining wildcat gene pool and prevent further hybridisation.

In general, wildcats prefer to live in the margins of mountains and moorland with rough grazing, often combined with forests and some crops. Although they may occur over 800m, as is perhaps reflected in hill names such as Beinn a' Chait above Glen Tilt, the lower ground is generally preferred due to the greater availability of shelter, rabbits and other small mammal prey. Like most cat species, they are essentially solitary except when mating, and home range size varies from around 2km2 in the eastern Highlands to more than five times this in the west, according to the quality of the habitat.

The wildcat has been persecuted in Britain since the Middle Ages and suffered a steady decrease in its range until around 1914, when it was believed to be confined to the north and west, where keepering pressure is traditionally less intense than elsewhere. A reduction in persecution following the First World War allowed the species to recolonise former parts of its range. Male wildcats tend to disperse much further from their natal area than females and this can bring them into contact with female domestic cats. As the wildcat population was recovering from this historic low point, the scarcity of female wildcats may have resulted in a rapid rise in hybridisation.

The hardy mountain, white or blue hare, as it is variously known is our only truly arctic-alpine mammal and, while it occurs from Ireland to Japan, it is almost entirely restricted to tundra, boreal forest or alpine habitats. Many hillwalkers, especially in the eastern Highlands, will have noticed them sitting upright in the heather keeping a watchful eye on their approach, or have 'spooked' one and watched it disappear over the horizon. However, in recent years, sightings have become much less frequent for many of us.

In Scotland, heather moorland actively managed for grouse provides an optimum habitat for the species, as rotational burning ensures that there is always young heather growth available. While heather forms the major part of the hare's diet, other dwarf shrubs and trees are also eaten. The ability to survive on poor quality vegetation has enabled mountain hares to flourish in areas where brown hares cannot, so they are generally restricted to ground above 300–400m, while their more widespread relative usually occurs below this altitude. Not surprisingly, the highest population densities occur on hills with more fertile soils, where better quality foraging can be found. Hare numbers are thus much higher over relatively calcium-rich rocks such as gabbros, and some schists, than over granites. The Monadh Liath and many grouse moors in the Eastern Highlands are particularly good places to see them, although heavy culling on some estates, often to reduce sheep ticks (carriers of the Louping Ill Virus that affects grouse), has led to hares becoming much scarcer in some areas than in the 1990s. In the best areas, hare numbers can exceed 250 per km², although typical densities elsewhere are between one and six per km².

Hare numbers fluctuate periodically by ten-fold or more, peaking approximately every ten years. It is unclear whether the current hare population is comparable in size to that of the Victorian era, but around 1900, their abundance was such that every winter, estate staff were provided with powder and shot in order to control them, as they were regarded as competitors with grouse.

Although mountain hares are often visible by day on the hill, they are most active at night, spending much of the day resting in their shelters, or 'forms', which usually comprise an enlarged cavity beneath dense heather. Sometimes they excavate short burrows in the peat or snow, but these structures are not extensive. At high altitudes, the options are more restricted and hares take refuge in boulder fields, or in simple shallow scrapes with good all round visibility. When disturbed, they usually flee uphill, perhaps because for such an agile animal, this is the best means of escaping ground predators. Hares are commonly preyed upon by stoats and foxes and, in the Central and Eastern Highlands, they form an important part of the diet of eagles. The females give birth to their first litter of 1–3 leverets in March, and two or three subsequent litters may be born in the following months, until early August. Lactating females may graze by day as well as by night in order to meet the demands of their young.

Mountain hares undergo two moults every year that result in obvious colour changes. The moult from brownish grey to white occurs between mid-October and January, and is largely complete by December. Curiously, despite the camouflage that the winter coat provides in snow, white hares can sometimes be seen sitting in dark patches of heather, where they are particularly conspicuous. There is some regional variation and at lower altitudes, for example in the Pentlands and Lammermuirs, the winter coat is rarely completely white. The Victorians were keen on moving various quarry species around, including hares, to "improve" the breeding stock. On Mull, for example, mountain hares have been introduced both from the Scottish mainland and from Ireland. Irish hares belong to a separate sub-species that rarely moults to a white coat, thus "piebald" (rather than white) hares have been reported from the Mull hills in the winter. However, genetic studies have failed to find evidence of Irish hare genes in the current population, so it appears that the prevalence of these Irish animals has declined and the population is now dominated by descendants of mainland Scottish stock. Between

The late Bob Scott of the Derry, gralloching a stag high on Beinn a' Bhuird

February and late May the winter coat moults back to brown, the rate being influenced by temperature, so hares on the tops remain white for longer than those at lower levels.

Of all the wild mammals encountered by the hillwalker, the red deer is the most familiar. Throughout the year, both physical and behavioural changes can readily be observed amongst the herds, providing a highly visible record of the passing seasons. The obvious physical changes involve moulting between winter and summer coats and the various stages of antler growth amongst the stags. The behavioural changes can be even more dramatic, particularly as the rut approaches and the glens resonate to the primordial roaring of the stags.

Red deer are essentially woodland animals, but the progressive loss of this habitat, followed by the creation of the stalking estate, has resulted in them becoming primarily animals of the open hill in Scotland; a remarkable adaptation. Nevertheless, they still use woodland for cover and foraging, particularly during the winter months. The generally poor quality of vegetation on the open hill results in lower body weights and antler sizes relative to their lowland forest cousins in southern England, or in more wooded countries such as Germany.

The Scottish red deer population is of international importance. However, in many parts of Scotland, this population exists at the expense of other key elements of our natural heritage, and human intervention is needed to control their numbers. Red deer occupy a unique position amongst Scottish wild mammals and occur over most of the country. Deer stalking is estimated to be worth £105 million per year to the Scottish economy and to support the equivalent of over 2,500 paid full time jobs. These concern the management of deer in the form of deer forests for stalking, predominately in the West and North-west Highlands.

As a field sport, upland deer stalking is traditionally undertaken by paying clients under the supervision of an estate stalker. Suitable animals are located on foot, and it is then necessary to use the contours of the ground to get as close as possible, and attain a position from which the quarry can be humanely and cleanly shot. The carcass then has its stomach and intestines removed in situ, a process known as 'gralloching', before being carried away by pony, or dragged to a point where it can be uplifted by all-terrain vehicle or boat to the estate larder. Large and mature stags between seven and ten years old, with impressive antlers, have always been favoured, although stags with less desirable characteristics are also targeted to try to improve the quality of the stock. Most hinds are shot by

Rutting stags frequently wallow in wet peat

estate staff for stock management purposes, rather than for sport.

Deer stalking is a skilled and time-consuming process, with a number of hidden subtleties. While the wind direction is critical when approaching deer, atmospheric conditions also play a crucial role in determining the distance that scent can be carried. A warm, moist atmosphere conducts scent better than a dry, cold one, and the olfactory system of animals requires a moist outer receptive surface in order to function properly. However, in misty conditions, the presence of tiny water droplets in the air presents a physical barrier to the rapid passage of scent, which is exacerbated because the temperature near the ground is lower than that above the mist, resulting in restricted air movement. In such conditions deer may not detect people until they are very close.

In common with all other deer species, except reindeer, only the stags grow antlers, and these become larger and progressively more branched with age. Antler size, however, is not necessarily related to dominance in the fiercely hierarchical deer society, as stags which fail to grow antlers, called 'hummels', can achieve higher body weights and successfully oust antlered stags from groups of hinds (harems). During late March and April, usually whilst still on low ground, stags shed their antlers and almost immediately start to grow a new set, coinciding with the relatively rich new growth of grasses and sedges in spring and summer. The shed antlers are also frequently chewed, as they are an important source of phosphorous and calcium. During this period, the growing antlers are covered in soft skin and are said to be 'in velvet.'

Spring is also the time when both sexes moult from their greyish-brown winter coats to their rich red-brown summer coats, and as the weather improves, they move up onto the higher ground to escape the unwanted attentions of biting flies. During mid August and September, the velvet dies and disintegrates with the aid of vigorous rubbing against trees, leaving the new antlers clean and ready for the rut. At around this time, the stags develop thicker necks and manes and begin to disperse from bachelor groups towards the 'hind grounds.'

October is the rutting season and a time when deer behaviour is fascinating to watch. The stags use their forelegs and antlers to create wet depressions or wallows in the peat, into which they spray urine and semen, rendering them highly pungent and more threatening to others. There is much roaring as each stag attempts to assert its dominance and intimidate others, whilst at the same time the nearby hinds are coming into oestrous, ready for mating. The stags approach groups of hinds which they then attempt to 'defend' from other hopeful males.

If roaring fails to intimidate a competitor, two stags may be seen 'parallel walking' on the hillside, assessing each other's physique. If they are closely matched, direct antler to antler conflict is likely to ensue. The stags spend so much time defending their harems that they have very little time to feed and lose condition rapidly, in turn making the task that much more difficult. By the end of October, the rut is almost over and the stags drift away, gradually regrouping into loose associations that move onto the lower ground as winter approaches. The winter coat starts to re-grow from September, and is generally complete by December.

For most of the year, the two sexes remain segregated, with quite separate areas occupied by groups of hinds and stags. These single-sex groups tend to remain within their traditional home range, and this 'hefting' behaviour is particularly marked amongst the hinds. Hind ranges generally comprise areas of richer grazing than those occupied by the stags, because of the high nutritional demands of the pregnant and lactating hinds and their followers.

After a gestation period of eight months, most hinds give birth to their calves between May and July. The calves are spotted or dappled in appearance and rely on this camouflage, especially in their first few days as they lie low in the undergrowth, seemingly abandoned by their mothers. If such a calf is discovered it is important not to intervene, as the hind will not be far away and any hint of human scent on her offspring could result in her deserting the calf. By August the young deer have lost their spots, but they remain with their mothers in highly-structured matriarchal hind herds for the rest of the year, the young males eventually dispersing to join bachelor groups elsewhere.

Hillwalkers on the northern slopes of the Cairngorms and nearby Cromdale Hills may come across the only free-ranging herd of reindeer in Britain. They are unmistakable, with heavy, almost bovine muzzles, large prominent hoofs and distinctive asymmetric antlers in both sexes. The herd was established from Swedish animals released in 1952, and provides a tantalising flavour of our original post-glacial mammal fauna, as the highest part of their range probably resembles the habitat which was present as the ice retreated 11,000 years ago. The herd is intensively managed and is currently maintained at around 150 animals by controlled breeding.

The other non-domestic hoofed mammal that hillwalkers may encounter is the feral goat. These animals occur in small, isolated herds across the Scottish uplands, generally on steep rocky ground above 300m. These sometimes have long histories, and the original animals on the slopes of Ben Lomond are thought

The Highlands are now the principal UK stronghold of the red squirrel

to have become established around the time of Robert the Bruce. However, the current herd may actually be the result of a later reintroduction. They are all descended from Persian domestic goats which were probably first introduced to Britain around 3,000 years ago.

Both sexes have horns and their coats vary in colour, but are usually black, brown or white, or a mixture of these. Like red deer, goats form single-sex groups for at least part of the year, with a matriarch heading each group of nanny goats. The billies possess a particularly pungent odour that can be detected from quite a distance downwind, and this may be related to the dominance hierarchy that also exists within each male group. The rut occurs in the autumn, with the kids born mostly between the following January and April.

Woodland

Native forest and some conifer plantations provide habitats for species such as red squirrels and pine martens, and also some small rodents such as bank voles and wood mice. Red squirrels are entirely dependent on woodland, but the others have also adapted, to a greater or lesser extent, to more open situations, although woodland remains their preferred habitat.

Bank voles are most likely to be encountered in areas with dense vegetation. Provided there is sufficient cover, however, they can be found in more open habitats such as grasslands, and have been recorded up to 800m. They feed on fleshy fruits, seeds, fungi, leaves, mosses and roots according to the season, with insects and worms also taken occasionally. Breeding may continue all the year round if the population is low and there is plenty of food available. Like other small mammals, bank voles are important prey for many predators such as owls, kestrels, weasels, stoats, pine martens and foxes.

Wood mice, also known as field mice, are very adaptable and agile animals with impressive jumping abilities, and despite their name, also occur in a range of habitats such as drystane dykes, and more rarely in rough grassland, heather moorland, blanket bog and even scree, reaching up to 1300m in the Cairngorms. In common with other small rodents and shrews, they are short-lived, with a maximum life span of just 18–20 months, and few adults survive from one summer to the next.

The Highlands are now the principal UK stronghold of the red squirrel, which occurs up to around 550m in the Cairngorms. Here, they are mainly associated with coniferous woods, especially of Scots pine, although they also occur in mixed and broadleaved woodland. Fortunately, red squirrels can also thrive in plantations of exotic conifers such as Norway spruce and larch, provided there are sufficient trees of coning age present. The availability of cones and seeds, however, can vary dramatically from year to year, so ideal forests include a variety of tree species of different ages, including broadleaves. They should also be sufficiently open to allow the development of a diverse ground flora, thereby providing a range of other seasonal foods, the most important being tree seeds, fruit, berries and fungi.

Although also primarily a forest dweller, the pine marten is considerably more adaptable than the red squirrel and will hunt on the open hill, though it is unlikely to remain at high altitude for extended periods. Martens are perhaps attracted to the tops in search of roosting ptarmigan, and their signs can sometimes be found on the highest mountain ridges, several kilometres from the nearest tree cover. Martens are mostly nocturnal, not least because daylight exposes them to the keen eye of the eagle, but they have been encountered by day on the summit of Ben Nevis, apparently scavenging on food scraps. Adult martens are mostly solitary and territorial, and the size of each territory varies according to the quality of the habitat, the sex of the animal and the season.

Martens are highly opportunistic animals and their diet is very varied. Voles and other small mammals form their main natural prey, with birds, beetles, squirrels, berries (notably rowan and blaeberries) and, in some areas, rabbits also eaten regularly. The marten's alternative names include 'sweetmart', which despite their apparent "sweet tooth" (martens can readily be attracted by baits such as jam) is more likely to relate to the animal's scent. This is much less offensive than those of its relatives, the mink and polecat, or 'foulmart'.

Martens were once found throughout Britain, but in the 19th century suffered one of the most dramatic declines of any British mammal as a result of persecution. On a single estate in the Cairngorms, 246 martens were destroyed by gamekeepers in the space of just three years and by 1900, they were reduced to isolated populations, mainly in north-west Scotland. In the last 50 years, as a result of legal protection and the expansion of commercial forestry, they have made a significant recovery, recolonising the rest of the Highlands and most of the area to the north of the Central Belt. There are also isolated populations further south, including Galloway and the Borders.

The badger is another, more widespread, carnivore that is usually associated with woodland and permanent pasture, but also occurs more rarely at high altitude. In common with other such species, badgers change their behaviour to survive in the uplands. In the lowlands, they live in social groups or 'clans', which are effectively extended families. Their most important food is earthworms, and the availability of these is a major factor in determining the territory size. The individuals within a clan co-operate to defend the territory, whose boundary is marked with latrines. This system appears to break down in wilder mountainous areas, where badgers often live singly or in pairs, roaming over vast tracts of unproductive moorland and not defending territories. In the lowlands, badger clans excavate complex and extensive tunnel systems to form setts. In the uplands, however, the absence of light, well-drained soils means that setts are rare, and alternative sites such as rock cavities are used instead.

Like pine martens, badgers are opportunists and will eat a wide variety of foods. Earthworms are scarce in the uplands, especially in areas dominated by peat, and carrion probably forms a major part of their diet, particularly in winter. At other times this is supplemented by fruit, berries, small mammals, birds and invertebrates.

Most of the species of deer that occur in Scotland are essentially woodland animals, and roe deer are the smallest of these. They are widespread and although they occur on moorland up to 760m, they are most likely to be encountered on the lower ground, where they can often be seen, especially in the early morning or evening, browsing amongst scrub on woodland edges and forestry tracks. Unlike red deer, roe deer do not form large single-sex groups, but are largely solitary between April and August, when the bucks defend exclusive territories of up to 0.5 or 0.6 km^2. These territories are marked with scent, and by fraying the bark of strategically important trees and shrubs. Females also occupy individual home-ranges during this period, but these overlap with neighbouring animals. During the winter months this territorial social system breaks down and small groups may be seen feeding together, often in fields.

Introduced sika deer are becoming increasingly widespread in areas with dense conifer plantations, and are rarely encountered far from thick woodland or scrub. The similar sized fallow deer also occurs in a few scattered parts of the country, and is likewise largely restricted to woodland.

Bats occur up to around 400m (exceptionally to 600m), and favour Highland glens with semi-natural broadleaved woodland and plenty of open water. The very similar common and soprano pipistrelle are the two most common species, distinguished by their different ultrasonic echolocation calls. They are best seen at dusk as they fly along linear features such as woodland edges, watercourses and even dams. Daubenton's bats are particularly associated with water and, although they emerge later, are often easily visible in the mid-summer twilight as they fly low in characteristic repetitive straight lines, catching flying insects or picking them directly off the water. All British bats feed exclusively on insects, with pipistrelles able to consume 3,000 midges in a single night.

Rivers and wetlands

Four mammals are particularly associated with watercourses and wetlands, and may be encountered in both the uplands and the lowlands; the otter, mink, water shrew and water vole. Of these, the water vole is increasingly restricted to the uplands, while the others are more common at lower altitudes.

Although traditionally associated with slow-flowing lowland rivers and canals, water voles can also occur in small mountain burns at 900m or above, and appear to be much more widespread in the Highlands than was previously thought. Nevertheless, water voles are still one of Britain's most threatened native mammals, and underwent a dramatic decline during the latter part of the 20th century. This was partly associated with the loss or degradation of good bankside habitat along many watercourses, but was largely due to the spread of non-native American mink which, if left unchecked, could wipe out many of the surviving highland populations.

A thick layer of peat and slow flowing water offer a prime habitat for water voles, as here on Mar Lodge Estate in the Cairngorms

Female mink are small enough to enter vole burrows and are efficient and systematic hunters. Fortunately, mink are scarce in open moorland and mountainous terrain, preferring the greater cover and abundance of prey that occur in lower-lying areas. This probably explains the current pattern of water vole distribution in the remote headwaters of many rivers, where they live in isolated colonies of rarely more than ten individuals. With such low numbers, these colonies are always at risk of being wiped out by chance events, such as sudden extreme flooding or occasional forays by mink. Recolonisation can only take place if there are other colonies reasonably close by; if not, then the species becomes extinct in that area, leaving any surviving colonies even more isolated.

Water voles need reasonably soft ground to excavate their burrow systems, so in the uplands, they are usually associated with areas where there is a thick layer of peat. Such areas also often provide their other key habitat requirement; slow-flowing or still water. As a consequence they are most likely to occur on small meandering burns and in flat marshy areas, such as Upper Glen Affric, near Allt-beithe. Lush, but not necessarily tall, bankside vegetation is also important, and areas with a dense growth of sedges and rushes are preferred. In common with field voles, their breeding success is low in the uplands, where they typically produce less than one third of the number of young that can be reared in the lowlands. In some years, females may only give birth to a single small litter.

As the presence of suitable prey is often restricted in the uplands, our two key semi-aquatic predators, the otter and mink, tend to focus their hunting effort in more productive watercourses at lower altitude. However, like any predator, both species will respond to seasonal changes in the behaviour of their prey. In the spring, otters may be attracted to marshy areas where amphibians are breeding, while in the late autumn, they follow salmon upstream to the shallow, gravelly burns where spawning takes place. Neither otter nor mink are often seen, but the characteristic signs of otters, in particular, can occasionally be found by upland lochans or on bealachs at altitudes of 600m or more.

Both species are largely solitary, territorial animals. Otters live at very low population densities, with each female typically occupying around 20km of watercourse. Males occupy larger home ranges of around 30km or more, and usually overlap the ranges of several females. Range sizes for mink are much smaller and are of the order of 1–4km, again with males occupying larger areas than females. In contrast to their largely nocturnal freshwater counterparts, coastal otters are mostly active by day and the plentiful supply of food in the inshore environment means that they are more abundant there. As a result, walkers' routes which follow sea lochs into some of the remoter parts of the Northern and Western Highlands, for example the path into Knoydart along the south side of Loch Hourn, are amongst the best places to see otters anywhere in mainland Britain.

The other aquatic specialist that occurs in some Highland burns is the water shrew which, like the water vole, may be more widespread than records suggest, given its preference for unpolluted fast-flowing watercourses. Like its two smaller relatives, the water shrew is a highly active and feisty predator, mainly feeding on aquatic invertebrates, but its larger size also allows it to tackle bigger prey, including small fish, frogs and newts. Water shrew signs are not easy to find or identify and perhaps the most visible are feeding remains, such as the cases of caddis fly larvae, or the shells of snails and other freshwater molluscs, which are left at feeding sites alongside burns.

Reptiles

Most British reptiles favour relatively dry heather-rich areas so, not surprisingly, some parts of the Highlands are very good places to find two of our hardiest species; the adder and the viviparous lizard. Our third native species, the slow worm, which is actually a legless lizard, is equally widespread, but is much less likely to be encountered as it is highly secretive, and is usually only found by turning over large stones. It is also less common in high open country, preferring instead the greater cover to be found at lower altitudes.

Although most reptiles lay eggs, all three native Scottish species give birth, in late summer, to live young. This adaptation may be advantageous to survival in a harsh, cold and unpredictable environment, and both the viviparous lizard and the adder are also widespread in Scandinavia, occurring well north of the Arctic Circle. The young reptiles still develop within individual egg membranes, but inside their mother, who effectively acts as a mobile incubator, basking in the sun to optimise the exposure of the developing eggs to external heat sources. At birth each egg membrane ruptures, freeing the offspring, which are self-sufficient and fully independent from that point on. The viviparous lizard gives birth to 3–11 almost black young, which look quite different to the predominantly brown adults, while adder broods vary from 3–18. The high cost of reproduction for reptiles at Scottish latitudes is such that for some species, notably the adder, adult females are unable to reproduce every year and must take every second year 'out' to recover. In Arctic Scandinavia, two of the short northern summers are required for every brood to develop, followed by another 'rest' year.

Although our reptiles are well camouflaged, they are only active by day, and those who know when and where to look may actually see the animals themselves,

Reptiles leave few obvious field signs, but the sloughed skins of adders can sometimes be found, especially in the spring. This a male; the females (and young) are brownish with a dark zig-zag, rather than grey.

rather than just field signs. The key to finding reptiles lies in understanding their basic biological requirements, in particular the need to regulate their body temperature. They achieve this by making use of the differences in microclimate that occur at ground level, basking in sheltered gaps in the heather or patches of ground at the base of grass tussocks, often with a south-facing aspect. Surfaces that heat up quickly and retain it well allow reptiles to absorb both radiant heat from the sun and conducted heat from below. Pieces of wood, flat stones, paths and small patches of flattened dead grass are commonly used, provided there is cover close by to retreat to if disturbed. Well-drained soils are also preferred, probably because they heat up more quickly than heavy, wet soils. However, lizards and adders are also common in blanket bog, where patches of dead purple moor grass provide an ideal dry natural 'straw' on which to bask.

Reptiles vary their activity patterns on both a daily and seasonal basis. From around October to March, they hibernate in frost-free holes and crevices underground. Spring is the best season to observe them, as they are often more sluggish than in summer and need to bask for longer because the air temperature is lower. Throughout their active period, and particularly in summer, the morning is the best time of day to see them. Although lizards are relatively tolerant of hot weather, adders tend to seek shade as the temperature rises from mid-morning onwards. The best conditions for seeing our reptiles are mild, overcast days with sunny spells, or those with interspersed sunshine and showers.

The viviparous lizard is the easiest to see, but is more likely to be heard first. Lizards make a characteristic rustle as they head for cover when disturbed, moving in short, fast bursts, and this is clearly reflected in the resulting sound. If you stop still as soon as you hear a lizard move, it will usually stop too and may then be easier to spot. In contrast, adders make a steady, continuous rustle as they disappear into cover. Lizards occur in suitable habitat over the whole of mainland Scotland and up to at least 900m. They feed on small invertebrates, notably spiders, which they actively hunt as soon as their body temperature is high enough. In some areas of lowland dry heath, lizards can occur at densities of one per 10–100m², but densities in upland Scot-

Rarely seen during the day, this palmate newt was photographed high in the Burn o' Vat, Deeside

land are probably considerably less than this. They are essentially ground dwellers, although a lizard may occasionally climb a little way up a drystane dyke or a slanting fence post to catch the last evening rays of sunshine.

Adders grow up to about 65cm, the biggest specimens being females. They are not aggressive snakes and will only attempt to bite if seriously provoked, that is, if touched or inadvertently trodden on, and they prefer to reserve their venom to kill their small mammal and lizard prey. The venom is quite potent and while bites are very rarely fatal to humans, hospital treatment is required. Areas of suitable habitat support roughly one adder per 1,000–10,000m², although densities may locally be much higher.

Amphibians

Amongst the three species of amphibian that occur in the mountainous areas of Scotland, the common frog is most likely to be encountered by the hillwalker. In lowland areas, outside the breeding season, frogs are rarely seen in the open during daylight. However, in many parts of the Highlands, it is not uncommon to see frogs active on hillsides even in bright sunshine, although overcast and damp days are preferred.

Alan Ross

If they can survive the many predators on the hill, toads may live for nine years

Frogs are known to occur at over 1,100m on Ben Macdui and seem remarkably unselective when it comes to sites for spawning; just about any piece of still, open water will do, even a puddle in an access track. Spawning dates vary across Britain, and in Scotland, this usually occurs in March. A typical clump of frog spawn comprises 2,000 eggs and, provided it is not exposed to particularly severe frost or excessive predation, 1,900 of the eggs might hatch. Of those, only between 20 and 100 will become froglets and, although life expectancy improves thereafter, only a handful of the original 2,000 will survive to breed at two to three years old.

In winter, frogs hibernate in the sediment at the bottom of pools and lochans. Here they can survive for months in a state of torpor, without breathing air, as dissolved oxygen is absorbed directly from the surrounding water through their highly permeable skin. It is unclear whether frogs hibernate at the highest altitudes in Scotland, but provided suitably deep pools are present, there is no reason to suppose that they cannot.

Toads can often be found on paths and tracks by torchlight, particularly on mild, damp nights, and take refuge by day under logs or rocks. Both frogs and toads are collectively known as 'puddocks' in Scots. This commonality is perhaps surprising in view of the association between toads and witchcraft, due no doubt to the hallucinogenic properties of their skin secretions, while frogs have no such deterrents against predators. In reality, the possession of a distasteful, toxic skin seems to be of limited benefit, and the remains of both amphibians can be found near breeding ponds following a visit by an otter. If they can survive the many predators on the hill, both frogs and toads can be surprisingly long-lived for such diminutive animals. Frogs may live for up to seven years in the wild, while toads may live to nine years.

The other widespread amphibian in the uplands is the palmate newt. Like toads, these secretive animals are unlikely to be encountered during the day unless a breeding pool is happened upon, and are most likely to be found under logs or stones.

Breeding sites are the best places to see amphibians, as both frogs and toads are then highly visible and audible, in large, lusty aggregations. Toad spawn is distinctive and quite different from that of frogs; the eggs are laid in long strings of spawn which are wrapped around the stems of pondweed. In contrast, newts lay individual eggs, which they attach to the leaves of pond plants, folding the leaf over the egg like a tortilla to conceal it.

Fish

Atlantic salmon and brown trout are the two fish species for which Scotland is renowned, and provide sport fishing in magnificent surroundings. Together with the arctic charr, these are the fish which are most likely to be present in the rivers and lochs of the Scottish uplands. All three belong to a group known as salmonids, which can be distinguished from other fish by the small, fleshy adipose fin situated between the dorsal and tail fins. Salmonids require cool, well-oxygenated water in the winter and spring for successful spawning and hatching of eggs, and in summer for growth and survival. Scotland's upland waters are therefore ideal, and many of them are designated as protected salmonid habitat under European environmental legislation (see map p265). Salmon and trout can often be seen keeping station above the gravel beds of shallow glides in streams where there is little surface turbulence, or rising to the surface of mountain lochs to feed on insects on a calm day.

Atlantic salmon, known as *Bradan*, or *Eog* by the Celts, migrate from the sea, generally from autumn through to early summer, to spawn in the gravelly beds of clean, fast-flowing rivers. Some fish reach considerable altitudes and in the Cairngorms, for example, they can be seen at 550m on the Avon and Feshie. Adult salmon are large, powerful fish, often reaching 40–100cm in length. During their spring and autumn migration runs they are often seen leaping spectacularly over natural cascades, known as 'loups', such as the Falls of Dochart in Perthshire and the Falls of Shin in Sutherland. Some insurmountable natural barriers have been removed in the past to allow passage to salmon, and in the mid-19th century the Duke of Atholl blew up a natural waterfall on the Tilt, 3km upstream of Blair Castle. Elsewhere, there has been extensive construction of fish ladders , as early as 1880 on the lower River Moriston and in the 1920s on the River Muick near Lochnagar, and there are now many such fish passes in use. Adult salmon do not feed in fresh waters and most die before they can return to the sea. Their offspring, known as 'parr', usually spend 2–3 years feeding and growing in fresh water before becoming 'smolts' and migrating to the sea. This process can often take twice as long in higher altitude rivers in the hills because their growth rates slow in the generally lower temperatures.

Brown trout live and spawn in similar habitats to salmon, but their natural range extends much higher and includes lochs and small streams down to only 50cm wide. The gaelic word for trout *breac*, meaning 'speckled', also applies to various species of the salmon family as well as being applied, with another gaelic word descriptor, to many other species of fish. So, for example, lamprey are known as 'easgann-bhreac'. Trout distribution is limited by natural physical barriers and the availability of suitable gravel beds for spawning, but they can otherwise be found throughout the upland rivers and lochs of Scotland. The highest recorded self-sustaining populations include those of the Dubh Lochainn of Beinn a' Bhuird, at 843m, and the Pools of Dee in the Lairig Ghru, at 810m, and they have also been reported from the Wells of Dee, at 1220m on Einich Cairn.

It is likely that Scotland's natural brown trout populations were derived from sea trout, which live in fresh waters, but migrate to the sea for one or more years before returning to spawn. Genetic typing has shown that the first trout to recolonise Scotland after the Ice Age came from southern Europe. Subsequent major advances and retreats of the ice-sheets, associated with changes in sea-level, have led to the isolation of some lochs and upper reaches of rivers along with these ancestral trout populations. Later, new stocks of trout, better adapted to northern waters, invaded all accessible rivers and lochs and displaced the previous populations. The ancient stock still occurs in many remote hill lochs and rivers above waterfalls, including the Crocach system of mountain lochs near Ben Hope. Ferox trout, 'dubh-breac', are spectacularly large, long-lived, fish-eating trout most often found in deep, glacial lakes such as Loch Rannoch and Loch Laggan. They are genetically distinct from normal trout and are thought likely by some fish ecologists to be a separate species. Ferox most often prey on arctic charr but will eat other trout if necessary. Loch Awe holds the rod-caught Ferox record at over 31lbs which is even heavier than the record sea trout in Scotland. The natural distribution of trout and salmon in the Scottish uplands has also been considerably influenced by man through stocking. In some cases, as at Loch Etchachan, this has been unsuccessful, but in many others, such as the Pools of Dee, the introduced populations have become established.

In hill lochs and streams trout diet mostly comprises of stoneflies, mayflies,

Fishing for brown trout in an upland loch. Water acidification has affected trout populations in some areas, but this should now decrease following international commitments to reduce emissions of sulphur and other pollutants

caddisflies and terrestrial insects but this food supply is often limited, contributing to their slow growth. At certain times though trout will gorge themselves on swarms of blackflies and midges. Loch trout populations usually migrate to inflowing streams to spawn, though gravelly loch shores are occasionally used.

The native arctic charr is a very attractive and colourful fish, the name being derived from the Gaelic tarr dearg, meaning 'red-bellied'. They prefer deeper, stiller water than other salmonids, and are usually found in lochs at medium to lower altitudes. Globally, the arctic charr is a threatened species and the Scottish Highlands are a stronghold. Charr vary greatly in size, feeding habits and preferred habitat, and different varieties have contrasting adaptations to suit their diets. Some open water charr that feed on tiny floating crustaceans have small heads and light jaws, whereas others that live close to the bottom of lochs, feeding on molluscs and other animals, have bigger heads and heavier jaws.

In Loch Rannoch, both these forms live as separate populations which do not interbreed. Recent genetic research suggests that they represent different historical colonisations. Although Scottish populations are largely natural, some artificial stocking has taken place, as well as accidental introductions. This has occurred, for example, in Loch Cruachan, where charr were introduced from Loch Awe through the pumped hydro-electric scheme. Unlike most loch-living brown trout, charr prefer to spawn on stony loch shores and rarely migrate into tributary streams for reproduction (though this occurs in Loch Insh on Speyside).

Eels, or Easg in Gaelic, can be found in lochs and rivers throughout Scotland, and reach moderate altitudes in the larger straths. Adult eels spawn in the

Caribbean and the juveniles drift to Europe on the Gulf Stream, a remarkable journey which culminates in the ascent of a river. Here, low temperatures mean that they are slow-growing, and they often reach extraordinary ages before migrating back to the sea. In Loch Pityoulish on Speyside, eels generally take 28 years to reach 50cm in length and in upper Deeside some eels take as long as 75 years to mature. In the past, eels were trapped and exported from Scotland for culinary purposes and fixed traps can still be seen on some lochs, with metal guidework on the lip of the outlet weir leading to large semi-submerged boxes. Numbers of eels have dropped dramatically throughout most of Europe in recent years. In Scotland there is evidence that numbers of juveniles, known as glass eels, are at only 2% of historic levels although, so far, our adult population remains relatively healthy. Possible reasons for this overall population crash include over-exploitation, pesticide pollutants, changes in ocean currents and an increase in exotic parasites.

A number of other fish can be found in upland rivers, though generally at lower altitudes. These occasionally include sticklebacks, which can tolerate salt water and colonised from the sea after the last glaciation. The small stoneloach, with distinctive sensory barbels on its upper jaw, can be found in southern hill areas. Pike have been introduced by man to many highland lochs and Loch Callater, near Braemar, is the highest water body in the British Isles with this fish species. Other introduced species include perch, American brook charr and the easily cultured rainbow trout, although this fish is not well adapted to the Scottish climate and self-sustaining populations are very rare. Minnows can also be found in some mountain lochs, often in great abundance. In most cases they have almost certainly been introduced by anglers as bait fish and there is increasing concern that they will compete with native brown trout for food, as has happened in Norway.

Two species of freshwater whitefish, vendace and powan, are very rare survivors from the ice-age. Natural populations of powan are restricted to seven locations in the British Isles and only two, Loch Eck and Loch Lomond, in Scotland. Conservation efforts have led to the transplanting of powan to Loch Sloy and the Carron Valley Reservoir, as pressures in Loch Lomond, including the invasive ruffe which eats powan eggs and fry, and reduced water quality, are a concern for long-term viability of these scarce fish. Vendace were extinct in Scotland until recently, but have been reintroduced to Loch Skene, above the Grey Mare's Tail near Moffat. This may have occurred just in time, since they may now be extinct in Bassenthwaite Lake, Cumbria, where this rare stock originated.

Fish in our uplands are now greatly influenced by various human activities. In the recent past acidification from sulphur-rich power station emissions caused significant damage, especially in the Southern Uplands and in the Cairngorms, but this has largely receded due to better controls. Some of the most significant impacts in our upland areas are due to artificial barriers to fish migration and there is considerable historical legacy of such structures with some 3000 km (16%) of rivers and 125 km² of lochs (13%) in Scotland being rendered impassible due to weirs and dams constructed for hydro-electric schemes or drinking water supply. Good examples include the entire Markie catchment, whose headwaters lie just east of Geal Charn in the Monadh Liath, and much of the upper Garry, draining southward from the Drumochter hills, which became impassable to migrating fish when hydro-electric catchment transfer schemes were built in the 1930s. Indeed, some 20 km of the Garry is dry in low flow conditions. Many recent small-scale

Dry rivers are a problem in some Scottish rivers due primarily to hydro-power schemes. These should reduce in the future as all such schemes are being licenced so that low flows are avoided

hydro-power schemes have had to comply with strict design regulations to ensure fish passage. These pressures are being slowly addressed under the European Water Framework Directive which requires that all waters should reach good ecological status, including healthy fish populations, by 2027 at latest.

Climate change is likely to be the major problem for the future. Salmonids are sensitive to rising temperatures and extreme floods and droughts, all of which are predicted for Scotland by a warming of the climate. Mitigation efforts are already focusing on widespread planting of bankside trees to keep rivers and streams cool and slow evaporation. There is also a concern that increasing carbon dioxide dissolving into freshwaters will lead to acidification all over again, especially in the uplands of Scotland, where relatively acid soils and waters are naturally widespread.

The fish in Scottish upland lochs and rivers provide important food for various predators, including otters and fish-eating birds such as mergansers and divers. Over the centuries these and other natural resources may also have helped to influence successive phases of human colonisation of the uplands. The legacy of these activities is considered in the next chapter.

Red deer (fiadh; daimh/stag, eilid/hind) *Cervus elaphus*

Red Deer are only likely to be confused with sika deer. Both species have similar antlers, but sika are slightly smaller, and during the summer, have white spots arranged roughly in rows; these are absent from the winter coat. The calves of both species are spotted. The rump in red deer is creamy coloured, but in sika is whiter with a dark outline. Fallow deer are similar in size to sika and also have white spots on the back, but the antlers of the bucks are palmate like those of a moose. They are restricted mainly to central Perthshire, the Trossachs, parts of Argyll and Dumfries & Galloway, with isolated populations elsewhere.

Derek McGinn

Prints are often seen and although those of red deer stags are larger, the prints of red, sika and fallow deer look similar. Forefeet are slightly larger than hindfeet, and the footprints of females are slightly smaller than those of males. Droppings are left in piles where the animals have been feeding and are often acorn-shaped and slightly pointed at one end; the opposite end is either rounded or has a slight depression. They are blackish and shiny when fresh, fading to a dull dark brown with age. In summer, the pellets are often softer and lump together. Red deer leave various signs in woodland including fraying and bark stripping and other traces include shed antlers and wallows.

Mark Wrightham

Red deer droppings are about 2–2.5cm long and 1.3–1.8cm wide. Roe deer droppings are smaller (about 1–1.4cm x 7–10mm) and of similar size to those of sheep and goats

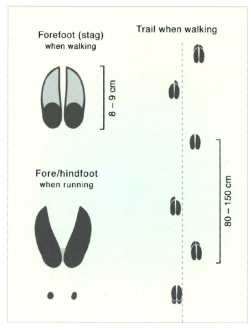

Forefoot (stag) when walking

Trail when walking

8 – 9 cm

Fore/hindfoot when running

80 – 150 cm

Red deer tracks; the footprints of sheep are about 5–6cm long with blunter tips, while those of cattle are broader and appear roughly circular

Roe deer (earb; boc/buck, maoiseach/doe)
Capreolus capreolus

Roe deer are readily distinguished from red and sika deer by their small size, short muzzles, more compact physique and the buck's short, pointed antlers. The white rump patch is particularly prominent when fleeing. Droppings resemble those of red deer and, in common with those of other deer, are often found in piles at feeding sites or as lines of pellets discharged when moving.

Alan Ross

All deer leave characteristic signs in woodland and remove the velvet from their newly-grown antlers by vigorously rubbing them against trees or bushes, causing branches and bark to be ripped off or left hanging. The velvet is usually eaten so is rarely found, but there may be hair amongst the debris. Roe deer do this throughout the spring and summer, as it serves a territorial function, while red deer only do this in late summer in preparation for the rut. Other woodland signs include browsing of shoots and bark-stripping, especially in winter, with teeth marks usually evident. In contrast to red deer, roe deer do not appear to use wallows. At their overnight 'lairs', roe scrape away surface vegetation to expose bare earth and unlike other deer, do not simply leave an area of flattened vegetation.

Andy Dugmore

Bark stripping by deer is a feeding sign. Deer fraying can sometimes appear similar, but usually includes damaged branches, due to the persistant rubbing of the antlers

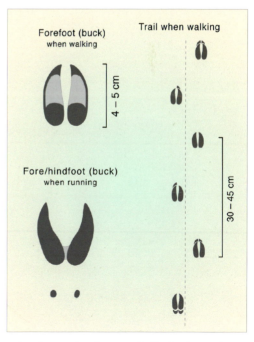

Forefoot (buck) when walking

Trail when walking

4 – 5 cm

Fore/hindfoot (buck) when running

30 – 45 cm

Roe deer tracks; these are similar in size to sheep and more pointed than those of young red deer, but distinction is often hard on appearance alone

225

Water vole (lamhallan)
Arvicola amphibius

Water voles are about the size of a rat and in Scotland many have black fur, rather than the brown which is usual for this species. They are active by day and can occasionally be glimpsed, but rarely away from a watercourse.

Water vole burrows are distinctive and are often the most obvious signs of their presence. They are typically 4–8cm across and may horizontally penetrate a peat bank or, if within two metres of a watercourse, go vertically down from the surface. If recently occupied, they are surrounded by characteristic grazed 'lawns'. 'Runs' may also be seen in the surrounding bankside vegetation, and are 5–9cm wide. Feeding stations with neatly chopped pieces of sedge, grass, rush or conspicuous white rush pith, typically 8–10cm long, can sometimes be found along the voles' runs and beside burns.

The droppings are cylindrical with blunt ends and vary from greenish, when fresh, to brown or black. They are usually deposited in small groups, often near burrow entrances, at various points alongside a burn, such as flat stones or areas of bare peat, or on prominent rocks within the watercourse itself.

Water vole droppings are about 7–10mm long x 3–4mm wide; those of field voles are smaller (about 6–7mm x 2–3mm) but of similar appearancee

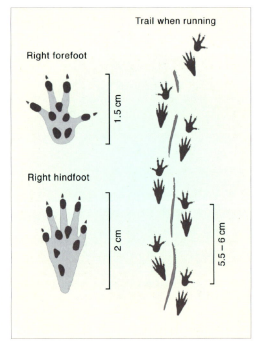

Water vole tracks. The footprints of field voles are somewhat smaller but the two are often difficult to distinguish in practice, for example in soft snow

Field vole (luch-fheoir)
Microtus agrestis

The greyish-brown field vole is markedly smaller than its aquatic relative, and is approximately mouse-sized with a short, inconspicuous tail. The similar-sized bank vole is more reddish in colour and has a longer tail.

Peter Lancashire

Field voles are active both by day and night, using regular runways that form tunnels as the vegetation grows over them. These are typically up to 5cm wide and are usually most visible in rough grassland, where they form complex, partially concealed networks, punctuated by occasional roughly circular entrances to underground burrow systems. In the spring, winter runs made under the snow become exposed and can be very obvious. The females construct roughly spherical nests of finely shredded grasses for breeding, which are often located at the base of grass tussocks. Field vole droppings are deposited along runways, and are greenish oval pellets 6–7 x 2–3mm in size, which are of similar appearance to those of water voles.

In common with water voles, field voles also leave chopped fragments of vegetation at associated feeding sites.

The signs of these two species bear many similarities, but can often be separated on the basis of size, although caution is needed here, as an overlap exists and field voles may also be found near water.

Nick Picozzi

A field vole feeding station; the chopped fragments are typically around 4cm long; less than half the length of those left by water voles

Nick Picozzi

A field vole run. These are much more widespread than those of water voles and can be seen well away from the nearest watercourse

Mountain hare (maigheach-gheal) *Lepus timidus*

Mountain hares are visibly smaller than brown hares, and are further distinguished by their much greyer colour in summer, and by their white winter coats. Brown hares are also unlikely to be found above 400m. Mountain hares leave a variety of easy to identify signs. The hares' regularly used paths are often clearly visible through the heather, and usually run up/down hill corresponding with the hares' instinctive escape response. Hares do not normally burrow, but create a partially concealed scrape under the heather or in the snow, where they crouch with their hind quarters inwards. Their droppings are usually greyish-green and composed of course fragments of vegetation, and are commonly deposited in groups on their runs. Prints are also frequently seen in snowy conditions.

David Whitaker

Hares frequently browse woody vegetation, notably including tree seedlings. In common with rabbits, their sharp incisors usually bite off stems and twigs cleanly and obliquely. The cut ends appear quite different from those produced by deer, which lack upper jaw incisors and browse with a partial tearing action; stems bitten off by deer are usually uneven and frayed, at least at one side.

Rob Raynor

Mountain hare droppings are roughly spherical, in contrast to those of deer, and are about 1.5-2cm across; larger than those of rabbits

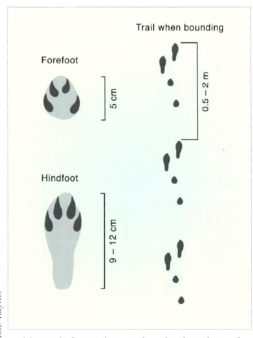

Mountain hare prints are broader than those of brown hare and may sometimes be distinguished by altitude, while rabbit tracks are considerably smaller. Typical bound is 1m

Fox (mhadaidh) *Vulpes vulpes*

Foxes are unmistakable if seen on the open hill, but more often betray their presence indirectly through their footprints or droppings, which are known as scats. Fox footprints can easily be confused with those of similar-sized dogs as both have four toe pads and show obvious claw marks, but fox pads are smaller and not as close together. Furthermore, the two central toe pads are positioned further forward, leaving a clear gap between their rear mar-

David Whitaker

gins and the front margin of the larger pad. Overall a fox's footprint is longer and more pointed at the front than a dog's and can appear almost diamond-shaped.

The pungent scats vary enormously in colour according to diet, but are often greyish, and can be white if old and a lot of bones have been consumed. They usually contain fur, feathers and bone fragments, but may also include the remains of berries and the hard, shiny parts of insects. Foxes use their scats as territorial markers and deposit them in prominent locations such as grass tussocks, cairns, narrow ridges or forestry tracks. Foxes are one of the few animals that humans can detect immediately from their 'foxy' or sour sharp scent, which results from urine marking.

Alan Ross

A fox scat; these are typically about 2cm in diameter, whereas pine marten scats are usually narrower and more twisted

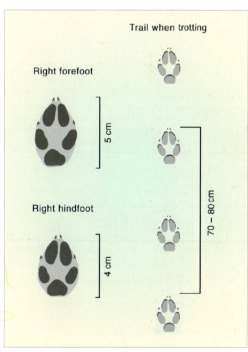

Trail when trotting

Right forefoot

5 cm

Right hindfoot

4 cm

70 – 80 cm

Fox tracks. The trail is typically more neat, regular and purposeful than that of a dog

Otter (dobhran) *Lutra lutra*

Otters are rarely seen, except on coasts, and the field signs most likely to be encountered on the hill, almost invariably near water, are the droppings (known as spraints) and, less often, footprints and feeding remains. The spraints are usually black and tarry when fresh, and are full of small fish bones. They have a distinctive, not unpleasant smell, sometimes likened to jasmin tea! In moorland

David Whitaker

areas, spraints can sometimes be found in dark recesses under overhanging heathery river banks. Sprainting sites can be used for many years and the constant input of nitrogen at such points often results in the formation of bright green grassy mounds which, especially in peatland areas on the west coast, contrast strikingly with the surrounding vegetation.

Footprints can occasionally be found in soft sediment at the water's edge. Like their relatives (such as martens and stoats), otters often adopt a bounding or jumping gait, leaving groups of footprints which are irregularly spaced and frequently lack any obvious pattern. Feeding remains are particularly conspicuous when otters have preyed on breeding amphibians. Otter dens, known as holts, are usually located in natural cavities under tree roots or amongst piles of large boulders and are often marked with spraints. Otters also lie-up above ground, where sufficient cover exists.

Alan Ross

Otter spraints are usually deposited at prominent points along watercourses, such as large in-stream boulders, confluences or bankside tussocks

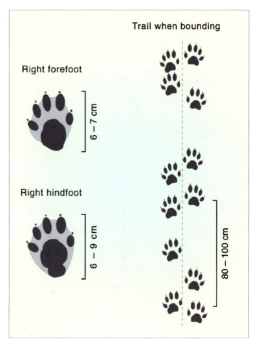

Trail when bounding

Right forefoot

6 – 7 cm

Right hindfoot

6 – 9 cm

80 – 100 cm

Otter tracks appear very round overall and of similar dimensions to those of a medium-sized dog, but with the toes splayed out widely. They are often very irregular in pattern

Pine marten (taghan) *Martes martes*

Rarely seen, the agile pine marten superficially resembles a dark, cat-sized weasel, but with a longer, more bushy tail. The most obvious field signs are the droppings (known as scats), which are typically twisted and taper to a fine tip at one end. They are usually blackish and full of fur, feathers, small bone fragments or, in late summer and autumn, blaeberries and rowan berries. They possess a distinctive musky aroma that is not unpleasant, unlike the droppings of mink or polecat. Older scats from animals that have consumed a lot of feathers are often grey with a clay-like texture. Scats are usually deposited in very prominent locations, ranging from the middle of forestry tracks to the crests of narrow ridges.

David Whitaker

Marten tracks are much less likely to be found except in good snow cover and, while clear footprints may show all five pads and claws, in common with its relatives only four are often visible. The marten's characteristic bounding gait is reflected in its tracks which, in snow, are often 'triple', where one of the hindfeet is placed on top of one of the fore prints, or 'paired' where both hind feet cover the fore prints.

Rob Raynor

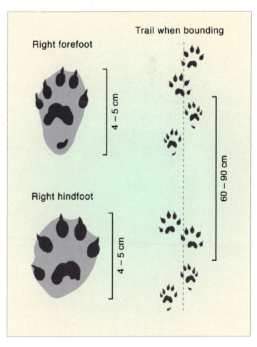

Right forefoot

Trail when bounding

4 – 5 cm

Right hindfoot

4 – 5 cm

60 – 90 cm

A pine marten scat; these are typically about 1.2cm in diameter and are therefore usually narrower than fox scats

Pine marten can adopt similar gaits to those of otters, but their prints are smaller. The trails of both species are highly irregular

Stoat (neas)
Mustela erminea

For much of the year, the stoat's fur is a rich chestnut brown above, with white on the underside and a distinctive black tip to the tail. The smaller weasel looks very similar, but lacks the black tip. However, during the winter months in more northerly latitudes, most stoats moult to a white coat ('ermine'), whilst retaining the black tail tip. They are then unmistak-

David Whitaker

able, as the stoat is the only British carnivore to do this. Ermine is used to decorate the robes of peers of the realm, the black spots on each robe being the ends of the tails. Animals from the south still moult to a winter coat but do not change colour and in Britain, there is a very broad transition zone where varying degrees of partial whitening can be seen.

Stoat scats are rarely found except by a den site, which is a small burrow or cavity amongst rocks. They are blackish, twisted and elongated, in common with those of other members of the weasel family, and about 5cm long by 5mm thick, containing fur, feathers and bone fragments. The footprints are also rarely found.

Wildcat (cat-fiadhaich)
Felix silvestris

Classic wildcat features include a blunt, relatively thick tail with a black tip, a lack of spots on the rump, a dark stripe along the ridge of the back (which does not extend onto the tail) and non-white paws. The available evidence suggests that most cats with this combination of features belong to a group of wild-living cats that are distinct from domestic tabbies.

Wildcat field signs are, for practical purposes, almost impossible to distinguish from those of other similar-sized domestic or feral cats. All cat footprints share three key characteristics: each print has only four toe prints; there is no sign of any claw marks (because the cat has retracted its claws); and the footprints fall more or less

Kerry Kilshaw/WildCRU

in a straight line in front of one another when walking. Fox and marten tracks often show some of these characteristics, but not all three. Cat droppings are usually about 6-8cm long and 1-1.5cm thick, and those of wildcats usually contain fur and bone fragments. Domestic cats generally bury their scats, but wildcats only do this within their own territory and deposit them conspicuously on territorial boundaries, on features such as tree stumps.

Common frog (losgann)
Rana temporaria

Frogs can grow up to 11cm long but are usually smaller, and females are larger than males. They are very variable in colour, being typically brown with black markings, but can also be yellowish, beige, greenish or reddish. Red frogs seem more common in the Western Highlands, which may be associated with the abundance of acidic peat. Breeding males have dark nuptial pads on their thumbs for gripping the female prior to spawning.

Tom Prentice

Frogs are readily distinguished from toads by their smooth, moist skin; toad skin is warty and relatively dry. Toads are also less variable in colour, and are typically mid-brown on the back, sometimes with a few small dark spots. Frogs readily jump and can move quite quickly, while toads are more sluggish, preferring to crawl.

Apart from their spawn, frogs leave few visible field signs except as the feeding remains of other predators. Otters usually dismember frogs and toads, eating only the hind limbs. Sometimes the skin of the hind limbs is left inverted or 'degloved', while still attached to the torso but with the limbs removed. Predators may also leave the oviducts, which resemble whitish lumps of slime.

Viviparous lizard (nathair chasach)
Zootoca vivipara

Viviparous lizards grow to around 15cm, more than half of which is tail. They are typically brown, and females often have dark sides and a dark stripe down the spine, while the males tend to be more uniform. The

Rob Raynor

young are almost black, with no obvious markings, and measure about 4.5cm at birth.

Although lizards superficially resemble newts, there are several obvious physical and behavioural differences. Adult lizards are covered in tiny granular scales giving them a slightly 'rougher' appearance, and are considerably larger than the palmate newt (8cm), the only newt likely to be encountered in the Scottish hills. Lizards are usually seen in relatively dry places, basking in the sun, while newts avoid direct sunlight and prefer damp places or water during the breeding season. Lizards move quickly on warm days, but newts are slow and laborious on land.

The sharp-eyed may notice tiny lizard droppings on rocks or logs in prominent sunny locations. These comprise the undigested parts of insects and other invertebrates. They are usually dark or blackish with a white tip, resembling small bird droppings, but tend to be more solid and sausage-shaped.

Human Traces

Andy Dugmore and Ian Ralston

Human traces may be obvious ruins like this former estate building beneath Sgurr na Ciche, Knoydart, or they may be much more subtle

Introduction

When venturing into the hills, it is easy to feel that they represent a more wild and pristine world. Key boundaries are crossed. There are no more cultivated fields, and few roads or houses, and the landscapes and vegetation are not ordered or regimented. In a very real sense, the hills are more natural and freer places. However, human traces still abound, including the occasional isolated lodge or bothy, rough gravel roads and tracks and the paths made by other hillwalkers. Indeed, taking the long view, the reach of human impact has been surprisingly extensive, affecting virtually all the glens and lower slopes and extending, in some degree, to most summits.

The signs of successive phases of human activity are overprinted on one another in the present-day hill landscape. The names of summits and corries sometimes suggest past use, although their origin is often hard to discern through the mists of time. Human activity is also widely recorded in upland vegetation and wildlife, which are described in Chapters 4-7. These signs are accompanied by much less extensive direct traces in the form of surviving physical structures that are still visible. Upstanding remains may become buried by peat accumulation, or attract later modification and reuse. Some structures, long since abandoned, have survived by chance; others are deliberate monuments built to last. The emphasis here is on a selection of these structures, including older, more subtle features and those of historical interest, as recent signs of human activity are generally obvious and need little description.

Identifying older human traces is not always straightforward, not least because of general degradation through time. Often, all that remains are minor irregularities in the ground surface, which can be picked out by low-angled winter sunlight, frost or light snow. Elusive features can also be highlighted by changes in the vegetation, often including shifts from dwarf shrub heath to richer grassland due to various combinations of improved drainage, soil enrichment and grazing. More recent structures are often reduced to a few courses of stone work surrounded by tumble, although some abandoned shielings may have virtually complete external walls.

The map may help, although marked features can vary greatly in their degree of preservation. The symbols used on OS maps still distinguish between 'antiquities' that are Roman and non-Roman, and the latter are generally indicated by Gothic script. This guide can, however, be misleading and Iron Age, Bronze Age and even Neolithic cairns, for example, may be labelled in normal script. The mapping of archaeological sites is also influenced by other cartographic factors, and many features considered less important will be omitted from 1:50,000 maps. In the case of cairns, for example, major burial monuments are much more likely to appear on the map than lesser heaps of stone. Coverage can be patchy for other reasons, too, even within a single glen, as the surviving field archaeology of some areas has been recorded in greater detail than others, and because of land use changes, such as afforestation, since the map was made. The OS map, of course, can only provide a general guide, and more detailed information on specific areas can be obtained through local histories, regional museums and specialist publications, as well as from online resources such as the *Canmore* database (see further reading).

The visible traces of past human activity frequently represent a long history of use, abandonment and re-use. In the hills near Peebles, for example, prehistoric settlements including house platforms and their stonework have been reshaped as sheep pens, while on the Strone, north-east of Balmoral, the depressions and walls of ancient round houses have been modified to form shooting butts. When searching for a perfect lunch spot, our footsteps may be drawn to that convenient windbreak or small patch of grass in a sea of heather. It is worth taking a second look, as this may be the site of an ancient building, a long-forgotten monument or even a grave. Building a casual cairn may be altering an ancient site, so it is worth dwelling on that famous homily to 'take nothing but photographs and leave nothing but footprints'; and to leave stones unturned.

The boundary between cultivated land and the open hill has been very fluid through time, as settlement has ebbed and flowed against the mountain slopes, and it is interesting to consider how far the physical environment has determined these limits. The environment clearly creates constraints, and without extreme intervention, fruit trees will not grow on the Cairngorm plateau. But these limitations do not explain all of the changes that have taken place. To take a modern illustration, the success or failure of present-day upland farms has comparatively little to do with the climate and is more directly influenced by non-environmental factors such as rural policy, the price of wool, the cost of fuel, the availability of labour and the health of the tourism industry. Another modern land use, downhill skiing, expanded greatly during the late 20th century, despite a general trend towards milder winters, because of increasing leisure and personal mobility and, in some instances, public subsidy. Although the environment provides general constraints, social, cultural, economic and political factors can therefore strongly influence upland land use, and probably also helped to determine whether settlement or other human activities extended into or retreated from the mountains in the distant past.

Our picture of past settlement in the hills is far from complete. Much evidence has been destroyed and of that existing today, only a small proportion has been thoroughly investigated. In general, since sites at lower altitudes are most often threatened by destruction through new development, much more archaeological effort has been devoted to them. We now know a great deal about the past occupants of the Scottish mountains, but there is still much to learn, especially about the interactions of past cultures with the environment and their role in shaping the landscape of today. Observant hillwalkers could contribute to this process, and need only learn to recognise the clues that survive in the landscape.

Historical background

The land that is now Scotland was first colonised by hunter-gatherers of the Upper Palaeolithic during a warmer stage late in the last glacial period about 15,000 years ago. Traces of people from this period remain very rare, but soon after deglaciation, much more evidence of hunter-gatherer-fisher groups has been recorded. The term 'Mesolithic' is generally used to describe the period from this early colonisation until the introduction of agriculture, called the 'Neolithic'. Archaeological evidence, such as tools from Mar Lodge Estate in the central Cairngorms, shows that Mesolithic people ventured into the uplands from these early times, and both followed the animals which roamed across hill country and exploited the upland vegetation.

The first known Neolithic sites in Scotland, in the eastern lowlands and Orkney, date from about 6,000 years ago, although 'Neolithic' agriculture and 'Mesolithic' hunting and gathering probably co-existed for some time in different parts of the landscape. Early Neolithic farming communities also used the uplands for subsistence, and exploited particular rock resources to make tools, such as those found at Creag na Caillich above Killin, at the west end of the Tarmachan Ridge. There may also have been all sorts of non-utilitarian reasons, now difficult to guess, that drew ancient people to such high-altitude places. We do know that Neolithic burial monuments were some of the first major artificial features in Scotland's upland landscapes. There are also some major early prehistoric earth- or timber-built structures in the uplands, including a long-known major enclosed site at Blackshouse Burn near Thankerton in Lanarkshire, and the newly-discovered ends of an upland cursus monument (like that near Stonehenge) at Broomy Law in the same county.

We have evidence of the use of metals from well before 4,000 years ago, initially in a copper-using phase now called the Chalcolithic. The 'Bronze Age' is a convenient shorthand to describe the period from about 4,200 to 2,800 years ago, and is based on the dating of bronze tools and objects such as the so-called 'Migdale hoard' from southern Sutherland. During the latter part of this period, around 3,500 – 2,800 years ago, settlements spread into upland areas in greater numbers than at any earlier time, reaching altitudes of about 400m, and beyond the limits of today's farm buildings. The traces of these prehistoric cultures can be seen in field systems, the subdued remains of circular buildings and slighter burial monuments usually less than 5m in diameter, such as 'kerb cairns' which have an outer kerb of disproportionately large stones.

Multiple lines of defence isolate Cademuir hillfort, Peeblesshire, to the right. Upright stones set into the gully slope were to disrupt a frontal assault

It is not clear why people moved into the uplands at this time, and this trend was set against a backdrop of generally deteriorating climatic conditions. Woodland was already in retreat due to natural processes, but the availability of this resource could have helped to encourage settlement further into the hills. The clearance of woodland would also have made relatively fertile soils available for agriculture, at least in the short term. It is therefore possible that the expansion and subsequent contraction of the settlement frontier were driven by the exploitation and depletion of natural resources. Other potential influences include economic innovation, population growth, migration or warfare. Some of these processes leave physical traces such as weapons or fortifications, but others may leave no lasting evidence. Whatever the reason, it seems likely that the lower slopes of at least some hills were more densely settled during this period than at many other times in Scotland's past.

The 'Iron Age' began in Scotland some 2,800 years ago, with the first traces of iron working, and was also marked by the appearance of enclosed settlements, ranging in scale from individual stockaded farms to major hillforts, such as that on Tap o' Noth, Aberdeenshire. In England, the Iron Age ended with the Roman invasion of 43 AD, which set wholesale social and economic changes in motion. In Scotland, Roman influences were far more limited and variable, and were generally confined to the south and the lowlands. In the Highlands, the Iron Age effectively merged into the early historic period in around 500 AD.

A complex political and cultural mix existed during the 1st millennium AD, and the Picts north of the central lowlands shared what is now Scotland with the Britons of Clydesdale in the south-west, and the Gododdin in the south-east. The Scots are first mentioned in Argyll around 500 AD, although they may have been present there long beforehand, and in the mid 9th century, unification of the Picts and the Scots formed the kingdom of Alba. This unification may have been stimulated in part by Norse incursions, as Viking raiders sacked the Columban monastery of Iona in 795 AD, and by 850 AD significant numbers of Scandinavians had settled in northern and western Scotland. Over the first three centuries of the 2nd millennium AD, normally known as the early Middle Ages, the Scots of Alba, the Angles of Lothian, the Britons of Strathclyde, the Vikings in the west and the Normans were brought together to form the Kingdom of the Scots. This process culminated in the Wars of Independence, starting in 1286 AD.

Despite frequent social and political changes, there were some continuing themes in human use of the uplands over this great sweep of time. Hunting was probably always important, but its status gradually changed from a practical necessity, through a quest for variation in the diet, to a testing pursuit for young men preparing for war, and eventually to a sport and prestige activity. Agriculture was also widespread. Prior to the Clearances, this was commonly based on the system of seasonal livestock movement known as transhumance, in which animals were moved uphill to summer grazings. These historic phases are recorded by various archaeological remains, and 'shieling' settlements associated with transhumance are among the most common built traces in the hills.

After the Union of 1707, written records relating to the uplands become more frequent, not least as a result of the military survey and records of estate seizures following the 1745 Jacobite uprising. The density of settlement in the glens was once again comparatively high, but by the mid-18th century, the draw of urban centres and emigration to North America had begun a depopulation of the Highlands. This process was compounded by the Clearances that began in 1785, as people were driven out of the uplands to make way for sheep, and which intensified in 1812 with the depopulation of Strathnaver by the Duke of Sutherland. Across most of the Highlands, this phase was rapidly succeeded by the development of large estates managed for deer stalking or grouse shooting, and large scale sheep farming became concentrated in the more productive southern hills. The industrial revolution provided the mass produced wire and metal for fences that made their appearance in the uplands, dividing and enclosing extensive tracts of land in a new way. With the growth of afforestation, the conservation movement and outdoor recreation during the 20th century, plus more localised changes due to electricity generation from water power and wind, and the development of telecommunications, the present-day pattern of upland land use was established.

Treasures lost and found

The former presence of people can be marked by objects which they made, left and lost in the hills. The earliest evidence consists of scatters of flint debris, or individual flint items such as arrowheads. The essential feature for locating these is disturbed ground and many finds are made by chance alongside paths, as on Mar Lodge estate, or around the eroding margins of rivers and lochs. One of the earliest and most surprising is a bone harpoon head of hunter-gatherer type, reputedly from Strath Avon in the eastern Cairngorms, which suggests that Mesolithic people were already venturing into the heart of mountain country.

Occasional stone axes have also been found well into the uplands, suggesting the activities of Neolithic colonists making inroads into the woodland cover. Some fine examples seem, however, to have been deliberately deposited in the ground, for reasons that we can only guess. Such 'hoarding' continues into the Bronze Age, and may have been intended to ward off the retaliation of the gods, or to demonstrate the status of the giver by putting precious items out of reach.

These were sometimes left in places where walkers or climbers may come across them. A pair of hardly-used bronze flat axes was placed in scree at the Pass of Ballater some 4,000 years ago, and a remarkable hoard of such items was recovered from Dal na Caraidh, just at the foot of Ben Nevis. Much later in the Bronze Age, a hoard of bronze fitments was placed under a large boulder in scree at Horsehope Craig, above the Manor Valley in Peeblesshire. Some of these were intended for a wagon, one of the earliest to be archaeologically attested in Scotland, although such vehicles were not equipped with brakes and would have been liabilities in this sort of terrain. A remarkable and 'international' Iron Age hoard has been found in the same county, in moorland below the summit of Shaw Hill, Netherurd, Peeblesshire. This consisted of the gilded and elaborately-decorated terminal of a neckring or 'torc', three other torcs of twisted gold wire, and some 40 gold coins from north-east France; the association of coins and torcs is also known from several continental hoards.

In some cases, it is extremely hard to envisage how items ended up at the places concerned, although there is no reason to doubt that they are

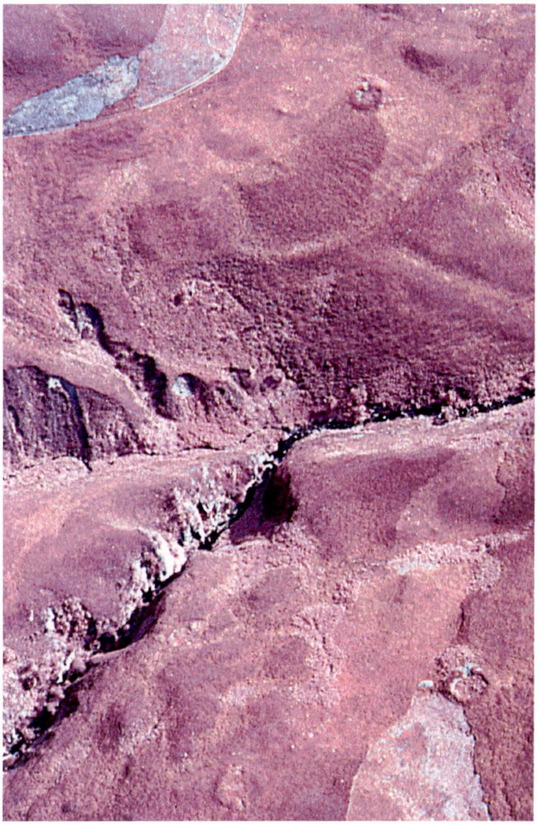

Ian Ralston

Ancient traces of upland settlement are often subtle and scattered. This oblique aerial photograph in infrared shows round houses (bottom right and centre, and top right) in the Strath of Kildonan, north-west of Helmsdale, Sutherland. Stripes formed by past cultivation can be seen below the round house top right

genuine ancient deposits. An Iron Age stone cup or lamp, believed to be a rustic, bigger and cruder version of Roman pottery oil lamps, was found high on Schiehallion, which was the sacred mountain of the Caledonians, a tribe of the Roman period. But who took the lamp up there and why? And are there more such lamps lying unrecognised on Scotland's mountains? Some of the modern artifacts lost in the hills have also acquired historical interest and have a story to tell. Odd items of old ski gear have been found in the peat on the slopes of Beinn Ghlas, where competitive Scottish skiing began in the 1930s.

Built traces

These are perhaps the most obvious and enduring signs of human activity, and can take a wide variety of forms.

Settlements

In general sites of ancient settlement are found in glens and on lower slopes, and can be marked on the OS map as *settlements, hut circles* or *enclosures*. 'Hut circles' or 'round houses' occur across much of upland Scotland at altitudes of up to 400m and on occasion higher, and sometimes correspond to quite complex buildings. In the Bronze Age, these settlements were generally open, without an enclosing ditch, stockade or wall. 'Enclosures', or enclosed settlements, reflect an overlapping phase of construction extending from about 2,800 years ago until early historic or medieval times, and were surrounded by a ditch, bank, wall or palisade with one or more entrances. More recent sites of this type may be indicated as townships, denoting the remains of a group of buildings which may or may not have been simultaneously occupied.

Round houses were variously built of stone or more ephemeral materials such as turf, and the latter may long since have become indistinguishable in the landscape. In some upland areas, notably the Border hills, it is still possible to recognise the remains of former timber round houses by slight irregularities in the ground surface, particularly where this consists of a closely-grazed 'sheepscape'. These were formed by the parts of the structures that were set into the ground, such as their outer plank-built walls, and are well seen, for example, in the Meldon Hills and Manor Valley of Peeblesshire. In such areas, timber houses were sometimes also built on levelled platforms, which can be seen scarped into the hillsides. Round houses which included more stone tend to be better preserved, and are ubiquitous through the glens and lower slopes of the Scottish hills, especially north of the Central Belt. These are the standard archaeologically-recognisable houses of many areas during the Bronze and Iron Ages.

The earliest rectangular buildings in the Scottish uplands generally date from no more than about 1,400 years ago. A distinctive series of broadly rectilinear turf- and stone-footed longhouses has been recognised in the Perthshire uplands, including the moors above Pitcarmick, in Strath Ardle. These byre-houses, defined in part by their slightly rounded ends, occur in much the same locations as stone-walled round houses, and radiocarbon dates indicate that they were built in the last centuries of the first millennium AD, towards the end of the Pictish period. In the far north, and along the Atlantic seaboard, are Norse houses, which were also generally rectangular, with lower walls of dry-stone construction, although grander halls could also be bow-sided. The general area of Norse influence included mountainous islands like Jura, Arran and Skye, and often extended to the landward ends of the western sea-lochs (including the Fort William area).

During the last 1,000 years, upland architecture has been predominantly rectangular, and surviving remains are widespread in rough grassland or heather moorland. As with round houses, structures built largely of turf may have become unrecognisable through decay. Sometimes the more prominent remains might not have been the actual dwelling places, as byres may have been built from stone and houses built from turf, which would have been warmer. In Eskdale, Dumfriesshire, rectilinear buildings were set onto prepared platforms cut into the slope, and these, rather than the buildings themselves, are conspicuous today. The footings of whole fermtouns, or grouped farming settlements, survive in some upland areas. A well-laid out example datable to around the 17th century, surrounding a fortified farmhouse or bastle house, survives at Glenlochar in Clydesdale. Not all structures set in farmed upland landscapes were necessarily roofed and buchts, as on Bucht Knowe in Lanarkshire, were simply walled enclosures where sheep were penned for milking or shearing.

A remarkable archaeological site crowns the 580m summit of Ben Griam Beg,

Part of an abandoned settlement in Glen Lui, Cairngorms. The improved land of the valley floor field systems still forms grassy areas beyond the stone dyke that crosses the picture left to right

overlooking the wild, rolling moorland of Sutherland where Strath Halladale meets the Strath of Kildonan. Described on a number of occasions and mapped once, the series of archaeological sites on this isolated block of sandstone and conglomerate is the highest set of coherent traces of early human settlement yet found in Scotland. It is likely that the aspect of its southern slopes, combined with the relatively rich soils derived from these rocks, enabled settlement here, perhaps at a time of more favourable climate. In the absence of excavation, however, the site is undated. All the known archaeological evidence is confined to the western peak, consisting of a series of stone-walled enclosures looping downhill from the summit, a detached dyke running for several hundred metres along the contour just below 500m, and six sets of rather ragged stone-walled plots and likely house sites which extend down the steep southern and western slopes of the Ben to about 420m. It is likely that these remains, which include traces of both rectangular and round buildings, reflect several periods of activity, although this has not been confirmed. Aside from the expansive outward views, the visitor is rewarded by very clear archaeological traces, for much of this exposed northerly site is above the limit for heather growth and is not masked by vegetation, although some stretches of walling have been distorted by frost action and solifluction. Elsewhere, it is likely that further structures are buried below deep peat, accounting for the incomplete pattern of some of the evidence on this remarkable hilltop.

A recurrent feature of the Scottish uplands, including the main island ranges, is the occurrence of shieling settlements, originally made up of stone- and turf-walled huts. These buildings are relics of transhumance, in which cattle, goats and other livestock were moved to higher pastures in summer, with numbers of people (usually the younger and more active) accompanying them. This tradition is hinted at in mountain names which include buachaille (herdsman) or airigh (shieling), such as Beinn Airigh Charr. The walk up to the summer quarters was known as the imrich, and is commemorated, for example, by the Allt na h-Imrich below Toll Creagach in Glen Affric.

These summer residences were not merely bunkhouses, and more elaborate buildings may have been subdivided, with part used for making and storing dairy produce, especially cheeses. Other important activities included the spinning of wool, and on occasion the remains of an illicit whisky still may be found discretely set amongst the shieling remains, as at Carn Bhithir on Mar Lodge estate. These buildings are also frequently accompanied by traces of enclosures for livestock. Many have settings enjoying wide outlooks, including those beside the headwaters of the burns above Ardcharnich on the east side of Loch Broom. They generally occur below 500m, but are sometimes found at high altitude, and a cluster of shielings reaches up to 670m below Meall Greigh, at the head of the Lawers Burn in Perthshire. Here archaeologists from Glasgow University have produced evidence for a dairy and for use of the site in the 16th and 17th centuries, based on discarded pottery. The highest known shielings in the Highlands occur at 800m on the southern side of the Monadh Liath.

Shielings normally occur singly or in small clusters, but bigger groups are known, and about 40 have been recognised at the foot of Garbh-bheinn on Skye. Where remains of isolated buildings lack permanent field systems they are likely to be shielings but, because of the fluctuating use of the uplands, abandoned farms may subsequently have become shielings. As a result, shielings are sometimes mixed with the remains of other more permanent-looking rectilinear buildings from the medieval period or later, indicating areas once permanently inhabited, but subsequently depopulated and only occupied seasonally. Since shielings usually represent the most recent intensive settlement of the locations they occupy, they often survive in relatively good condition.

The Clearances ushered in a new generation of buildings in the hills, which were constructed during the 19th and early 20th centuries to support the newly dominant land uses of sheep farming and deer stalking. Small cottages were frequently built, often in very remote locations, to provide permanent accommodation for shepherds, stalkers or other estate staff. These small, one storey buildings often had just two rooms, an outer room (or but) and an inner room (or ben). In turn, most of these structures have also passed into disuse, owing to a combination of factors including the use of vehicles to access remote areas, and changed social expectations which have ushered the 'but and ben' lifestyle into history. These buildings now remain as more substantial ruins, often wholly or partially roofed, with gable-end chimneys, and have sometimes been renovated for use as bothies. Comparatively recent rectangular buildings are often superimposed on earlier sites with circular ones, and the traces of decayed walling the walker sees can result from episodes of occupation separated by hundreds if not thousands of years; the triumph, on the grand scale, of hope over experience.

Where odd fragments of artificial structures exist, the building materials may give a clue as to their antiquity, although some relatively recent structures may have been built to look old, or reuse very old materials. From the Middle Ages to the 19th century, construction used rather weak and erodible lime mortar. In the 19th century, concrete (where an aggregate of sand, gravel or crushed stone is bonded together with cement) was used more widely, until by the 20th century it had become a ubiquitous building material.

Field systems

In places that have seen little recent use, early settlements can be surrounded by

Traces of former cultivated field systems can be seen on the southern flanks of Dunsyre Hill in the Pentlands, on higher, steeper slopes beyond the current limits of enclosed farmland

the remains of quite complex agricultural landscapes. For obvious reasons, these usually occur on relatively gentle gradients, and are marked by field boundaries defined by rickles of stone (the remains of walls), or pock-marked with low heaps of stone which have been cleared from the tilled land. These may be accompanied by small plots of richer grassland, trackways or cultivation terraces. Not all of these types of remains necessarily occur together, and many are enduring types of feature which are rather difficult to date with any precision.

These sites are sometimes indicated as *field systems* on OS maps, and can occur well above the present limit of enclosed farmland. The oldest traces of this kind belong to the Neolithic period, and include a drystane dyke buried below peat on Hill of Shurton, in Shetland. There are signs of similar activity to sub-divide upland landscapes during most periods thereafter, variously reflecting periods of more favourable climate, transhumance, unbridled optimism or desperation. Indeed, older sites often include visible signs of more recent activity, including more substantial field dykes, areas of later cultivation and rectangular buildings placed within them.

The most obvious traces of cultivation consist of alternating furrows and raised strips or ridges, which occur at a variety of scales. The narrowest of these are referred to as 'narrow rig' and 'lazybeds', and were dug with hand-tools. Narrow rig is particularly associated with the Border Hills, where associations with settlement sites suggest that some narrow rig cultivation may date to the Iron Age; good examples of such traces can be identified to over 300m in the Cheviots. Lazybeds or feannagan, by contrast, are characteristic of Highland Scotland, with a variant type occurring in the south-west of the country. Sometimes now encroached on by the spread of peat, such systems can still be very visible features of some moorland areas, such as on Harris. Steep hillsides were sometimes cultivated by creating artificial terracing, which continues to be used, for example, in the Himalaya, and some Scottish examples may date back to the pre-Roman Iron

Age. The best-preserved such system in Scotland occurs near Romanno Bridge in Peeblesshire, but the best-known is probably the now rather eroded set on the slopes of Arthur's Seat, in Holyrood Park in Edinburgh.

By far the most extensive signs of early cultivation, however, are of a type referred to as broad-rig, which was carried out using ploughs pulled by cattle and occurs in a variety of forms. This style of strip cultivation developed from the medieval period, apparently spreading northwards, and continued in less elaborate form on more marginal land into the 18th and locally the 19th centuries. All of these systems provided strips of better-drained ground on which cultivation could take place, and have since been superseded by the use of buried drains, or 'underdraining', which was developed during Victorian times.

Some related features can be seen in wilder places that may never have been intensively managed. Linear drains, or 'grips', have been excavated in recent centuries in an attempt to improve the grazing value of wet heath and blanket bog on the open hill, creating partially concealed trenches that can be hazardous to walkers and, more particularly, to young lambs. Much blanket bog also carries the distinctive signs of peat cutting, usually for fuel, with characteristic steps in the bog surface corresponding to the faces from which peats were removed. These can be seen in many parts of the uplands and often extend to moderate altitudes, for example on the eastern slopes of Quinag below the Bealach a' Chornaidh.

Early field systems were generally surrounded by turf or stone banks, which were intended to keep livestock in or out, or simply to subdivide the land. These may have been very temporary, as with the *faulds* of medieval times, in which livestock were corralled so that their dung could improve the land. Earlier sites such as hillforts or other enclosures may also have been adapted for this purpose. In later field systems, a substantial stone 'head dyke' separated the enclosed land, or 'in-bye', from the less intensively-used hill ground beyond, which was seldom cultivated. The cultivation of Scotland's relatively thin soils, either using hand-tools or simple and manoeuvrable ards or ploughs, dislodged stones which would then be removed by hand. While some went into walls, others were simply stacked into piles, called stone clearance heaps. Large numbers of these little piles of stone are distributed across parts of the uplands at various altitudes, especially on areas with broadly southerly aspects and relatively low gradients. Some of these sets of little cairns date from the Bronze Age, and they often occur around the footings of round houses. Others overlie areas of broad-rig cultivation and thus postdate medieval times.

A special type of artificial mound known as 'burnt mounds' may also be encountered in the glens and on lower slopes. Their name comes from their defining characteristic – the fire-crazed or shattered rocks they contain. With 1,899 Scottish sites currently recorded in the Historic Environment Scotland Canmore database, they are common if enigmatic features of the archaeological landscape. In the mounds small quantities of domestic debris may be mingled with the stones, including pottery fragments, stone tools, charcoal or animal bone, and excavation has occasionally uncovered other associated features. These may include a substantial trough, normally built of stone slabs but occasionally of split timber, a hearth and sometimes traces of stone walls, effectively amounting to a small building. Dating suggests that these mounds are of widely variable antiquity, spanning both the Bronze Age and Iron Age, while others may be more recent.

There are two preferred explanations for burnt mounds, which are invariably found close to water. They may have been cooking places where fire-heated stones were dropped into a water tank to raise its temperature, thus explaining the shattered rock. It is argued that this ancient version of 'boil-in-the-bag' cuisine would have been particularly useful in the absence of vessels that could withstand direct heat, and when peat was a major fuel. Early Irish literature and archaeological records clearly indicate that such sites existed, and were used to prepare feasts after hunting expeditions. An alternative explanation also focuses on heated water, but sees the burnt mounds as evidence for saunas or sweat-lodges, and parallels for this can also be found among European and native American cultures.

Burnt mounds were once thought to be confined to the Highlands, the Northern Isles and the Hebrides, but during the last 20 years they have been found in increasing numbers elsewhere, including the Rhinns of Galloway and the skirts of the Lammermuirs. Many probably remain to be identified by watchful hillwalkers near burns and lochs throughout the Scottish hills.

Mining and quarrying

Mining and quarrying has a long history and while recent activity may be obvious (such as track side excavation of building materials), old examples may be hard to identify, sometimes requiring a process of elimination where holes in the hillside (and associated spoil deposits) are unlikely to be of geological or geomorphological origin.

Early traces of the winning of stone by quarrying can occur in surprising places, none more so than in amongst the dolerite screes of Clash na Bearnaich on St Kilda, where stone for prehistoric tools was extracted. The most famous upland area involved in the extraction of minerals is perhaps the Wanlockhead – Leadhills sector of the Lowther Hills, where lead continued to be mined into the 1950s close to Scotland's highest village (at about 450m). Other upland areas of Scotland also show traces of mineral extraction including spoil heaps, horizontal passages known as adits, and bell-pits – a type of shallow working in which mineral deposits are reached by a short vertical passage. These sites include the lead mines near Tyndrum which extend to over 500m, the bell-pits for coal on Harran Hill, near Ballingry (Fife) or the 18th century and later remains associated with the quest for antimony along the slopes above the Glenshanna Burn in Eskdale, eastern Dumfriesshire. Mineral workings continue in some places to the present day including, for example, a barytes mine on the Corbett Meall Tairneachan above Aberfeldy.

Burial structures

While they are by no means confined to the uplands, various types of prehistoric and early historic funerary monuments can occur in the Scottish hills, sometimes on conspicuous summits. The oldest date to the Neolithic period, most famously including the megalithic (literally 'big stone') chambered cairns, so-called because of their use of imposing slabs and the presence of internal cells or chambers in which the dead were placed. In the Bronze Age, further burials were either inserted into earlier monuments or placed in or under new ones, including stone-built 'round cairns' and earthen barrows. Some of these also occur in upland settings. A substantial Bronze Age round cairn stands on the summit of Tinto Hill at an altitude of 712m, and is visible over a wide swathe of the Clyde valley and surrounding countryside. This massive heap of surface-gathered stone is some 6m high and 43m in diameter, and although its upper part has been disturbed, most of the mound, which has not been excavated, seems to be intact. A number of other archaeological sites can be seen on the lower slopes of Tinto.

Rab Anderson

The 3.7m high Nether Cairn at North Muir in the Pentland Hills. It probably dates from around 4,000 years ago, although it could be older

Such cairns generally cover burials or cremations, often accompanied by various types of pottery or other grave goods. They usually occur at lower altitudes, and conspicuous summit cairns such as this may have been more than simply cemeteries, perhaps initially erected to fulfil some symbolic or ceremonial function, or to convey a message to those who could see them. Some other types of Bronze Age burial also occur in upland settings, including enclosed cremation cemeteries and burials marked by small cairns, as on the moor above Monzie in Perthshire.

More recent hilltop memorials range from the ostentatious 30m high tower and statue of the Duke of Sutherland built on the summit of Beinn a' Bhragaidh after his death in 1833, to modest plaques often commemorating people who have died in the hills. In Assynt, a recently emplaced memorial stone to an aircrew buried at the site of their crash in 1941 is officially recognized as a war grave. The recent practice of scattering human ashes on the high peaks can leave noticeable traces where repeated frequently because of their high content of calcium and phosphorus, which may potentially alter the composition of alpine plant communities. On Ben Nevis potential impacts are now minimized by scattering ashes away from the summit cairn and the north face. The memorials placed on Ben Nevis, along with a large number of recent cairns, have been removed and in a very 21st century development are now recorded on a website.

Some lower hills are marked by follies, which are buildings constructed essentially for ornament. They may take many forms, from obelisks, arches and towers to sham castles and deliberately built ruins. These were largely constructed from the late 17th century onward and were generally built to be seen, occupying conspicuous places within the landscape which are not necessarily summits. The Watch Tower, Dun Na Cuaiche, was built in 1748 and was positioned to create a silhouette against the sky when viewed from Inveraray. Kilpurney Tower stands within a much earlier unfinished hillfort on the hill of the same name in Angus, and was built in 1774. With its crenellated walls over 13m high and its three stories with infilled upper windows, it forms an unconvincing observatory (its original purpose) but a rather impressive folly.

Military activity

Occasional hill names hint at military activity, such as Carn an Fhreiceadain (cairn of the watch), but their true origins are frequently obscure. Various physical traces can also be found in the uplands, and provide more or less convincing evidence of turbulent times in the past.

Iron Age hill forts are often marked on OS maps and are most abundant on lower summits south of the Highland boundary, particularly in the eastern Southern Uplands. Despite the name, their military function is sometimes open to question, and the lack of obvious defensive strength at some substantial sites, combined with changing ideas about Iron Age and early historic societies, raise the possibility that they may on occasion have fulfilled similar roles to those claimed for earlier stone circles and henges. A well-known example occurs on the conspicuous granite tor of the Mither Tap (493m), which crowns the much-loved Aberdeenshire hill of Bennachie.

Some such remains are of a distinctive type known as 'vitrified forts', consisting of hill-top stone structures built with a drystone wall and internal timber lacework, which was then set on fire. Examples include Dun Deardail, which sits at 340m below the north ridge of Mullach nan Coirean, overlooking Glen Nevis, and Tap o' Noth (564m) in Aberdeenshire (see p254). We may never know why these sites were burned, although it is evident that the characteristic remains are the product of the destruction, rather than the construction, of these sites. One interpretation is that they are a by-product of a violent confrontation, in which the walls of a captured fort were systematically destroyed for reasons of ritual and display. In an age before street lighting, these fires could have created beacons glowing red against the night sky, which would have remained visible for some time – certainly one way to impress the neighbours.

The first armies to leave unambiguous military traces in the Scottish hills were those of Rome, during a century or so of incursions beginning about 2,000 years ago. The resulting signs are almost all to the south of the Highland boundary. So called 'glenblocker' forts were built at the mouths of several glens in the Southern Highlands, such as Fendoch, in the Sma' Glen in Perthshire. These are believed by some to have been the springboards for an advance into the mountains that never took place, and are interpreted by others as an attempt to corral the troublesome Highlanders. Further south, a well-preserved Roman fortlet survives at Durisdeer, where the Roman road from Nithsdale to Clydesdale cuts along the flanks of Ballencleuch Law. Its rectilinear outline, with two internal timber blocks to house the garrison, can be seen on a slight spur above the Kirk Burn.

A network of barracks was established in the Highlands in the wake of the risings of 1715 and 1745, and some of these, such as Tigh nan Saighdearan (the 'Soldiers' House') at the west end of Loch Arkaig, stand guard over very rugged hill country. These barracks were generally linked to the system of military roads established during this period by Caulfield and Wade. The pre-existing 'arterial' route network had consisted largely of drove roads, which were created by the movement of stock and pack animals, often traversing high ground with sections of fearsome gradient. Many of these are still famous routes through the hills, such as Jock's Road and the Minigaig, which crosses the remote plateau above the head-waters of the River Feshie, passing just below the summit of Leathad an Taobhain. The advent of the military road network started the transformation of communication in the Highlands, establishing, for example, the route through the Central Highlands now taken by the A9.

Mark Wrightham

The northern gable is the most obvious remnant of Tigh nan Saighdearan at the head of Loch Arkaig, a barracks built by the Government at the time of the 1745 Jacobite rebellion

The Second World War saw renewed activity in some upland areas, famously including commando training around Spean Bridge. There are some surviving traces of the defensive lines established by Scottish command in 1940-1, and the remains of a concrete pillbox and three stone-built machine gun emplacements can be seen above the Meeting of the Three Waters, in the Pass of Glen Coe. Anti-tank blocks were also constructed in many strategic locations, including at high altitude around the Devil's Elbow below The Cairnwell. A number of high summits and corries are strewn with fragments of twisted debris from war- and peacetime plane crashes, including the remains of a Lancaster bomber around the Far West Buttress of Coire Mhic Fhearchair on Beinn Eighe, on the winter climb known as *Fuselage Gully*. The small stone El Alamein bothy on the slopes of Strath Nethy was built to commemorate the 1942 battle in Egypt, and is marked by a line of small and now mostly degraded cairns that lead towards it.

Map making

Cartography has often been driven by military objectives, and the first map of the Highlands was created in 1744-55 by General Roy. While comparatively crude by modern standards, Roy's map still provides an important historical record of the distribution of settlements, landuse and woodland at this time.

More accurate mapping began with the Ordnance Survey (OS) in the 19th century, and was based on triangulation. From any one survey site, in good visibility, it is possible to see at least two other triangulation (or 'trig') points, and so define precise triangles which formed a fundamental basis for map making. Survey teams camped close to summits across Scotland in the 1840s, establishing temporary bases known as 'Colby Camps' (after Major General Thomas Colby, who was the OS director from 1820-1846).

As survey work required good visibility, some of these camps were occupied for weeks and even months on end and left behind a series of lasting traces typified by the structures on the summit ridge and in the eastern corrie of Beinn an Oir, Jura, and on Creach Bheinn, Morvern. On Creach Bheinn the most striking features are the windbreak walls, which are up to 2.5m high, and shelter low circular stone footings for tents and a rectangular stone building that may have been an officers' mess or cook house. A well-made path leads from the encampment to the summit survey point, where holes would have been bored into a substantial, partially buried rock to record the survey instrument location.

After the initial survey was completed, cairns were raised over the survey points; a later generation of trig points established during surveys after 1935 was marked by the familiar concrete pillars. Eight examples of Colby camps are currently recorded in *Canmore* and generally duplicate the pattern of remains on Creach Bheinn. The 'Sappers' Bothy' near the summit of Ben Macdui was also built by a military survey team in 1847. Satellite-based GPS has now made most trig points redundant, but some are maintained as locations for GPS base stations.

Hunting

Hunting has probably been one of the most widespread human activities in the uplands, and is likely to have occurred, in some form, ever since people first ventured into the hills. Some place names make enigmatic references to this pastime, including Sgurr nan Conbhairean (peak of the keeper of the hounds), and a number of built features testify to these activities at different times in the past. Hunting probably began as a communal and collaborative activity from the initial arrival of people in very late Palaeolithic and Mesolithic times, and it seems likely to have soon extended onto high ground, particularly once dense forest spread over much of the lowlands. Few traces of hunting have been recorded, although subtle signs such as flint arrowheads probably lie undiscovered in remote corners of the hills. Some Pictish stones illustrate the use of the bow and hunting from horseback, which is often depicted with considerable panache. The quality of the horses in these sculptures, and details of dress, suggest that by the early historic period hunting had become an activity for the elite – a surrogate, and a training for war.

Some kinds of early evidence are linked to the traditions of reserving hunting of certain species, or within certain areas, to a privileged few. Pressure on resources in medieval times resulted in the encroachment of farming onto areas previously used for hunting, and led to the creation of hunting reserves called 'deer parks'. These were large areas of upland fringed by an embankment with a ditch on its inner margin. The bank would originally have been crowned by a fence or 'pale', and served both to define the limits of the reserve and to contain the deer within it. A good example is provided by the Buzzart Dykes, within the former Royal Forest of Clunie in upland Perthshire. This feature is indicated on the OS map and much of its circuit, enclosing nearly a square kilometre, remains clearly defined in the rough moorland. Another hunting tradition of this time was to drive the quarry to a place where they could more readily be taken, and large scale deer drives are documented from various parts of the Highlands. Deer were sometimes cornered between pairs of dykes converging, often downhill, towards a narrow neck which provided a funnel or cul-de-sac, and good examples of these features have been recognised around Orval on Mull. This style of hunting, known as 'tinchel', is also recorded in historical descriptions.

More modern signs of hunting correspond with the availability of guns to bring down the game. At the same time as the country was being opened up to 'romantic' tourism, others were coming to shoot and to fish, a process greatly facilitated from the mid-19th century by the development of railways. These activities left various built traces in the Highland landscape, as well as widespread imprints on vegetation, and continue to do so today.

The most conspicuous buildings are the shooting lodges, the successors of earlier hunting lodges. Shooting lodges reached their architectural apogee in high Victorian times, and often included subsidiary buildings to accommodate servants, kennels for dogs and stables for ponies. Although mock-baronial or similar creations are often considered typical, not all were necessarily as grand. At Ruigh-Fionntaig, beside the Allt Lorgaidh in Alvie, to the south of Aviemore, Ordnance Survey staff of the 1870s recorded 'a number of houses chiefly of wood and used as a shooting-lodge', and four unroofed structures were still mapped here a century later. Shooting lodges were sometimes built at moderately high altitudes, and one of the highest, Delnadamph, was sited at 430m on the Balmoral Estate, until it was demolished more than 20 years ago.

The development of deer stalking, from hunting with hounds to rifles, was accompanied by the development of new infrastructure in the hills. To facilitate access, the Victorians built large numbers of stalkers' paths, many of which were superbly constructed and are still used today. To help protect deer, particularly from poaching, they created 'watchers' huts' such as Blackrock Cottage near Buachaille Etive Mor and small shelters on the tops. The cast iron fences which stretch for kilometres along some summit ridges also date from around this time. More substantial constructions still survive in a few places, including the large stone wall that marks the summit ridge of Garbh Chioch Mhor above Glen Dessary.

Land management for grouse shooting frequently leaves distinctive traces in the form of muirburn patchworks, where fire has been used to manage the growth of heather and thus support the grouse. Many grouse moors are also marked by rows of grouse-butts in which the guns and their retrievers conceal themselves as the game birds are driven towards them.

In recent decades, grouse shooting and deer stalking have become increasingly dependent on motorised access, a trend which at least partly reflects changed expectations of paying clients, and the availability of powerful 4x4 vehicles. This in turn has resulted in a proliferation of bulldozed hill tracks, a development which has been particularly pronounced in the Eastern Highlands. These tracks sometimes extend onto very high ground, including the plateau of the Moine Mhor to the east of Glen Feshie, and can be visible from a considerable distance as sinuous scars in the landscape. Tracks which have been built to access grouse moors are commonly associated with muirburn and are frequently used as firebreaks, so that burnt strips appear to radiate outwards from them. Hill tracks are not, however, exclusively associated with stalking and grouse shooting, and have also been constructed for access to forestry plantations and upland sheep grazing. A further relatively recent feature associated with deer management has been the appearance of deer fences, which are intended to protect commercial conifer plantations and planted, or regenerating, native trees. These fences also create linear or angular shapes which can be very prominent, particularly when accentuated by contrasting vegetation growth on either side.

Recent use of the hills

The emphasis so far has been on the older, more subtle human features, which are usually the most difficult to recognise and interpret, and on some features of historic interest. In many mountain areas, however, the traces of modern human activities are much more prominent, reflecting recent land uses and a variety of social, economic and technological changes.

The most conspicuous modern features are large scale forestry plantations,

Set between the 'Tarmachans' and the Ben Lawers range, the dam at Lochan na Lairige is part of the extensive hydro-electric system surrounding Loch Tay

hydro-electricity schemes and wind turbines. Many larger glens now contain dams which date from the 1940s, '50s and '60s, and the associated reservoirs are rimmed by conspicuous bare 'drawdown' zones resulting from fluctuating water levels. In contrast, the pumped water storage systems, notably at Cruachan, Argyll, are hollowed out of the mountain and thus make less visible impact on the landscape. More recent hydro-electric schemes are generally smaller and typically consist of a weir and intake in the upper reaches of a burn, from which water is transported by pipe to a lower turbine house. Windfarms are becoming increasingly widespread and tend, by their nature, to occupy exposed and prominent locations, as on the northern edge of the Monadh Liath. Conspicuous transmission lines such as that from Beauly to Denny are often used for power distribution and sometimes penetrate remote country, for example around Kinlochhourn.

Communications technology has left a widespread imprint on the hills, and conspicuous mobile phone masts are dotted along major transport corridors. Masts and their associated equipment may be concealed in a variety of ways, with some of the more imaginative including buildings that have been specifically restored for the purpose. Some hilltop masts that were originally developed for the emergency services are now hosting the telecommunications equipment of mobile phone operators. Downhill ski developments have a relatively localised but considerable individual impact, meanwhile the widespread recreational use of the mountains for hillwalking and climbing adds minor visible traces in the form of cairns and path erosion, and perpetuates a legacy that stretches back to the earliest times that people ventured into the hills.

The increasing prominence of built features in the hills has been a source of growing contention, and the future implications of such development for Scotland's mountains are considered in the next chapter.

Ancient artefacts

Ancient stone tools and other small artefacts can occasionally be found in eroded areas beside paths, in stream banks or in peat. The most common objects are probably chipped stone tools, while polished stone axes or metal items are less likely finds.

Positive identification of stone tools is a specialist job, but obvious surface features can be diagnostic. Size and shape are not necessarily good guides, but small scallop-

Neolithic and early Bronze Age arrowheads

The Orkney Museum, Orkney Islands Council
© Hugo Anderson-Whymark

shaped gouges across the surfaces and 'nibbling' of the margins to form a more or less sharp edge are excellent clues. There may be a small flattened area at one end – the remains of a 'striking platform' where the tool was flaked off a larger piece of stone – with a bulge below the point of impact. A uniform surface patina indicates that the shape is old, and not formed by a series of disconnected events.

Any finds should be left in place unless they are at risk, for example beside a busy path. In such cases, only remove loose items without dislodging further material, as subsequent excavation may reveal more information. Record the exact location and report finds to the local authority archaeological service, a museum or the Treasure Trove Unit in Edinburgh *www.treasuretrovescotland.co.uk*

Cairns and burnt mounds

Cairns have been formed for many reasons and come in all shapes and sizes, although most are roughly circular. Burial cairns often occur on hilltops and other prominent places, while clearance cairns are found at altitudes where farming of some sort is, or was, possible, and are often associated with more obvi-ous agricultural traces. Burnt mounds always occur near

Burnt mound above Gruting Voe, Shetland

Andy Dugmore

water. Cairns may be more recent route or boundary markers, which are often obvious from their location. Cairns or burnt mounds are sometimes identified on OS maps.

Older cairns do not necessarily appear as neat piles and may have been reduced to low spreads of stones or subtle mounds in which the stones are entirely or partly concealed by peat or other soil, or by vegetation. They can therefore merge with natural features, with their detection requiring a very sharp eye.

Burnt mounds are irregular, sometimes kidney-shaped, heaps of fire-cracked and dis-coloured rocks (with red-orange surface oxidation) mixed with charcoal, and may be only a few metres across and less than a metre high; relatively few are over 10m in diameter. They are sometimes revealed in cross-section above the eroding banks of burns and are commonly found close to lochs.

HUMAN TRACES

Round houses

Round houses, sometimes marked on OS maps as *hut circles*, are among the most common prehistoric archaeological remains in Scotland, with more than 2,000 in Sutherland alone. They vary in form across the country, and are found over much of the uplands up to about 400m.

Stone round houses can appear as low banks of stones, usually much less than a metre high, defining roughly circular areas generally at least 5m, frequently about 10m and exceptionally almost 20m in diameter.

The stone wall of a round house on Kinrive Hill, Strath of Kildonan, Sutherland, can be seen in the foreground

These are the wall-footings for houses originally principally built of wood, with internal posts sunk into the ground to support a conical thatched roof. The stone footings (sometimes also including turf) have generally become covered with peat or other soils that have formed since the buildings were abandoned, and there may be little or no visible stonework. Under these circumstances, round houses may be defined by little more than a circular patch of contrasting vegetation, often bent-fescue grassland (see p98), perhaps with subtle hints of a raised circular 'rim'. The circular base of the wall is usually breached by a single doorway, commonly facing between north-east and south-east. Round houses may also have been built entirely from turf or timber, leaving very little visible trace.

Round houses with platforms or enclosures

Sometimes, especially in the Southern Uplands, round houses are found on level platforms, more or less the size of the building itself, which were cut into a sloping hillside. These platforms can be quite subtle and may be blanketed, along with the adjacent hillside, in a more or less continuous cover of

Shadow highlights the bank enclosing round house remains on a terrace above Meldon Burn, Peeblesshire

heather or bracken, but can also be defined by an obvious change of vegetation. At Lintshie Gutter in Upper Clydesdale, platform houses were built at least 3,500 years ago and on Green Knowe in Peeblesshire they persisted until about 2,800 years ago.

If the remains of a round house are closely surrounded by visible banks or ditches, it is probably more recent, dating from the Iron Age. These later, enclosed settlements may be marked on the OS map as enclosures and can occur in isolation, but are more often associated with some type of field system (see p255), which may or may not be visible in the modern landscape. The resulting arrays of subtle ground features are often best seen from a slightly more distant vantage point, such as a neighbouring slope or ridge, in low angled sunlight and under frost or light snow.

253

Hillforts

Hillforts are larger forms of Iron Age enclosed settlement and consist of stone walls, earth banks or ditches enclosing an upland site, which can be very extensive. They are generally found below about 400m, usually (but not necessarily) on low summits. Hillforts are mostly found on foothills in the east, through the central belt to Kintyre and in the Southern

Tap o' Noth, Aberdeenshire

Ian Ralston

Uplands, where they are particularly common, but they do occur elsewhere, including the north of Skye. Not all are marked on OS maps, and where recorded, they can be labelled as *forts, settlements, enclosures* or *earthworks*. It can be difficult to immediately relate markings on the map to traces on the ground, as these can be relatively subtle features defined by quite modest banks and ditches, sometimes appearing as a narrow shelf running across the slope. Do not necessarily expect major earthworks!

Vitrified forts, although broadly similar to other hillforts, are an intriguing special case. Their present appearance, the result of the destruction by firing of their timber-laced enclosing walls, is marked by melted and re-solidified rock, sometimes showing glassy 'runs' where molten rock has begun to flow. In the 18th century the vitrified fort on Tap o' Noth was even suggested to be an extinct volcano. An online *Atlas of Hillforts* is now available.

Rectangular buildings

Remains of rectangular buildings are probably less than 1,400 years old and are most likely to be comparatively modern. They may still have visible stone work that could be dry-stone wall footings (originally accompanied by timber or turf) or the remains of later, mortared walls, sometimes with chimneys in their gable-ends. Timber features are less easy to recognise from surviving traces as they have usually been scavenged

Shieling remains above Grey Mail's Tail, Moffat Dale

Andy Dugmore

from the buildings or rotted away, but the lower walls of some upland buildings contain stone emplacements for cruck-construction – massive curved timbers that carried a thatched roof. Wall footings can be distinctly irregular, commonly as a result of re-building.

Remains of shielings, that were commonly in use in the uplands into the 18th century, can be rectangular in plan, although it is important to note that not all shielings were this shape. They typically sit on level but decently-drained areas and are associated with patches of better bent-fescue grassland, usually, though not always, with a stream nearby. They can sometimes be distinguished from former permanent settlements by altitude, or by the absence of field systems, but some sites may have seen both permanent and seasonal use down the years.

Field systems

Former fields are generally found below 500m altitude and may be recognised by distinctive combinations of key elements; they may be surrounded by a low bank formed by the remains of turf or stone walls or dykes, or an enclosing ditch, but may also have no clear boundary other than where cultivation stopped. This

Stuart Rae

Traces of post medieval cultivation

may still show as a vegetation change, commonly with a tendency to grassland over the former field. The ground may also be irregularly dotted with clearance cairns (see above).

Various surface markings may have been left by cultivation with spades, hoes or ploughs, appearing as parallel raised ridges that are more obvious when viewed from a moderately distant vantage point, and in low-angled light. The oldest of these are known as 'narrow rig', 'cord rig' or 'lazybeds', and consist of very narrow ridges, about a metre wide, occurring in relatively small patches. These were hand-dug and can be very sinuous when necessary, for example to avoid rock outcrops. Broad rig is of wider gauge and can be very extensive, running across or along contours. This was generally cut using ploughs pulled by cattle, and such fields often have relatively wide uncultivated margins where beasts and ploughs could be turned.

Boundary head dykes and stock pens

Enclosed areas of more intensive arable cultivation and pasture were separated from rough upland grazings by boundary 'head dykes', which served to keep livestock away from growing crops. These took the form of low walls constructed from stone, turf or both, which were sometimes associated with shallow ditches. These features may still be marked by rickles of stones, raised banks or shallow ditches running

Ian Ralston

Head dyke in Glen Shurig, Arran

across hillsides, often associated with traces of cultivation. Head dykes have, however, moved with the fluctuating upland boundary of more intensive agriculture, and so may not always lie at the limit of visible rig markings. Changes in the position of this boundary may still be visible in present-day vegetation, and may be recorded by differences in the proportions of grassland and dwarf shrubs along relatively clearly-defined but artificial lines, which are not obviously linked to the underlying topography.

Open hill ground above the head dyke may contain stock pens where animals grazing summer pastures, such as sheep and goats, could be gathered for lambing or milking. These are often marked by dykes or stone walls enclosing much smaller upland areas, in the order of 10m diameter or less, and are frequently associated with shielings.

Peat cuttings

Recent peat cuttings are easy to recognise but older traces, whose age may be measured in centuries, can also be seen in the hills. These mirror the distribution of peat itself and are particularly common in the west. They are generally associated with areas of blanket bog in the floors of glens, but can also extend to moderately high levels.

Andy Dugmore

Older peat cuttings tend to appear as straight-sided depressions in the peat surface, edged by steps up to a metre high, which may form one or more open-ended rectangles, sometimes linked in a 'castellated' pattern. Conversely, extensive cutting may have reduced the peat cover to isolated upstanding 'baulks', whose regularity distinguishes them from natural haggs. Cuttings may also be accompanied by small mounds of dried-out, granular peat, which mark the positions of former peat stacks, though these may be hard to differentiate from natural features. Blanket bog can sometimes recover relatively fast in the wetter west, and the vegetation above and below the step may be indistinguishable. Old cuttings of this type are commonly close to existing or, in the hills, former settlements, but may also be found in remoter areas, suggesting that this valuable resource justified the walk.

Grouse butts

These generally take the form of enclosures roughly 2-3m square with walls of turf, drystone or wood close to waist-height. They are built to give cover to shooters lying in wait for grouse driven over their position and are found in single lines of about ten or so, positioned just over a ridge line or running up a slope, where the birds will fly along the contours. The butts are often individually numbered

Tom Prentice

(or sometimes named) and each has a single entrance facing away from the anticipated arrival direction of the birds. The rows of butts are often served by obvious tracks which have been either built for or created by estate vehicles.

Grouse butts are most likely to be seen on larger estates in the Central and Eastern Highlands and, if the moor is being actively managed, will normally be associated with patchworks of heather burning. More subtle traces include small piles of fine grey medicated grit, often placed on small areas of bare ground or upturned slabs of peat. A few grouse moors in the Eastern Highlands are encircled by conspicuous electric fences which are intended to exclude deer and can be awkward obstacles for walkers to cross.

Historic hill paths

People have walked through the hills for millennia, often taking obvious routes through bealachs and glacial breaches, and many of these are still used by modern hillgoers. These routes may never have been formally constructed, with few visible traces apart from an informal 'evolved' path. The most obvious indications of

Parallel walls marking the drove road over Craig Head and Kailzie Hill, south of Peebles

long use are often the green signposts of the Scottish Rights of Way & Access Society.

Many well-known routes were once drove roads used to drive cattle to market, or coffin roads used to carry bodies to consecrated ground. These often crossed surprisingly high ground, such as the Bealach Duibh Leac (721m), west of Creag nan Damh in Kintail. In the Southern Uplands, some drove roads developed into formal routes sandwiched between walls, which still remain.

18th century military roads were deliberately constructed and generally take straight lines, except on steep sections like the Devil's Staircase in Glencoe. These are therefore easier to detect, unless covered by later developments. From the 19th century, many paths were built for stalking. These seek out high ground, taking broad zig zags at a steady gradient up steeper slopes. They were often superbly constructed, with drainage ditches on the uphill side, and now provide important hillwalking routes.

Aircraft crash sites

The remains of crashed aircraft are surprisingly common in our hills. They vary in size from an almost complete wing on Carn t-Sagairt Mor to scattered fragments of metal; any otherwise unidentifiable metal debris is quite likely to be of this origin. The remains may become covered by peat, as happened to a Lancaster recovered from Conic Hill. The quantity and spread of wreckage reflects the speed and angle of impact and how much was recovered at the time or later removed by trophy seekers. In many locations, the impact scar remains visible, along with

Undercariage legs, burnt debris and melted aluminium on the east flank of Braeriach above Sròn na Lairige

charred wood, melted aluminium and often a strong 'burnt' smell. Aircraft crashes peaked in the Second World War, causing many deaths. They reflect the limited navigation technology at the time and are clustered around flight paths, with over 20 in the Eastern Cairngorms associated with flights from RAF Kinloss and Leuchars, and over 30 in the Galloway hills.

Some of the new navigation technology that has helped to prevent air crashes is located in the hills, including an air traffic control beacon on Broad Law and an air traffic radar station on Lowther Hill. Despite this there was a major civilian crash on Ben More, Crianlarich, in 1974 and two US Air Force jets crashed on Ben Macdui in 2001.

The Future of Our Mountains

Nick Kempe

Stuart Rae

Looking towards Ben Cruachan from the windfarm on Beinn Ghlas

As old as the hills

The rocks of our mountains are, compared to human life expectancy, incredibly ancient but even Scotland's oldest rocks, the Lewisian gneisses, are – at 3,000 million years – only two thirds the age of the earth itself. In geological timescales, our most recent rocks, the volcanic rocks of Ardnamurchan and the Inner Hebrides created when Scotland split from North America, are young at c59 million years.

In contrast to our rocks, everything else about our mountains is very recent, and much easier to grasp in terms of human lifespans. Apart from the pattern of our major river systems, almost all our mountain scenery is a legacy of the last Ice Age, or only 11,700 years old at most. Many of the plants and animals that now live in our mountains arrived much more recently than that.

The rate of change in Scotland, since the ice receded, has been considerable. The sea level has risen further, isolating land to create islands and forming our western mountainous seascapes. As the land and sea have warmed up, a succession of new plants and animals have colonised them and species capable of tolerating harsh frosts and severe winters have been replaced by ones better able to thrive in a warmer wetter climate. What all these species have had in common is an ability to colonise relatively quickly – slower dispersing species, such as snakes, either never reached the British Isles or in certain cases, such as the adder, only reached the mainland and some inshore islands.

The most important thing to appreciate about the natural history of our hills, therefore, is that like other areas that were ice-covered, almost everything is relatively new and, because Scotland became part of an island, there are fewer species. The paradox is that, for many people, part of the attraction of the mountains is

258

that they appear unchanging and old compared to our more urban environments. Yet on reflection, cliffs crumble even in our lifetimes and rock features which were part of mountaineering lore, such as the Gendarme on the Skye Ridge or the bottom of Parallel B gully on Lochnagar, are now fading from memory. Rapid global warming is likely to make the changing nature of our mountain environment ever more obvious.

The importance of Scotland's mountains

Globally, mountains are weather makers for large parts of the world, the main source of water for humanity, and have become important refuges for other species as human activities have come to dominate less inhospitable areas. They have also played a large role in the human imagination across many different cultures.

Scotland's mountains, and the experience they offer, are distinctive because of their particular combination of climate, geology and scenery, with their accompanying mix of arctic, alpine and temperate species. Their distinctiveness ensures they retain a special place in the affections of people brought up with them and makes it easy to argue that there is nowhere like the hills of home – an argument that is, however, repeated by mountain peoples all over the world!

In global terms, Scotland's mountains are probably most important for their geology, providing within a small area evidence of half the history of the world, a remarkable range of rocks and world class examples of a number of geological processes, including the Moine Thrust and caldera subsidence in Glen Coe.

By contrast, our mountains are home for a relatively limited range of species, although the resulting habitats, such as blanket bog, are in many ways unique. This is partly because once the sea rose to create the British Isles, further colonisation by natural means became difficult or impossible for many animals and plants. Extinctions then greatly reduced the number of species, most noticeably mammals. So, in Scotland there is only one true mountain mammal, the mountain hare, whereas the Alps have the ibex, chamois and marmot, not to mention various alpine mice, shrews and voles. Meanwhile, on the continent natural recolonisation by mammals, such as the wolf's move back west into the French Alps, is always possible whereas in the British Isles this would require a political decision. Since it took 10 years to approve the re-introduction of the far from fearsome beaver in 2016, widespread re-introductions of top predators like the lynx or wolf appear a far-off prospect.

The significant exceptions to Scotland's limited mountain biodiversity are Scotland's mosses and liverworts. These reproduce partly by means of spores, which are easily carried considerable distances, and therefore can overcome the island effect. They are also particularly well adapted to our climate, so Scotland has probably the finest range of liverworts in the world. Until recently, these remarkable plants were known only to the specialist, and they have only been touched on in this book (see p96), but introductory guides are now available.

While geographic isolation tends to result in reduced overall biodiversity, it can also facilitate the evolution of new species – as is illustrated by the unique wildlife of the Galapagos. Scotland's isolation is too recent as yet for significant species variation, and the likelihood of this is reduced further by our proximity to the European mainland. However, there are some signs of species evolution in Scotland, such as the Scottish crossbill, the St Kilda wren and the divergence between the red grouse and its European cousin, the willow grouse. How much variation develops in future will largely depend on how far humans allow nature to take its own course but also on the unpredictable impacts of global warming. Scotland's mountains are therefore potentially a significant ecological resource, because they offer large areas of wild land where natural processes could develop relatively uninfluenced by people.

They are, as well, an increasingly important social resource. Our mountain scenery has been a source of inspiration to many and plays an important part in our cultural imagination and identity. It also provides a challenging setting for recreational activities. These special qualities have brought substantial benefits to, and in some places underpin, the rural economy through tourism and outdoor recreation.

The use and management of our mountains

Historically, while humans have played a major role in determining our mountain flora and fauna, few decisions about land use have been informed by respect for natural processes or our mountain landscapes. Most have been driven by other economic and social priorities which, more often than not, have involved overcoming nature rather than working with it and exploiting nature's 'capital' while putting little or nothing back.

The hostile nature of the environment and relative lack of exploitable resources has however also constrained the economic use that could be made of hill land compared to the lowlands. Agriculture in this environment has always been marginal and in many hill areas you can see ruckles of stones, evidence of past habitation and subsistence farming.

Scotland's mountain landforms and habitats continued to be strongly influenced by natural processes long after people settled in the glens. The wet climate interacted with human exploitation of natural resources, sometimes impoverishing the land but sometimes with interesting consequences. Deforestation, for example, contributed to the formation of blanket bog which has become a valuable ecosystem in its own right.

The history of land use in Scotland's mountains has however taken a distinctive course. Until the last 50 years and the development of mass mountain tourism, most societies across the world made little or no use of the higher and more hostile mountain areas or, like in Scotland, agriculture only moved uphill when times were hard. Mountainous country has generally not been worth owning and been left to nature or to native peoples. Consequently, in many parts of the world, mountains have been treated as common land or belong to no-one at all. However, in Scotland, the topography and early development of the British economy, meant financially valuable uses were found for hill land at a relatively early date: first sheep farming and then hunting by the new leisured classes. Both contributed to the Clearances and helped shape the present-day system of private ownership based on large estates.

While the balance of land use between farming, deer stalking and grouse shooting has varied over time, large estates have remained dominant in mountain areas and Scotland as a result has one of the most unequal patterns of landownership in the world.

The state has only sought to acquire land for specific reasons, usually relating to perceived national strategic needs. The creation of the Forestry Commission after the First World War to increase wood production was followed by the development of hydro-electricity schemes and some military use, from training areas to

Blanket afforestation, as here below Corserine in the Galloway hills, has restricted access, destroyed eagle territories and created an unnatural landscape

communications infrastructure, but little else.

The creation in 2002, under the Land Reform Act, of a community right to buy land has so far had little impact on the concentrated pattern of ownership of our mountains. This is partly because in most hill areas, local communities are tiny or non-existent and do not have the funds required. It is also because ownership of land is increasingly through companies and trust funds, designed to avoid death duties and legal provision like the right to buy. Land use in much of the Highlands therefore is still under the control of private estates.

These estates were for a long time unresponsive to changes in public subsidy for agriculture and forestry, the main means by which the state has influenced rural land use elsewhere. This is because most have not been run on a commercial basis and their primary interest has been hunting.

That is now changing as technological developments combined with new subsidies have resulted in a further phase of development in our mountains. First came communications masts, then another phase of renewable energy developments, including both wind and micro-hydro schemes. New technologies have also made it much cheaper to develop hunting infrastructure, such as bulldozed tracks for vehicles.

While the historic imperviousness of private estates to outside influence had some positive effects, such as protecting many upland areas from the mass conifer afforestation of the 1970s and 1980s, it also acted as a barrier to the adoption of conservation friendly practices. Estates may have been generally unprofitable to run, but their capital value has increased markedly. The value of stalking estates has been based in part on numbers of stags, which has provided an incentive to increase stag numbers. Meanwhile hinds, which are not shot for sport, have been subject to limited culls. This helps to explain the continued increase in deer numbers and consequent grazing pressure, which has had a detrimental effect on our upland habitats, particularly native woodland, and has contributed to the lack of a natural tree line in Scotland.

values between these groupings has led to very different responses to issues such as the development of windfarms.

Most nature conservation, as currently practised, sits within the context of ever increasing human intervention in the natural environment. Areas are set aside for conservation to protect what is valued, whether this be a landform, habitat or species, and then are managed to benefit whatever is being protected. This can result in apparently contradictory actions, such as trees being cut down in one part of the country to recreate or preserve moorland or bog, while in another part of the country the priority is to enable trees to recolonise moorland. It can also result in interventions that cut across natural processes. While targeted action is needed to protect certain species and habitats, this approach leaves little room for nature to take its own course and can conflict with the 'wild' feel to the landscape that many people value in the uplands. Moreover, in the face of global warming, it may make little sense trying to save our alpine plants if it becomes so warm that the tree line rises above Munro level.

This has led, in the last 10 years, to a shift in conservation thinking, particularly in our hills, from targeted management of defined sites for particular habitats and species to more open-ended approaches based on natural processes. These could allow habitats and species to shift in response to climate change and are sometimes referred to as re-wilding. This concept is now well established, even if subject to much debate, with a few people claiming that a deer dominated eco-system is the outcome of natural processes while others see large numbers of deer as a human construct and the greatest threat to nature reasserting itself. The more radical of these argue for the re-introduction of top predators such as the wolf as a natural means of controlling herbivore numbers.

While nature conservation is based on science, conservation priorities are strongly influenced by cultural perspectives and the political process. Perceptions of species change over time, with golden eagles and other raptors now being regarded by the public as creatures of wonder, rather than pests that prey on other creatures, while birds and mammals still attract more public concern than an unassuming moss or liverwort. While what is valued in conservation terms influences current conservation priorities, political boundaries and the relative power of institutions at the local, regional, national and supra-national level also play an important role. The EC for a time was the main driver for conservation in Scotland and its priorities changed with its boundaries: for example, the total number of dotterel in the EC was very low until Sweden joined, after which the number increased several thousand-fold and it became common in the EC. However, it still remains rare in Scotland.

The establishment of the Scottish Parliament in 1999 created a new political context which had an immediate impact on conservation in Scotland, with the establishment of National Parks, the passing of the Nature Conservation (Scotland) Act 2004 and a raft of other environmental measures. It also made local 'political' lobbying easier, which since then has played a significant role in how these laws have been implemented.

Current means of protecting mountains in Scotland

Since 1950, the main means of protecting Scotland's mountains has been to designate areas considered to be of particular conservation importance. The different types of designation, which are at first sight bewildering, have arisen because

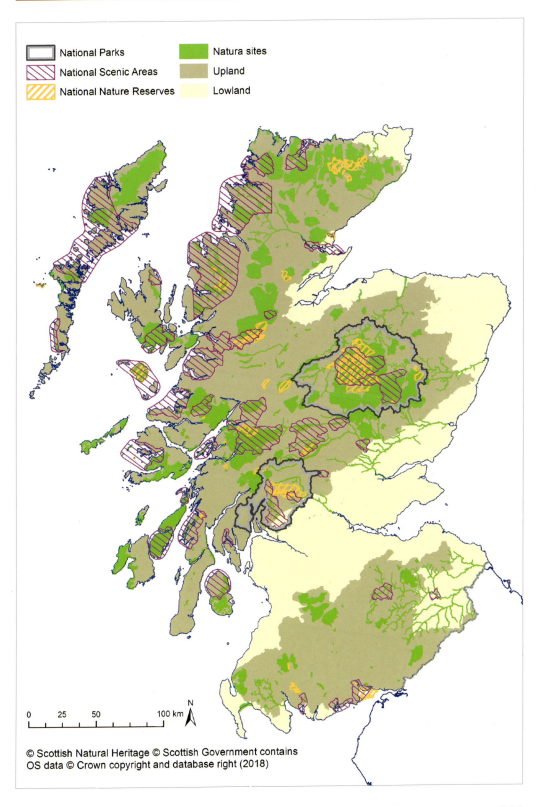

National Parks
National Scenic Areas
National Nature Reserves
Natura sites
Upland
Lowland

0   25   50   100 km
N

© Scottish Natural Heritage © Scottish Government contains
OS data © Crown copyright and database right (2018)

Creag Meagaidh NNR has demonstrated how native woodland regeneration can be achieved with high deer culls (see p204)

they are designed to protect different things and at different levels of government, whether local, national or international. In Britain, unlike much of the continent, landscape and nature conservation are treated separately and the mechanisms to protect them are largely distinct. While specific laws and regulatory mechanisms have developed to protect nature conservation sites most landscape protection has been through the planning system.

National Scenic Areas (NSAs) are Scotland's main landscape designation, cover almost a sixth of Scotland and focus largely on upland areas, including much wild land. NSAs allow recognition of landscape values within the planning system and enable greater control of some developments, such as vehicle tracks and phone masts. Planning guidance for NSAs has been gradually strengthened since they were created in 1978. Unlike Areas of Outstanding Natural Beauty in England and Wales though, they have no dedicated resources and the development of management plans to protect them has been minimal. More recently the Scottish Government has recognised wild land in planning policy, linked to work undertaken by Scottish Natural Heritage (SNH) to map such areas.

Sites of Special Scientific Interest (SSSI) provide the foundations for our nature conservation designation system and underpin a number of other types of protected area. SSSIs are designated for specific geological features, landforms, habitats or species and impose constraints on land management activities that might damage these. These controls have been controversial, being viewed as unduly restrictive by land managers, while many conservation interests have considered them to be insufficiently effective. The Nature Conservation Act revised this regulatory system and tasked SNH, with developing positive management plans for each SSSI in partnership with land managers, in return for public funding. SSSIs are often focused on very specific management for particular habitats and species that were present when the site was first designated, and there is now growing debate about more adaptive management approaches to help accommodate the effects of climate change. SSSIs provide no means to address external factors that damage them, such as airborne pollution, and only limited means to address overgrazing. Moreover, being site based, they can offer only limited protection to species with wide territories or which migrate, such as many of our mountain birds and animals.

EC legislation created, through the Birds Directive and Habitats Directive, Special Protection Areas for Birds and Special Areas of Conservation for other species and for habitats. Together these are known as Natura sites. In the UK these have usually been selected from SSSIs, and conferred protection under European law and access to European funds for positive management. The rationale behind Natura sites, which was to dedicate 10% of land to nature in a European wide network of sites, was excellent. However, in practice they share many of the inherent limitations of site-based conservation, are weighted towards birds rather than other species and leave out geology and landforms. Their future is likely to remain uncertain for several years following the Brexit vote in 2016.

Scotland's National Nature Reserves (NNRs) take a more holistic approach. Some of the best known are mountain reserves such as Beinn Eighe, Creag Meagaidh and Ben Lawers, and they have played important roles in the development of conservation policy and practice.

NNRs on private land depend on the voluntary co-operation of the landowner and a number of mountain NNRs such as Inverpolly, Inchnadamph, and Caenlochan, have had to be de-designated over the years because their private owners did not accept the principle of primacy of nature. Gradually the policy emphasis has changed and NNRs are now promoted as places for people to enjoy nature. In 2015 the Great Trossachs Forest NNR, at 18,000 hectares Scotland's largest, was established in the Loch Lomond and Trossachs National Park not to protect what was there already, but because of its potential for both nature and people.

In the last 30 years, the time and effort spent on deciding what areas to designate has been significant and arguably has diverted effort from conservation work on the ground, and the needs of the wider countryside. Moreover, conservation funding has tended to follow designation so that where there is no designation, there is little money. This has had consequences for mountain land, much of which is not covered by other forms of public subsidy, such as support for agriculture and forestry.

The creation of the Loch Lomond & The Trossachs National Park in 2002 and the Cairngorms National Park in 2003 introduced new mechanisms which could allow a more holistic approach that bridges the gap between nature conservation and landscape and conservation and human use. While the National Parks have provided the setting for a number of specific projects, which have demonstrated how such new approaches could work, they have yet to replicate this at anything like a landscape scale.

Besides designating sites, the other main means of protecting wildlife is to protect individual species, including those which have historically been persecuted. While it has been an offence since the 1981 Wildlife and Countryside Act to kill listed species of animal, pick protected flowers or uproot any wild plant, the Nature Conservation Act 2004, greatly increased penalties. It also created an offence of reckless behaviour, which applies to both land managers and visitors to the countryside. Despite this, and high profile condemnations of wildlife crime,

Footpath work, as here on the Allt a' Mhuillinn path below Ben Nevis, often depends on funding from organisations such as the Scottish Mountaineering Trust

persecution has continued and upland birds of prey, for example, are still absent from many mountain areas because of it. This, and a continued loss of species through habitat destruction has led to action plans being developed for declining species, including a number featured in this book, from hen harrier to red squirrel. This has had both successes and failures but it's unclear at present to what extent it will prevent the decline in species diversity.

In response to a perceived failure of government to protect mountains and their wildlife, the alternative has been to buy them and many important mountain areas in Scotland are now owned or managed directly by conservation bodies. This approach was pioneered through Percy Unna, a mountaineer, whose efforts and donations were responsible for the National Trust for Scotland (NTS) acquiring Glen Coe, Torridon, Ben Lawers, Goatfell and the Five Sisters of Kintail to protect wild land and public access. After a lull in activity, a reinvigorated conservation movement started in the 1980s to purchase a significant number of mountain areas. Recent years have seen an ongoing process of land reform and efforts to encourage greater community involvement in the ownership and management of land, and NGOs are increasingly working in partnership with community groups and other interests to manage particular mountain areas.

The management of mountains by NGOs has on the whole been a success and there have been significant achievements, particularly the efforts of NTS and RSPB to facilitate regeneration of Caledonian Forest in the Cairngorms. They have, however, been unable to acquire some areas of land which are high priority for conservation management, and their ability to do so in future appears limited without significant land reform as many of the large private estates have converted themselves into trusts or complex company structures whose purpose is to manage the land in perpetuity. More significantly, the NGOs have generally failed to influence other landowners, for example by encouraging Deer Management Groups to increase deer culls, while frequent attempts over 40 years to change government land use policy have had mixed results. While there has been a general move towards more conservation-friendly approaches to land management in the uplands, progress has often been painfully slow and failed to keep up with changing technologies and management practices.

As the purchasing activity of the conservation sector waned, a new type of seriously rich conservation-minded private landowner appeared. Among the estates purchased was Glen Feshie, a former target for conservation organisations, which has been transformed in 10 years through large deer culls which have enabled native woodland to recover. These landowners have been associated with a European movement for re-wilding.

Recreation and the natural heritage

Although hunting is not usually classed as a form of recreation in the UK, but rather as a land use in its own right, it has through the leisure pursuits of deer stalking and grouse shooting provided the dominant human influence on the mountain environments of the Highlands over the last 120 years. Unlike other parts of Europe where hunting is a mass recreational activity, in the UK it is far more socially exclusive, although those who hunt in Scotland, such as the Danish billionaire Anders Holch Povlsen who bought a string of estates in the decade starting from 2006, often share many of the values of outdoor recreation, such as enjoyment of physical challenge and a love of wild places. This has resulted in a complex and sometimes contradictory relationship between hunting and other forms of outdoor recreation, which has ranged from mutual support to antagonism.

In Scotland, for 20 years this relationship revolved around the debate about access rights before these were enshrined in law in 2002. Access rights continue to be subject to debate, particularly in respect to the impact of specific activities on the natural heritage, which raises questions of the relative impacts of visitors compared to those who own and manage the land.

Informal outdoor recreation can have impacts such as trampling, path erosion, disturbance to wildlife, pollution of watercourses, noise and litter. However, these are impacts that can equally result from land management or other activities and, just as with good land management, many can be avoided entirely with a little thought. In general, the presence of people in itself has very little impact on the natural environment, it is what people do that matters. While concerns are sometimes voiced about recreational disturbance to nesting upland birds, the available research indicates that this does not significantly affect their overall populations. In a historical context, our birdlife was a lot richer in the past when more people lived in the glens. For example, estate records for Glengarry from 1837-40 show that birds shot included 27 white tailed eagles, 15 golden eagles, 18 ospreys, 63 goshawks, 285 common buzzards, 375 rough-legged buzzards, 63 hen-harriers and 78 merlin. Persecution by hunting interests continues to have a far greater influence on the distribution of birds of prey than disturbance of birds by walkers. However, the key challenge if we are to increase birdlife in our mountains is not just to prevent such persecution or avoid recreational impacts but to change the way that the land is managed to benefit a wider range of habitats and species.

Probably the most significant recreational impact in the hills is path erosion,

Before the vehicle track from Glen Feshie, the principal hillwalkers' route up the Munro Mullach Clach a' Bhlair followed the ridge over Meall nan Sleac in the background

which results from the propensity of most hillwalkers to get to the top, following obvious 'lines' such as ridges and choosing the 'easiest' ground. This concentrates people onto certain routes, and increases erosion. Even so, the effect of human feet is slight compared to the natural erosive forces of wind, water and gravity, which shift far greater amounts of material downhill each year. It is also far less significant than the impact of grazing animals, which affect vegetation and soils both through nibbling and trampling. Indeed, where a grassy top has been over-grazed, the impact of human feet will be exacerbated.

While some types of recreation can have particular impacts on specific species, the effect will often depend on the health of the species population. Winter climbing on frozen turf, for example, could potentially affect certain very rare plants now confined to specific cliff faces. Summer climbing, however, is unlikely now to affect the overall health of the peregrine population, which has recovered in the last 30 years, even without the excellent best practice guidance that has been developed on how to avoid disturbing nesting birds.

While some knowledge of natural history is helpful to an understanding of recreational impacts, particularly for those involved in implementing the access legislation, our response to recreational impacts ultimately depends on values as much as science. Paths may, to varying degrees, scar the landscape but this is relatively minor in historical terms, and are trivial when compared to the erosive power of ice. People have always walked over and through our mountains, and have done so without lasting impacts. Most paths, if left unused, would be reclaimed by vegetation within a few years and even vehicle tracks at lower altitudes could disappear within human lifetimes, as has happened to unused sections of old single track road throughout the Highlands. Where one draws a line in terms of the acceptability of erosion will depend on whether one has recre-ational or more utilitarian values. In the case of paths, a small amount of invest-ment across the country, as has happened, for example, in Glen Coe, Torridon and the Cairngorms, would do much to reduce perceived impacts. While there are some excellent examples of good practice in Scotland, these have been limited because of funding. The debate is being complicated by the emergence of new forms of recreation, which either use or depend on technological developments, such as mountain biking or the use of All Terrain Vehicles for stalking. Further research, debate and thinking is required about where and when use of such machines in our mountains is appropriate and what investment is needed to support this.

There are a number of sources of advice available for walkers and climbers on how to reduce impacts which link to the Scottish Outdoor Access Code (see further reading). As well as reducing impacts, however, recreational visitors can, as John Muir put it, "do something to make the mountains glad". Ways of doing this vary from conservation and footpath work to contributing to citizen science and there are now various projects for mountaineers to record what they find in the hills, from spiders to birds. This data is being collected into one geographical information system, the "Atlas of Living Scotland", a great resource for people who want to learn more about specific areas in the hills.

What future for Scotland's mountains?

Human induced climate change, pollution, unsustainable use of many of the world's resources, whether oil, forests, soils or fish, and the destruction of natural habitats have created a global environmental crisis. Yet for Scotland's mountains the current crisis is probably of less importance than a history of degradation.

While we need to think globally, we need to understand and act locally. The main purpose of this book has been to help hillwalkers and climbers appreciate better what we have, and so make links between nature conservation and outdoor recreation. All the authors hope, though, that it also provides a stimulus to consider wider questions about what our mountain environments should be for, including the contributions they might make to a healthier global environment and a sustainable rural economy. While most readers are likely to have a particular interest in mountains, the health of upland environments cannot be seen in isolation, but is dependent on the health of other ecosystems, as is illustrated by the long migrations of many of our mountain birds. It is also linked to the well-being of the local and wider communities that depend on the mountains.

This chapter has attempted to place human impacts on our mountains in a wider context and to provide an overview of current attempts to protect them. It has hardly touched on some of the key current debates within the broad environmental movement, such as the acceptability and need for windfarms or the debates on whether natural woodland regeneration is preferable to fencing and tree planting. It is written in the belief that those debates should start from the wider questions of what the natural environment, including mountains, is for and what roles humans should play in them. What better ending, and starting point for debate, than W.H.Murray?

"Land and wildlife have their own being in their own right. Our recreation is an incidental gain, not an end in itself to be profitably pursued by exploiting land where that means degrading it. The human privilege is to take decisions for more than our own good; our reward that it turns out to be best for us too".

Further Reading

Climate

Introducing Meteorology: A Guide to Weather; Jon Shonk (2013). Dunedin Academic Press. ISBN 1780460023. An easily readable explanation of all aspects of meteorology.

Mountain weather; David Pedgley (2nd edition 2004). Cicerone Press. ISBN 1852842563. A practical guide for interpreting weather maps and local conditions in the British hills.

Environmental Change in Mountains and Uplands; Martin Beniston (2000). Arnold. ISBN 0340706368. A thorough review of research on causes, impacts, prediction and mitigation of climatic change in the major mountain regions of the world.

Met office data; *www.metoffice.gov.uk/public/weather/climate*; for mountain observation stations (Aonach Mor, Bealach Na Ba, Cairn Gorm Summit, Cairnwell and Glen Ogle) *www.metoffice.gov.uk/public/weather/mountain-observations/*

Geology

Geology and Landscapes of Scotland; Gillen, Con (2013). Dunedin Academic Press. ISBN 9781780460093. A detailed description of the geology of Scotland for the non-expert.

Volcanoes and the Making of Scotland; Upton, B.G.J. (2004). Dunedin Academic Press. ISBN 1903765404. A detailed account of how volcanoes shaped Scotland's landscape written in an accessible style.

The Hidden Landscape: Journey into the Geological Past; Fortey, Richard (1993). Pinlico. ISBN 0712660402. An exploration of the connections between the geology and landscape of the British Isles, by the UK's premier geological storyteller.

British Geological Survey 1:50,000 maps of Scotland are now available online and there is an app iGeology which allows you to see what rock unit you are standing on wherever there is a phone signal. *http://mapapps.bgs.ac.uk/geologyofbritain/home.html*

Edinburgh Geological Society produces geological excursion guides to various areas in Scotland including the NW Highlands. *www.edinburghgeolsoc.org/*

Landforms

Land of Mountain and Flood: the Geology and Landforms of Scotland; McKirdy, A.P., Gordon, J.E. and Crofts, R (Revised edition 2009). Birlinn, Edinburgh. ISBN 9781841586267. An accessible illustrated account of the shaping of Scotland's landscape.

Glaciers; Gordon, J.E. (2001). Colin Baxter, Grantown-on Spey. ISBN 1841070742. An attractive introduction to glaciology.

Classic Landforms of Skye; Benn, D.I. and Ballantyne, C.K. (2000). ISBN 1899085807. **Classic Landforms of the Assynt and Coigach Area;** Lawson, T.J. (2002). ISBN 1843770172. Two informative regional guides published by the Geographical Association, Sheffield.

www.fettes.com/Cairngorms/ an excellent website explaining the geology and geomorphology of the Cairngorms, including many photographs of mountain landforms.

http://qra.org.uk/ The Quaternary Research Association publishes technical field guides to the geomorphology and natural history of many mountain areas in Scotland including Skye, Western Sutherland, the Monadhliath, Glen Roy, Glen Affric & Kintail, the Cairngorms and Wester Ross.

Vegetation

Mountain Flowers; Scott, M. (2016). Bloomsbury Natural History. ISBN 9781472929822. A very readable and attractive description of selected species across the UK, with extensive reference to Scotland.

The Wild Flower Key; Rose, F and O'Reilly, C. (2006). Frederick Warne. ISBN 0723251754. A well-illustrated, user-friendly field guide to flowering plants, with some reference to grasses, sedges and rushes.

Grasses, Ferns, Mosses and Lichens of Great Britain and Ireland; Phillips, R. (1994) Macmillan, London. ISBN 0330259598. A large format selective photographic guide that covers a lot of ground rather well.

Scottish Wild Plants; their History, Ecology and Conservation; Lusby, P. and Wright, J. (2001). Mercat Press ISBN 1841830119. Superbly illustrated profiles of 45 less common, mostly upland plants, including many famous alpine rarities.

Invertebrates

Guide to Insects of the British Isles; Lewington, R. (2012) Field Studies Council ISBN 9781908819055. This 8-panel fold-out chart is a guide to the main groups of insects.

Bugs Britannica; Marren, P. and Mabey, R. (2010) Chatto & Windus. ISBN 9780701181802. A wide ranging chronicle of invertebrate life and its interactions with humans.

Collins Complete Guide to British Insects; Chinery, M. (2009). Harper Collins. ISBN 9780007298990.

Photographs and brief descriptions, covering most of the species that amateur naturalists are likely to find.

A Comprehensive Guide to Insects of Britain & Ireland; Brock, P.D. (2014). Nature Bureau. ISBN 9781874357582. Photographs of over 2500 species are included with clear succinct text.

Vertebrates

RSPB Handbook of Scottish Birds; Holden, P and Housden, S. (2016). Bloomsbury Publishing, London. ISBN 9781472927293. Attractively illustrated field identification guide with distribution maps of Scotland.

Bird Life of Mountain and Upland; Ratcliffe, D. (1990). Cambridge University Press. ISBN 0521331234. A superb overview, well worth seeking out.

Birds Britannica; Cocker, M. and Mabey, R. (2005). Chatto and Windus, London. ISBN 0701169079. A fascinating and comprehensive overview of the cultural links between humans and birds.

Birdtrack; Lets you record and see what birds have been recorded by others. ***http://app.bto.org/birdtrack/main/data-home.jsp***

Field Guide to the Mammals of Britain and Europe; Macdonald, D. (2005) Harper Collins. ISBN 0002197790. A comprehensive and well-illustrated guide.

Animal Tracks and Signs; Bang, P. and Dahlstrøm, P. (2001). Oxford University Press. ISBN 0198507968. An excellent non-technical guide to the more characteristic tracks and signs of European mammals and birds.

The Amphibians and Reptiles of Scotland; McInerny, C. and Minting, P. (2016). Glasgow Natural History Society. The PDF can be downloaded at ***www.dropbox.com/s/21hi4idrs0sepjd/aros_mcinerny_minting_gnhs.pdf.zip?dl=0***

Scotland's Freshwater Fish: Ecology, Conservation & Folklore; Maitland, Peter S. (2007). Trafford Publishing. ***www.snh.gov.uk/about-scotlands-nature/species/fish/freshwater-fish/***

Monographs offering more in-depth accounts of the ecology of various species or groups of birds, including golden eagle and peregrine; many published by T. & A.D. Poyser, London. ***www.acblack.com/naturalhistory***

Human Traces

The Landscape of Scotland: a Hidden History; Wickham-Jones, C. (2001). Stroud: Tempus. ISBN 0752414844. A useful introduction focusing on illustrated examples of a wide range of sites.

Scotland after the Ice Age; Eds. Edwards, K. and Ralston, I. (2003). Edinburgh University Press. ISBN 0748617361. An overview of the archaeological and environmental records to 1000 AD.

Historic Environment Scotland's online **CANMORE** database allows access to PASTMAP information on some 300,000 individual historic assets in Scotland, and while most are located on lower ground includes shielings, tracks and some old photographs from hill summits. ***www.historicenvironment.scot/ archives-and-research/archives-and-collections/canmore-database/***

General Reading and Conservation Issues

Scottish Hill and Mountain Names; Drummond, P. (2010). Scottish Mountaineering Trust. ISBN 0907521959. Particularly interesting because the majority of hill names reflect some aspect of the natural environment, past or present. Other SMT and SMC books are listed on the inside rear endpaper.

The Cairngorms; Nethersole-Thompson, D. and Watson, A. (1981). Melven Press, Perth. ISBN 0906664128. This classic and still authoritative review is out of print, but well worth tracking down.

The Highlands and Islands; Darling, F.F. and Boyd, J.M. (reprinted 1989). Penguin Books. ISBN 187063098X. Revision of Fraser Darling's earlier classic Natural History in the Highlands and Islands, whose central theme is human influence on natural processes, a large part of which is about Scotland's Mountains.

Scottish Natural Heritage website ***www.nature.scot*** includes various attractive introductory publications and topical material relating to Scotland's mountains and conservation, and the publications section can be searched for species, habitats and areas of interest. The section on Landscapes and Habitats includes a range of information on upland landscapes, including SNH's 2002 statement promoting greater recognition of and care for wild land.

The Atlas of Living Scotland ***https://scotland.nbnatlas.org/*** provides a gateway to data about species and habitats

Good Practice Guidance

Scottish Outdoor Access Code; Scottish Natural Heritage (2005). ISBN 1853974226. Sets the framework for responsible access under the Land Reform (Scotland) Act 2003. Further information can be found on the official website at ***www.outdooraccess-scotland.scot***

Mountaineering Scotland has published several codes of practice and information leaflets, including the **Crag Code, Wild Camping, Where to 'Go' in the Great Outdoors** and **A Brief Guide to 'Birds at Crags' for Climbers**. These are available at ***www.mountaineering-scotland.org.uk***

Notes on Contributors

Stuart Benn worked for the RSPB for nearly 30 years, largely in North Scotland and continues to monitor golden eagles. Stuart loves being out on the Scottish hills and has a particular affection for the much maligned Monadh Liath.

Andy Dugmore is Professor of GeoSciences, at the University of Edinburgh, and is a geographer with research interests in human-environment interactions in the North Atlantic Islands. Andy takes undergraduate field classes to the Scottish mountains to explore the shaping of upland landscapes and is also, when time permits, a hillwalker and mountaineer.

Richard Essery is a Reader in atmospheric modelling at the School of GeoSciences, University of Edinburgh, and has studied mountain climates in the USA, Canada, Switzerland, Wales and Scotland. He is a participant in the International Network for Alpine Research Catchment Hydrology and a member of the Snow and Avalanche Foundation of Scotland.

Jonathan Gregory works at the University of Reading and the Met Office Hadley Centre in climate change research, using computer models to study the effects of greenhouse gas emissions on climate and sea level. Jonathan is a hillwalker and rock climber in Britain and a summer Alpine mountaineer.

Kathryn Goodenough is a Senior Geologist at the British Geological Survey. She has made geological maps in the NW Highlands and several countries around the world, and she now applies her geological knowledge to understanding worldwide resources of the many unusual metals that are needed for new technology, from smartphones to electric cars. When she gets the chance, she still loves to walk, cycle and ski in the Scottish hills.

John Gordon is a geomorphologist with particular interests in mountain landforms, glaciers and geo-conservation. He is an Honorary Professor in the School of Geography and Sustainable Development at the University of St Andrews. John has studied or travelled in mountains from the Arctic to the Antarctic and has written widely about the landforms and glacial history of Scotland. He has walked, run and skied over the Scottish hills for many years.

Nick Kempe has been exploring Scotland's mountains since the age of six and enjoys all forms of mountaineering. He has a keen interest in our relationship to the hills and has served as President of the Mountaineering Council of Scotland, Chair of Mountain Leader Training UK and as a Board member of Scottish Natural Heritage. He currently runs a blog, *Parkswatchscotland*, and is finishing a book on natural and human history for walkers.

Keith Miller career in conservation has focussed on mountain areas. Now self-employed, Keith provides mountain environment, navigation and skills courses, undertakes upland plant surveys and is an avalanche forecaster for the Scottish Avalanche Information Service. Particular interests include the ecology of the alpine zone and invertebrates. Mountain natural history and all forms of mountaineering remain complementary passions.

Roger Owen was Head of Ecology for the Scottish Environment Protection Agency. Roger's PhD investigated fisheries management issues and, amongst other responsibilities, he oversaw the assessment of fish populations in rivers and lochs in Scotland. Roger is a founder member of Stonehaven MHC, has completed all the Munros and Corbetts, is a keen ski mountaineer and has climbed in many other parts of the world.

Ian Ralston is Abercromby Professor of Archaeology at the University of Edinburgh, and is an archaeologist whose principal research interests lie in eastern Scotland (prior to the medieval) and in the pre-Roman Iron Age of France. One of Ian's favoured subjects is the hill-forts of both areas. Ian regularly follows a labrador up local hills in Perth and Kinross.

Rob Raynor has worked as a species advisor and mammal specialist for Scottish Natural Heritage for over 23 years, and deals with conservation management issues associated with terrestrial mammals throughout Scotland. Rob has extensive experience of the Scottish hills and mountainous regions abroad.

Mark Wrightham is an upland vegetation ecologist and has worked in various policy areas which relate to the uplands. He is an enthusiastic hillwalker and climber in the UK and beyond, and was Secretary of the National Access Forum for the first 10 years after access rights came into force. He is currently Policy & Advice Manager (Recreation, Access & Tourism) with Scottish Natural Heritage.

Index

Index

Know the Code before you go ....

Enjoy Scotland's outdoors! Everyone has the right to be on most land and inland water for recreation, education and for going from place to place providing they act responsibly. These access rights and responsibilities are explained in the Scottish Outdoor Access Code. The key things are:

When you're in the outdoors:
- take personal responsibility for your own actions and act safely;
- respect people's privacy and peace of mind;
- help land managers and others to work safely and effectively;
- care for your environment and take your litter home;
- keep your dog under proper control;
- take extra care if you're organising an event or running a business.

If you're managing the outdoors:
- respect access rights;
- act reasonably when asking people to avoid land management operations;
- work with your local authority and other bodies to help integrate access and land management;
- respect rights of way and customary access.

Find out more by visiting **www.outdooraccess-scotland.com** or phoning your local Scottish Natural Heritage office.

SCOTTISH MOUNTAINEERING CLUB
SCOTTISH MOUNTAINEERING TRUST
Prices were correct at time of publication, but are subject to change

HILLWALKERS' GUIDES

The Munros	£23.00
The Corbetts and Other Scottish Hills	£23.00
The Grahams & The Donalds	£25.00
North-West Highlands	£22.00
Islands of Scotland Including Skye	£20.00
The Cairngorms	£18.00
Central Highlands	£18.00
Southern Highlands	£17.00

SCRAMBLERS' GUIDES

Skye Scrambles	£25.00
Highland Scrambles North	£19.00
Highland Scrambles South	£25.00

CLIMBERS' GUIDES

The Outer Hebrides	£29.95
Highland Outcrops South	£28.00
Inner Hebrides & Arran	£25.00
Northern Highlands North	£22.00
Northern Highlands Central	£25.00
Northern Highlands South	£25.00
Skye The Cuillin	£25.00
Skye Sea-cliffs & Outcrops	£25.00
The Cairngorms	£25.00
Ben Nevis	£22.00
Glen Coe	£22.00
North-East Outcrops	£22.00
Lowland Outcrops	£22.00
Scottish Winter Climbs	£25.00
Scottish Rock Climbs	£25.00
Scottish Sport Climbs	£28.00

OTHER PUBLICATIONS

Ben Nevis – Britain's Highest Mountain	£27.50
The Cairngorms – 100 Years of Mountaineering	£27.50
Munro's Tables	£16.00
A Chance in a Million? Avalanches in Scotland	£18.95
Scottish Hill Tracks	£18.00
Scottish Hill Names	£16.00
Mountaineering in Scotland (The Early Years)	£24.00
Mountaineering in Scotland (Years of Change)	£25.00
Ski Mountaineering in Scotland	£18.00

Visit our website for more details and to purchase, www.smc.org.uk

Distributed by: Cordee Ltd
(t) 01455 611185 (w) www.cordee.co.uk